Praise for *Dangerous Games*

'Larry Writer has delivered a gem in *Dangerous Games*, a story of the 1936 Berlin Olympics' impact on the lives of 33 Australian athletes. The peril and portent of that incendiary period of the 20th century was embedded in those Games with Hitler and the Nazis at their pre-war propaganda peak. The swift narrative puts the period and impact in a most readable, clear perspective, while showing the innocence, courage and honesty of Australian amateurs abroad.'

—Roland Perry, author of *Bill the Bastard* and
The Australian Light Horse

'Writer has faithfully recreated the 1936 Olympics—the most controversial in history—from the point of view of Australia's 33 competitors. Hitler, the host, represented the darkest evil . . . those Australians, the purest innocence.'

—Harry Gordon, author of *Australia and the Olympic Games*

About the author

LARRY WRITER is an award-winning author with an interest in sport, history and crime. He is author of the Ned Kelly Award-winning *Razor*, on Tilly Devine, Kate Leigh and Sydney's razor gangs of the 1920s, *Never Before, Never Again: The Rugby League Miracle at St George 1956–66 and the Lives of the Great Saints Since* and *Bumper: The Life and Times of Frank 'Bumper' Farrell*. He has also collaborated with high-profile sporting and arts figures on their memoirs, including Chrissy Amphlett and Rod Laver.

Other books by Larry Writer

Razor: Tilly Devine, Kate Leigh and the Razor Gangs
(winner of the Ned Kelly Award for True Crime 2002)

Rod Laver: Memoir

Bumper: The Life and Times of Frank 'Bumper' Farrell

Pleasure and Pain: Chrissy Amphlett

*Never Before, Never Again: The Rugby League Miracle at St George
1956–66 and the Lives of the Great Saints Since*

Winning: Face to Face with Australian Sporting Legends

Australia at the 1936 NAZI OLYMPICS

DANGEROUS GAMES

LARRY WRITER

ALLEN&UNWIN
SYDNEY·MELBOURNE·AUCKLAND·LONDON

First published in 2015

Allen & Unwin
83 Alexander Street
Crows Nest NSW 2065
Australia
Phone: (61 2) 8425 0100
Email: info@allenandunwin.com
Web: www.allenandunwin.com

Cataloguing-in-Publication details are available
from the National Library of Australia
www.trove.nla.gov.au

ISBN 978 1 74331 938 3

Internal design by Lisa White
Set in 12/16.5 pt Bembo by POST Pre-press Group, Australia
Printed and bound in Australia by Griffin Press

10 9 8 7 6 5 4 3 2 1

The paper in this book is FSC® certified.
FSC® promotes environmentally responsible,
socially beneficial and economically viable
management of the world's forests.

CONTENTS

For Basil Dickinson,
Ian Heads, John Devitt and Harry Gordon,
champions all

The most important thing in the Olympic Games is not to win but to take part.

The important thing in life is not the triumph but the struggle.

The essential thing is not to have conquered but to have fought well.

To spread these precepts is to build up a stronger and more valiant and, above all, more scrupulous and more generous humanity.

—Pierre de Frédy, Baron de Coubertin, founder of the modern Olympic Games

German sport has only one task: to strengthen the character of the German people, imbuing it with the fighting spirit and steadfast camaraderie necessary in the struggle for its existence.

—Joseph Goebbels, Nazi Propaganda and Enlightenment Minister

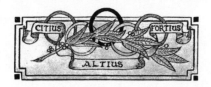

PROLOGUE
THE WATTLE AND THE SWASTIKA

The 33 athletes who travelled by ship and rattletrap train to Germany nearly 80 years ago to represent Australia at the 1936 Summer Olympic Games in Berlin—the so-called 'Nazi Games'— were innocents abroad, true amateurs in every sense. When these men and women departed Australia in May 1936 they, so apolitical, so young, were unprepared for what awaited them in the German capital: in Berlin itself, the despicable National Socialist regime that would just three years later spark World War II; and on the tracks and fields and in the pools, athletes from other countries who were leaving behind the amateur ethos of Olympism and competing with an expertise and intensity the happy-go-lucky Australians could not match. The lessons the Australian Olympians learned in Berlin would change them as people and as athletes forever.

Of course they'd heard that German Chancellor Adolf Hitler was a dangerous dictator leading a brutal regime, but they wanted to believe that sport and politics must never mix and that, win, lose or draw, what mattered was that they competed fairly and did their nation and loved ones proud. Wasn't sport the best antidote to tyranny?

'The Olympics were everything to me,' 1936 Olympian Basil Dickinson told me in an interview in 2013. 'I'd read that Hitler had dragged his country out of the great inflation and was trying to re-establish Germany as a world power. I'd heard rumblings about how he was persecuting Jews and rearming the army, navy and air force, but [I] didn't know enough to take him or his Nazis seriously, and most of the Australian team didn't either. We just didn't talk about it. We understood that the opportunity to represent Australia at an Olympics was a rare one that may never come again.'

So Dickinson and his teammates turned a deaf ear to calls to boycott Berlin, and packed rose-coloured glasses with their green and gold blazers.

As for Olympic competition, the Australians held no real hopes of topping the medal tally, but they expected to do well enough. They suspected their antiquated and poorly funded training regimes and shambolic state and national competitions, their lack of coaches, doctors and masseurs, would put them at a disadvantage when pitted against the athletes of Germany, the United States and Japan. Yet they assured themselves that they were God-blessed beneficiaries of the sunshine, salt water and fresh food that abounded in the wide, brown land, and trusted that, as in past Olympics, merely being Australian would compensate for any shortcomings.

No previous Olympics had been organised as efficiently nor staged with such breathtaking pomp as those Berlin Games in 1936. Of all the Olympic Games of the modern era, arguably only Sydney in 2000 and London in 2012 could match the Berlin Games' minutely calibrated efficiency and awesome pageantry. The athletes of Australia and the 48 other competing nations enjoyed warm hospitality and superb living and training facilities, and many athletes responded with fine—in some cases truly great—performances. But for all the high hopes and good intentions of the competitors, these Olympics had a rancid underbelly. Hitler, who had always despised sport, cynically used the Games to camouflage the malevolence of Nazism and trick the world into dropping its defences while he mobilised for war. His splendid international festival of athletics was a five-ring circus of smoke and mirrors to promote the 'New Germany' as a tolerant, strong and efficient country that deserved to be readmitted into the world community after being reduced to a pariah by the Treaty of Versailles following the Great War. Behind the Olympic bonhomie and the Games' glittering façade, the Nazi government was persecuting Jews and other non-Aryans, communists, socialists and liberals, intellectuals and creative people, the Church and anyone else whose beliefs opposed its own, and, in brazen defiance of Versailles, rearming to invade neighbouring lands. For the first and only time in Olympic history, the Games and its ideals were taken hostage by a political regime, and a terrifying one at that. Although Hitler and his henchmen's excesses were never able to diminish the athletic feats and camaraderie of the competitors, the 1936 Olympic Games are doomed to be known as a gala of Nazi propaganda and bloated militarism that was a portent of what the Führer would unleash on the world after the Games were over.

What the Australian athletes experienced in Berlin would change them profoundly in the years that followed. They revelled in competing in a magnificent stadium, in friendships forged with Berliners and rival athletes. They marvelled at grand old buildings and monuments, and sampled the customs and culture of a great European city. Yet with hindsight, a number, having witnessed Hitler, Göring and Goebbels coiled in their special enclosure in the grandstand and the jackbooted storm troopers goosestepping along the streets and the Reich Sports Field, were not surprised when Germany ignited a second world war. And they would remain forever saddened that the beautiful city of Berlin they knew that summer was destroyed and, worse, that so many of the young men and women they competed against, cheered on and caroused with later perished on the battlefields and in concentration camps. Also among the casualties were their own youthful illusions. After Berlin some of the athletes became disenchanted with the Olympic Games altogether—at least one refused to attend reunions or watch from the stands. Many were anguished that the Olympic ideals of sporting excellence, friendship and respect could be so easily perverted and used to achieve evil ends. They came to resent the nationalism, politicisation and commercialism that blighted the Games in 1936 and which continue in some respects to this day.

Dangerous Games is the story of the Australians who competed at the Summer Games of the XIth Olympiad in Berlin—who they were, what they achieved, and how their experiences in Berlin changed their lives. The genesis of the book is the intensive interviews I conducted with the last-surviving Australian Berlin Olympian, the remarkable Basil Dickinson, who passed away aged 98 in 2013. I also interviewed the descendants of many of the athletes, and utilised the athletes' diaries as well as documents and official reports and press coverage. I travelled to Berlin and was granted access to the Berlin Olympic archives, and given guided tours by local authorities of what remained of Nazi Germany and the Reich Sports Field.

This book has also been enriched by four extraordinary acts of generosity. Apart from giving his time and memories in our interviews, Basil Dickinson authorised me to consult his Berlin Olympics diaries and the lovingly accumulated collection of letters, memorabilia, programs and photographs that he had donated to the Mitchell Library. Harry Gordon, author of the landmark work *Australia and the Olympic Games*, allowed me access to his archive at the National Library and permitted me to mine interviews he conducted in the 1990s with the now-deceased Olympians Jack Metcalfe, Dunc Gray, Dick Garrard, Fred Woodhouse and Cecil Pearce. When those athletes are quoted in the pages that follow, mostly it is from the Gordon transcripts. British Olympic historians Stephanie Daniels and Anita Tedder granted me access to interviews they conducted with three of the four Australian women athletes in Berlin—Doris Carter, Pat Norton and Evelyn de Lacy—for their book *A Proper Spectacle: Women Olympians 1900–1936*. And Warren Whillier, grandson of de Lacy, passed to me her wonderful diary, in which her spirit, and that of her teammates on their great adventure, shines through across 80 years. Basil, Harry, Stephanie, Anita and Warren have helped me to bring the athletes and their era back to life.

CHAPTER 1
BERLIN WINS THE GAMES

'The winner,' declared the Belgian aristocrat, 'is Berlin.'

On 13 May 1931, Count Henri de Baillet-Latour, the 55-year-old president of the International Olympic Committee, rose from his seat at IOC headquarters in Lausanne, Switzerland, and declared the result of the ballot to determine which city would host the XIth Summer Olympic Games five years hence. The delegates of each member nation had placed their vote at the annual IOC conference in Barcelona the previous month, or by post or cable if they had been unable to attend.

The 1936 Summer Games would be staged in the German capital from 1 to 16 August, and Germany, as was custom, would also host the Winter Olympics, in the Bavarian alpine village of Garmisch-Partenkirchen, from 6 to 16 February.

Among the delegates who awarded the Olympic Games to Berlin over Barcelona, by 43 votes to 16, was Australian Olympic Federation (AOF) president and Sydney accountant James Taylor. Taylor was a hard-working, sometimes curmudgeonly fellow with white hair and thin lips and who wore rimless spectacles. He blended in well with his fellow Olympic committee and federation delegates who, to a man, were elderly, conservative and white sports administrators with past or current careers in politics, commerce, medicine or academia, or were minor European royalty. Having himself voted for Berlin, Taylor ventured, 'Australian athletes and officials look forward tremendously to competing in Berlin, and are confident of a good showing at what, I'm sure, will be a memorable Olympic Games.'

At his home in Paris, Pierre de Frédy, Baron de Coubertin, the 68-year-old founder and former president of the modern Olympic Games, was also pleased by Berlin's success. Germans, he declared, would be excellent stewards of the traditions of modern Olympism. In 1931, with Adolf Hitler's rabble-rousing Nazis still a divided and derided minority, there was no reason to believe Germany would not be such.

The revered president of Germany and World War I hero Paul von Hindenburg, though far more at home on a battle-field than a sports arena, threw his gravitas behind the Berlin Olympic Games. With his formidable belly and chest bedecked by medals, Hindenburg stood before an early prototype of the new Olympic stadium and, as reporters scribbled and flashbulbs popped, proclaimed that the spirit of the Games would be upheld as never before, and that in gratitude for the IOC bestowing the Olympics on the Fatherland he would personally see to it that throughout all Germany physical fitness would become a 'life habit'.

German Olympic Committee (GOC) president Dr Theodor Lewald stepped up and delivered the first of what would become a tornado of windy speeches about the Games of the XIth Olympiad. 'We have been entrusted,' he announced, 'with the only genuine world festival of our age, in fact, the only one since the begin-ning of time, a celebration which unites all nations and in which the hearts of all civilised peoples beat in harmony.' During the

Olympic fortnight, continued Lewald, 'the interest of the entire world is concentrated upon the results of the Olympic competition, each nation hoping for the success of its own athletes but nevertheless applauding the victor in a true sporting manner regardless of his nationality'. These Games, he fulminated, were the expression of 'a new outlook and a new youth. The world expects the German nation to organise and present this festival in an exemplary manner, emphasising at the same time its moral and artistic aspects. This means that all forces must be exerted, that sacrifices of a physical as well as financial nature must be made, and there is no doubt but that all expectations will be fulfilled for the advancement of the Olympic ideals and the honour of Germany.'

By the time the Berlin Games came to pass, many of Lewald's fine words rang hollow.

Around the world, the decision to award Berlin the Olympics was applauded by those who supported Germany's post-war government, a liberal-minded parliamentary democracy known as the Weimar Republic, named after the city where its constitutional assembly had taken place in 1919. The republic, under presidents Friedrich Ebert and then Hindenburg, who presided over a succession of chancellors, was a well-intentioned if hapless hodgepodge of conflicting factional interests, valiantly struggling to embrace democracy, address the ravages of the Great Depression, and restore Germany to its respected pre-Great War status even while it was being economically throttled by the rapacious reparation demands of the victorious nations who blamed Germany for causing the war. Under the War Guilt Clause, the Treaty of Versailles ordered Germany to compensate its conquerors to the tune of 269 billion gold marks. The treaty amputated 13 per cent of Germany's territory, including the Rhineland, Alsace and Lorraine. To ensure that Germany could never wage war again, its army could comprise no more than 100,000 men and there could be no conscription. There could be no air force, no submarines, and no navy vessels of more than 101,604 tonnes.

Many Olympic delegates who supported Berlin's bid were impressed by the creative and intellectual life in Germany's multiracial melting-pot capital. From 1918 when the Great War ended, in what are now remembered as the Weimar years, Berlin hosted a golden era of culture. An extraordinary group of artists, scientists, novelists, playwrights, actors, dancers, singers, musicians, philosophers and architects—many Jewish—gave the world a trove of treasures. Fritz Lang directed the film classics *Metropolis* and *M* starring the young Peter Lorre. Josef von Sternberg's *The Blue Angel* made a star of Marlene Dietrich for her portrayal of cabaret singer Lola Lola. The impressionist classic *The Cabinet of Doctor Caligari* starred Conrad Veidt, who would make a career portraying Nazis in Hollywood in the 1940s—most notably Major Strasser in *Casablanca*—after fleeing the real-life Nazis. Vladimir Horowitz played sublime grand piano with the Berlin Philharmonic Orchestra. Architect Walter Gropius founded the Bauhaus School and inspired artists Paul Klee and Wassily Kandinsky. Dramatist Bertolt Brecht and composer Kurt Weill's *The Threepenny Opera*, featuring the enduring hit song 'Mack the Knife', was the smash-hit musical of the period. The plays and musicals of directors Max Reinhardt and Erwin Piscator regularly sold out Berlin's theatres. Albert Einstein was a professor at the University of Berlin. The books of Christopher Isherwood (*Goodbye to Berlin* and *Mr Norris Changes Trains*), Erich Maria Remarque (*All Quiet on the Western Front*), and the Mann siblings Thomas (*The Magic Mountain*) and Heinrich (*Professor Unrat*) are still cherished.

In the Weimar years, Berliners promenaded down the great thoroughfares Unter den Linden and Kurfürstendamm, and in Potsdamer Platz and the verdant parklands of the Tiergarten, gossiping, flirting and exchanging ideas on politics and the arts. It was a gloriously decadent city—1920s and '30s writer Stefan Zweig called it 'the Babylon of the world'—with an uninhibited cabaret and cafe culture, and gambling houses, brothels and bars catering to every sexual preference and peccadillo. Berliners flocked to art galleries, theatres, museums and concert halls.

There were also some international observers who felt that Germany deserved a break. As well as the deprivations inflicted upon it at Versailles, Berlin had been selected to stage the 1916 Olympics but the Great War had put paid to that, and as punishment for its role in that war Germany had also been banned from competing in the Olympics of 1920 and 1924. Surely the great land of Goethe, Bismarck, Bach, Beethoven, Wagner, Brahms, Gutenberg and Martin Luther had done its penance and it was time for the community of nations to welcome Germany back into the fold.

Yet there were some who believed that awarding Germany the 1936 Olympics was too much, too soon. A number of those who opposed Berlin staging the Games were unable to forget or forgive Germany's role in the 1914–18 war. Others were concerned about its out-of-control inflation and burgeoning unemployment that could turn the Olympics into a financial fiasco. And there was the ceaseless political unrest, which often exploded into street fighting, that made Berlin in many eyes an unsuitable venue.

Through the 1920s, there had been a spate of left- and right-wing putsches, notably in March 1920 when the arch-conservative Freikorps paramilitary group installed extreme right-wing journalist Wolfgang Kapp as chancellor of Germany for all of four days before he, and they, were overthrown by the government and the trade unions. Then, on 8 November 1923, the fledgling fascist National Socialist German Workers' (Nazi) Party, 35,000 members strong, sought to overthrow the Weimar Republic. Some

600 Nazis, led by a scruffy yet charismatic 34-year-old Great War veteran named Adolf Hitler, attempted to seize Munich by storming the Bürgerbräukeller beer hall when Bavarian commissioner Gustav von Kahr was addressing 3000 supporters. Hitler leapt onto the stage brandishing a pistol and, in the hoarse shout that the world would come to know too well, declared, 'The national revolution has broken out!'

Hitler's time would come; for now he spoke too soon. The so-called Beer Hall Putsch ended the next day when Hitler and 2000 followers were fired on by police and the army. Eighteen died in the fighting, many were wounded, including flying ace and future Reichsminister Hermann Göring, who was shot in the leg. The Nazis fled, and Hitler was arrested and sentenced to five years in prison. He served just twelve months, but that was long enough for him to plot his next moves and dictate *Mein Kampf* (*My Struggle*), his nationalistic and racist manifesto, to his acolyte and fellow prisoner Rudolf Hess.

The German economy had been in a parlous state. Across Germany in the 1920s, businesses failed, millions starved. Hard times spawned more political strife, and tens of thousands were victims of political murder. There were strikes as workers demanded a wage sufficient to pay rent and feed their families. To placate the strikers, the government simply printed more money. The result was rampant inflation. At the outset of 1923, one US dollar bought 4.2 reichsmarks; by November it bought 4.2 trillion marks.

Then, in 1930, just as the government was beginning to wrestle hyperinflation under at least a semblance of control, the Great Depression laid waste to the economies of the world and certainly did not spare Germany's already ailing one. The disaster saw Hitler's National Socialists win favour among disenchanted conservative Germans, war veterans, farmers and the struggling lower and middle classes. Tired of what they believed—with some justification—was a weak and incompetent government that had wrought crippling taxes, unemployment and civil mayhem, they embraced the Nazis' hardline autocratic panaceas.

In the 1930 general elections, the National Socialists won 18.7 per cent of the vote and claimed 107 seats. Adolf Hitler found himself leading the second-largest political party in Germany. A significant part of Hitler's appeal was his fiery rhetoric demanding what he termed 'a New Germany', rearmed, implacable in the pursuit of its—*his*—ideals, and with the resolve and power to smash those at home and abroad whom he blamed for Germany's defeat in 1918 and its present predicament: the Jews, communists, democrats, France. His spellbinding speeches created in Germans a persecution complex, a belief that they had been victimised by inferior races, subjected to international hatred and envy, plotted against, stolen from and laughed at, and that the only valid response was revenge.

'Like most great revolutionaries, [Hitler] could thrive only in evil times, at first when the masses were unemployed, hungry and desperate,' wrote William L. Shirer, Berlin-based American correspondent and author of *The Rise and Fall of the Third Reich*. And Ian Kershaw, biographer of Hitler: 'Without the great depression, without the crash of 1929, without the disintegration of the bourgeoisie, the liberals and the conservatives, Hitler would have remained a nut case on the political sidelines.'

Had Germany had a leader powerful enough to slap him down before he and his cohorts gathered momentum, Hitler may never have risen to prominence, but in 1931, the year Germany was awarded the 1936 Olympics, President Hindenburg was 83, ill and senile. Though Hindenburg scoffed at Hitler's apoplectic harangues, his ragbag appearance and uncultured ways, the once mighty warrior was no longer a match. Hitler considered

Hindenburg easy pickings, and schemed, cajoled and bullied to usurp him as leader.

Hitler ran against Hindenburg for the presidency in 1932, and while he lost again, this time he won more than 35 per cent of the vote. Like it or not, the old lion could no longer denigrate Hitler as a lightweight without support.

Berlin's bid to stage the Olympics could not have succeeded in 1931 without the efforts of GOC president Dr Theodor Lewald and secretary Dr Carl Diem. Seventy-one-year-old Lewald had devoted his life to the German Olympic movement, administering its finances and serving as GOC president since 1919. It was he, more than anyone, who had won the Games for Berlin in 1916, only for the Great War to thwart his plans. Lewald stoically endured his country's banishment from the 1920 and 1924 Games, and was proudly front and centre when Germany was reinstated to compete at the Amsterdam Olympics in 1928, and won eight gold medals, seven silver and fourteen bronze. Capitalising on Germany's performance, Lewald went all out to secure the Games of the XIth Olympiad for Berlin.

Diem was a 58-year-old newspaper athletics writer who knew his subject. A good middle- and long-distance runner, he captained the German team at the 1906 Athens Olympics and was general secretary of the aborted 1916 Berlin Games. Industrious and dedicated to German sport, Diem toiled to improve training facilities for athletes and establish centres of sporting excellence for budding champions. Diem can take credit for reinstituting in 1936 the Olympic Torch Relay, which had been first run in Athens in 80 BC but had not been a feature of the Olympics since the modern Games began in Athens in 1896.

Lewald's and Diem's hearts were in the right place. Their grand ideals would be corrupted by Hitler, but in 1931 they agreed with Coubertin that sporting competition not only built healthy bodies but also had a positive 'moral influence' on participants and could promote friendship between nations. Like Coubertin, they believed that the Olympic Games should be conducted with due pomp and ceremony but should never be sullied by crass commercialism or aggressive jingoism nor used for political or militaristic ends. When Berlin was chosen to stage the 1936 Games, Lewald wrote to Coubertin saying that it was his most ardent desire to arrange the Olympics in the spirit desired by their founder. When he uttered those words, he undoubtedly meant them. He could have had no inkling that Hitler and his followers were gathering forces to take power and five years later would hijack the Games and trample Coubertin's lofty ideals. (Sadly, the founder of the modern Olympics would turn out to have feet of clay. Shortly before the Berlin Games, Coubertin was so troubled by Hitler's usurping of the Olympics that he refused to give the festival his blessing. Refused, that is, until he was slipped 10,000 reichsmàrks from Nazi coffers and promised that he would be nominated for the Nobel Prize. He *was* duly nominated in 1936 but missed out, and died the following year.)

It took energy and determination to get the bid for Berlin 1936 to the starting line at the 1931 IOC conference in Barcelona. One not inconsiderable problem was that with Berlin broke, the city council was baulking at supporting the bid because they knew that an Olympics would be hugely expensive. It took an impassioned campaign by Lewald and Diem to persuade the burghers of Berlin to sign off on the massive project on the grounds that the Games would turn a profit for the city, perhaps as much as 10 million reichsmarks, and provide work for thousands. With the City of Berlin finally onside, Lewald and Diem travelled the globe shoring up delegates' support for Berlin's bid.

When critics reminded Lewald and Diem of Berlin's financial woes and political unrest, the duo reminded *them* that Berlin's main rival, Barcelona, was enduring civil strife of its own—in the form of a rent strike in which, with the backing of unions, socialists and communists, unemployed tenants were refusing to pay rent to their landlords; the army had been brought in to rectify matters.

When Berlin was awarded the Games, the nation applauded Lewald and Diem's tireless efforts. They were national heroes. In 1931 it mattered not that Lewald's paternal grandmother was Jewish, nor that Diem's wife had a Jewish grandparent. There would come a time when these things mattered a great deal.

On 30 May 1931, the GOC formed the Olympic Organising Committee, chaired by GOC president Lewald, to fine-tune every aspect of the Games and work with the City of Berlin to ensure their success. The estimated cost then of staging the Games was four million reichsmarks, and it was calculated in 1932 that this sum would be raised through a government donation of one million reichsmarks, the sale of three million reichsmarks' worth of tickets, a national lottery, contributions from business and citizens, the proceeds of advertising billboards, the sale of specially minted Olympic postage stamps and, instigated by Diem, a small surcharge on the price of all Olympic admission tickets to be known as the 'Olympic penny'. Organisers attended the Los Angeles Games in 1932 to study how the Americans staged their Olympics and so, combining the best American sports administration methods with Germanic attention to order and detail, to prepare for Berlin.

The Olympic Organising Committee in October 1932 published a document, *Our Expectations*, and it was not all to do with athletic achievement. In part it stated that for the success of the Games to be assured, the event must not be regarded as the exclusive affair of German sporting circles nor of the City of Berlin, 'but must command the interest and support of the entire

German nation'. If this was achieved, the Games of 1936 'will be the most outstanding Festival of modern times', venerating German art and culture as well as sport. At the first official meeting of the Organising Committee, in Berlin Town Hall in January 1933, President Hindenburg consented to be the patron of the Games. With Hindenburg's blessing and the best intentions of the organisers, it seemed the Berlin Olympics were right on track. In Germany and around the world, elite athletes limbered up.

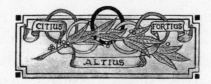

CHAPTER 2
ON YOUR MARKS

Today, Australia is a Summer Olympics powerhouse, with a swag of medals and new records expected, and achieved, at each Games. Yet while there were meritorious, and occasionally world-beating, performances by Australian Olympic competitors dating from the first modern Olympics in 1896, it was only after World War II that Australia emerged from the shadows of the United States, Great Britain, France, Japan, Germany and the Scandinavian countries. Amateur athletics in Australia—that is, track and field, swimming, boxing, wrestling and cycling—was impoverished. Even if not true to the amateur spirit of Olympism, other countries had always found ways to raise money to pay for their Olympic teams, including hefty government grants, under-the-table corporate funding, and donations from wealthy private benefactors. Australian amateur sport relied on what little money the various sporting associations could eke from balls and dances, smoko nights, raffles, picnics, the occasional miserly government handout, and the few hundred pounds or so that might result from newspaper campaigns encouraging the public to support a worthy competitor. This paucity of funds doomed Australia's teams to be small and ill-prepared.

Any Australian competitor who succeeded at the Games did so despite Australia's outdated, or sometimes non-existent, training facilities. There were a few qualified swimming, rowing and boxing coaches, but track and field coaches and masseurs were a rarity—no officially appointed coaches accompanied Australians to Olympic Games until after World War II—and there were no dietitians or doctors; competitors were largely left to coach and treat themselves.

With few exceptions, Australian sporting administrators were well-meaning and enthusiastic part-timers, their expertise limited to firing a starting pistol, marking lanes and organising sing-songs and chook raffles. They were also unashamedly parochial. When it came time to select a national team, state officials chose sub-standard competitors from their own neck of the woods over better competitors from other states. In the lead-up to the 1936 Olympics, this approach to selections threatened to leave a number of our best competitors at home and became a national scandal.

The 33-strong Australian team of four women and 29 men who attended the 1936 Berlin Olympics was our ninth Olympic squad. The first, for the inaugural Summer Games of the modern Olympics, in Athens in 1896, had comprised just one athlete. Victoria-based Englishman Edwin 'Teddy' Flack did Australia proud, although strictly speaking he was representing Victoria, as the federation of the states was still five years away and Australia technically did not exist as a nation. Erect of bearing, with an extravagantly dimpled chin punctuating a handsome face, the Melbourne Grammar School-educated track and tennis star won gold medals in the 800m and 1500m, competed unsuccessfully in the doubles tennis, and was leading the marathon when he collapsed, shaking and vomiting, at the 37km mark and had to withdraw. His appearances on the winner's dais were heralded by the raising of the Union Jack and the playing of 'God Save the

Queen'. For his efforts, Flack was mobbed in the street in Athens and back home in Melbourne, and was grandly nicknamed 'the Lion of Athens'. In his book *Australia and the Olympic Games*, Harry Gordon called Flack Australia's first sporting hero: 'the first to compete, the first to win'. His exploits in Athens 'gave Australians their first real awareness of the Olympic Games'.

The Paris Olympics in 1900 may well have been the most bizarre ever. As well as traditional sports, competitors tried their hand at firefighting, fishing, tug-of-war, boules, cannon shooting, pigeon racing, ballooning and underwater swimming. The two Australian athletes, Freddy Lane and Stan Rowley, confined themselves to swimming and running respectively—and excelled. Lane placed first in the 200m freestyle final and the 200m obstacle event; though by the time his races were won, all the gold medals had been handed out and he had to be content with bronze statuettes of a horse and a peasant girl. Rowley claimed bronze medals in the 60m, 100m and 200m, and was a member of Britain's gold-medal-winning 5000m cross-country team. The 200m result rankled the cantankerous Rowley. 'I really should have won the race,' he bleated. 'On a fair course I would have won easily!'

St Louis hosted the 1904 Games, where Australia's sole competitor was Corrie Gardner, a prominent Australian Rules footballer. He failed to survive the heats of the 110m hurdles and the broad jump. (In early modern Olympic times, including in 1936, the broad jump was the official term given to leaping after a run-up. Today such a leap is known as long jumping, whereas a leap from a standing position is called a broad jump.) It was scant consolation that Australia's US-based, soon-to-be American citizen Frank Gailey won three silver and a bronze medal in swimming for his adopted homeland.

Four years later at the London Olympics, Australia's representation soared to 37 (numbers were bolstered by the inclusion of the Wallabies rugby union team, which was touring Great Britain at the time, and three Kiwi athletes, in an 'Australasian' team), competing across seven sports. The team returned with five medals. The Wallabies won gold; there were no preliminary matches as only Australia, England and France fielded rugby teams and France withdrew without playing a match. Middleweight boxer Reg 'Snowy' Baker—who also competed in the swimming and diving—won a silver medal. As did seventeen-year-old Frank Beaurepaire in the 400m freestyle. Despite a heavy cold, he also took bronze in the 1500m. New Zealander Harry Kerr placed third in the 3500m walk. Surprisingly, considering Britain's reputation for fair play, the London Olympics was a shamefully provincial Games tainted by hometown decisions, with British officials openly cheering for their athletes, and even coaching them during events. Understandably, the United States and Sweden were insulted when local organisers failed to fly their flags at the stadium at White City. The Irish, too, were angry when ordered to march behind the Union Jack, not the Irish Republic's flag, as part of the British team. The cash-strapped Australian team arrived in London without uniforms, and it took a last-minute and begrudgingly deposited cash injection by the federal government to purchase 37 cheap singlets and shorts on which green and gold piping was hastily sewn. Even an Australian flag for the athletes to march behind had to be rustled up at the eleventh hour. 'The overall makeshift effect was embarrassing to some, particularly measured against the tailored splendour of some of the European contingents,' wrote Harry Gordon, 'but it reflected accurately enough the do-it-yourself status of sport in the Antipodes, unsubsidised by associations, governments and the public.'

In 1912, again competing as Australasia, a 26-strong team established the region as a gallant minnow of world sport by returning from Stockholm with seven medals. This was the first Olympics in which women were allowed to compete, though in swimming only; it wasn't until 1928 that they could participate in track and field. Apparently Baron de Coubertin considered it unseemly for women to indulge in sweaty competition. (That attitude still prevailed in some quarters in 1933 as the Berlin Games loomed. Bruno Malitz, sports spokesman for Hitler's Sturmabteilung, or stormtroopers, declared, 'We oppose women's sports . . . Women should remain womanly. Look at the girl athletes who have reached the age of 30. They look 50: manly, the spirit of battle written on their faces, bony and bare of womanhood.') Sydney swimmer Sarah 'Fanny' Durack proved that women's place *was* at the Olympics when in Stockholm she easily won the gold medal in the 100m freestyle despite colliding with the side of the pool. The men's 4x200m freestyle relay team also won its final, and team members Cecil Healy (who would be killed just four years later at the Battle of the Somme) and Harold Hardwick each enjoyed individual success, with Healy taking the silver medal in the 100m freestyle, and Hardwick placing third in the finals of the 400m and the 1500m freestyle events. 'Australasian' Tony Wilding of New Zealand won bronze in the men's indoor tennis singles.

The war that took Healy's life put paid to the Olympic Games scheduled for Berlin in 1916, and when the Games resumed in Antwerp in 1920, the twelve-strong Australian team won three medals. The redoubtable Beaurepaire, today regarded as one of our finest-ever swimmers, at the age of 29 won two of those. He was a member of the silver-medal-winning men's 4x200m freestyle relay team, and took bronze in the 1500m freestyle. George Parker came second in the 3000m walk.

Beaurepaire and fellow swimmer Andrew 'Boy' Charlton were Australia's stars at the 1924 Paris Games, playing their part in four of the six medals won during one of the City of Light's hottest summers, the temperature soaring some days to 45 degrees Celsius.

Charlton won the 1500m freestyle in which Beaurepaire, now 33, claimed the bronze medal, and also won bronze in the 400m freestyle. Both Beaurepaire and Charlton were members of the silver-medal-winning 4x200m freestyle relay team that was bested in the final by a red-hot United States outfit anchored by future Tarzan movie star Johnny Weissmuller. Dick Eve won the gold medal in the men's plain high diving. Anthony 'Nick' Winter won the men's hop, step and jump (today the triple jump). The successes in Paris captured the imagination of a previously blasé Australian public. On the team's return, thousands gathered at Sydney's Circular Quay to greet their ship RMS *Tahiti*. Reported the sporting newspaper *The Referee*: 'Never in the history of sport have the citizens of Sydney displayed such spontaneous enthusiasm.' At the quay, Charlton and Beaurepaire received more cheers than anyone. Charlton had a fabulous swimming career but it's thought he could have achieved more had his heart been truly in his sport. Although an Olympic gold medal eluded him, Beaurepaire lived an epic life. After rescuing a swimmer who had been attacked by a shark at Sydney's Coogee Beach in 1922, he established the Beaurepaire car tyre company, was knighted, and served twice as lord mayor of Melbourne.

Charlton, who won silver in the 400m and 1500m freestyle, and rower Henry 'Bobby' Pearce, who took gold in the single sculls, were Australia's stand-outs in Amsterdam in 1928. Pearce hailed from a renowned sporting family. His grandfather and father were champion scullers, brother Sandy played rugby league for Australia, Sandy's son Cec rowed at the Berlin Games, and Cec's son Gary rowed at the Tokyo, Mexico City and Munich Olympics. The Amsterdam Games were also notable for the debut of arguably Australia's greatest cyclist, Edgar 'Dunc' Gray, who, aged 22, won a bronze medal in the men's track time trial. Gray's was Australia's first cycling medal.

By 1932, when Los Angeles hosted the Games, the Great Depression was biting hard in Australia. Sports funding was even harder to come by than usual. Australia's squad of twelve nevertheless returned with three gold medals, a silver and a bronze. Gray won the men's 1000m time trial, and Pearce again left rival rowers in his wake in the single sculls. The sixteen-year-old prodigy Clare Dennis took gold in the 200m breaststroke. Backstroker Philomena 'Bonnie' Mealing placed second in the 100m event, and wrestler Eddie Scarf won bronze in the freestyle (as opposed to Greco-Roman) light heavyweight division. It was a groundbreaking Games, with the introduction of electronic time-keeping, and the victory ceremony we recognise today, with winners standing on a dais, medals ceremoniously draped around their necks, flowers proffered, national anthems played and flags raised. Radio broadcasts, teletype communications and updated bulletins printed and distributed event by event made the media's job easier than ever before. Los Angeles boasted the first designated Olympic Village to accommodate athletes.

Immediately after the 1932 Games concluded, the race for inclusion in the Australian team for the Berlin Games began. Over the next four years, places in the team were fiercely contested.

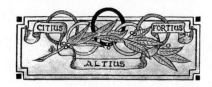

CHAPTER 3
THE CLASS OF '36

In the late 1920s and early '30s, starry-eyed young athletes all over Australia were running, jumping, swimming, rowing, boxing and wrestling, with the Berlin Olympic Games their Holy Grail. One such hopeful was a self-effacing and serious-minded track and field athlete named Basil Dickinson. He was born in Queanbeyan in south-eastern New South Wales on 25 April 1915, at the very moment when the Diggers were storming the beaches at Gallipoli. 'I dreamed of being an Olympian from my early teens when I started winning sprints, high and broad jump, hurdles, and hop, step and jump at school and for my local club and state,' Dickinson reminisced in his 98th year. 'I followed the Olympic exploits of Dunc Gray and Bobby Pearce, and while there was not the instant and blanket coverage of the Games that exists today, I read the cabled reports in the newspaper and listened to wireless updates. To win an Olympic medal, I thought, what a thing that would be.'

At primary school in the 1920s, Dickinson seemed anything but Olympic material. 'In my pre-teen years, I was just Joe Blow.' He won a few school events but was not up to the mark in district, city and state meets. 'Once I came home from an athletics carnival complaining that I'd not done well and wanting to quit. My father, Perce, who'd have been happier had I been more studious, called my bluff. "Well, why *don't* you?" Thank goodness I persevered. It wasn't until later, when my family moved to [the southern Sydney suburb of] Hurstville . . . and I joined St George Athletic Club and attended Cleveland Street High School and then Sydney Boys High, that I came into my own. It was all so basic then. We ran on grass tracks in bare feet or sandshoes. I didn't know what spikes were, or, heaven forbid, cinder tracks . . . There were no coaches either. The lads coached each other. There was a marvellous camaraderie.' At St George Athletic Club, Dickinson put sprinting, hurdles and high jump on the backburner to concentrate on the broad jump and the hop, step and jump.

At Sydney Boys High, Dickinson blossomed. He began to win regularly in Greater Public Schools (GPS) broad jump and hop, step and jump events. 'I was suddenly good. Well, not suddenly. I was a slow starter and with practice and competition I built up to my best over a period. It helped when I learned to reduce the pressure on myself. I didn't set goals that were unattainably high, and I discouraged my parents and sisters from watching me compete because their presence put me on edge. I definitely performed better when I was relaxed.'

This was the time of the Depression and his was not a wealthy family, so Dickinson left school before completing his leaving certificate to earn a wage. 'I was disappointed because I'd had my heart set on matriculating and attending university, and my father was disappointed too because he wanted me to have the education he never had, but in the Depression this simply wasn't an option.' He found work as a junior clerk with the Royal Insurance Company in Sydney.

When writing and filing insurance policies permitted, Dickinson continued to compete in athletics. 'I did very well in the national championships in Adelaide in 1934 and Melbourne in 1935. By then I was the second-best broad jumper and hop, step and jumper in Australia, behind Jack Metcalfe, who was three years older than me and also a Sydney Boys High old boy. Jack's father told Dad it was a shame that Jack was around because I was among the best jumpers in the world and if not for Jack I would have been the best in Australia.'

Royal Insurance begrudged its young employee taking time off to compete. When he applied for Friday and Saturday leave to attend the Melbourne centenary athletics carnival in 1935, his superiors scowled and made him stew before they signed the holiday chit. 'With four or five other coves I caught the early morning Friday train from Central . . . and arrived in Melbourne at 11.30 p.m. without having eaten. Starving and exhausted, I gulped down a sandwich and went to bed at the NSW team's pub, the Carlyon, and woke next day, the day of the championships, feeling crook. Even so, I gave Jack Metcalfe, who by then was considered the best hop, step and jumper in the world, a fright. He jumped 50ft 4½in [15.35m], and I managed 49ft, 11⅞in [15.24m]. The buggers wouldn't even give me the extra eighth of an inch so I could break 50ft! Jack won, I came second, and that was that.'

Jack Metcalfe was born in Bellingen, northern New South Wales, in 1912, the son of a senior executive at Kodak. He attended Sydney Boys High and Sydney University, where he studied law while working as an articled law clerk. Although he had left Sydney Boys by the time Dickinson started, the school connection, the sports they excelled at, and a natural empathy between two thoughtful, decent young men enriched their friendship. Metcalfe was a friendly, generous fellow, quick to offer advice to rival athletes. He filmed athletic meets and screened them, with his own commentary, to young athletes at the YMCA. If Metcalfe had a fault, it was that he spread his talent too thinly. Noted *The Referee*: 'Metcalfe is an excellent combination of fine physique, keenness, intelligence and natural ability. When he sets out to reach an objective, his methods are the result of close study [but] he endeavours to reach too many objectives. For instance, he would, if time permitted, compete in a high jump, a broad jump, and a javelin throw on the one day. He might even attempt a [shot put] or a hop, step and jump as well. It is all an outlet for his tremendous enthusiasm for field games. But supposing all this energy and enthusiasm were diverted into one channel . . . What might we not expect from Metcalfe in such circumstances? There we would find a real Olympic possibility.'

Stocky, broad-shouldered and with massive legs (his thighs were 61cm around), Metcalfe's party trick was to walk 100m on his knees. He is widely regarded as one of Australia's best-ever jumpers and finest all-round track and field athletes. Like his younger rival Dickinson, he bloomed late. He told Harry Gordon: 'I was six when we came to Sydney and I attended a number of primary schools in quick succession. Accommodation was hard to get in Sydney at the time. I basically went from Daceyville School to Sydney High, having played practically no sport at all. I'd never even played football and the nearest I'd got to cricket was rounders with the family in the backyard.' In his first years at Sydney High he competed at the annual sports day and came nowhere. 'I was a trier. I competed in everything but was very much an also-ran until in third year I won the under-sixteen high jump with a very poor jump of about 4ft 8in [1.42m]. This was quite an enjoyable experience.' Metcalfe's high jumping improved, and at the Combined High Schools athletics carnival in his final high school year in 1930, he won the event, beating the existing record by 3½in (9cm).

After starting with the scissors jump, Metcalfe taught himself the eastern cut-off—he studied the style in a textbook, there being no one to instruct him—which he used thereafter. 'I'd read up on the various overseas [high jump] styles and it was quite obvious that the western roll was having more success than the eastern cut-off but the western roll needed a pit to land in and we didn't have one—we jumped on hard ground . . . I learned the eastern cut-off and my first success with it took me to 1.88m and that was at the Sports School at Manly on the day Sydney Harbour Bridge was opened.'

At the University Championships in 1933, 21-year-old Metcalfe blitzed the field in every event he entered. He set new records for the high jump, the broad jump, the hop, step and jump, the shot put and the javelin. His high jump of 6ft 5in (1.96m) beat the existing Australian record by 1.73in (4.4cm). At a meet in December that year he high jumped 6ft 5.9in (1.98m), which smashed the Olympic record and was just 1.18in (3cm) below the world record of American Harold Osborne. Early in 1934, at an athletics meet in New Zealand, Metcalfe won all his events and set an Australian broad jump record of 23ft 11.7in (7.31m). In analysing Metcalfe's prowess, the *New Zealand Truth* praised his muscular physique and natural athletic ability, but reckoned that the key to his success in 'the leaping business' was that he approached it meticulously, 'measuring his run-up, and in every way concentrating on the job to make certain his action is machine-like in its accuracy'. The reporter discerned 'something very engaging about this unassuming, ever-smiling young Wallaby. He has been described as a freak jumper, but a more apt summing up of his qualities would be that of a serious young athlete who has brought his natural jumping ability to a high degree of perfection through a deep study of its technique . . . Metcalfe is a sheer delight to watch, even to those unversed in the arts of leaping.'

Metcalfe was a civilised man, as interested in the arts and philosophy as he was in sport. All his life he cherished a letter written by George Bernard Shaw to Sam Gudsell, social secretary of the New Zealand Amateur Athletic Association in Auckland, who had invited Shaw to attend the athletics meet where Metcalfe was competing, promising the playwright that Metcalfe would astound him with his high-jumping ability. Shaw responded: 'I take athletic competitive sports very seriously indeed as they seem to produce more bad feeling, bad manners and international hatred than any other popular movements. Possibly I may look in unobtrusively on Saturday if I am not otherwise engaged, but if I meet Mr Metcalfe I shall certainly try to dissuade him from shortening his life by jumping the height that you mentioned. He should use a step ladder.'

After world-class performances in the high jump, broad jump and the hop, step and jump, 'Jumping Jack' Metcalfe was hailed as a certain 1936 Olympian, and was selected in Australia's 1934 British Empire Games team bound for London.

At London's White City stadium, Metcalfe won a gold medal in the hop, step and jump, after which *The Sydney Morning Herald* raved, 'Metcalfe was the first Australian to send our flag to the top of the flagstaff with a sensational win in which he eclipsed 14 competitors . . . He was bronzed and impressive in physique compared with the other competitors . . . His best effort in the first round was 50ft 1in [15.26m], 2ft better than his opponents despite the fact that he found the run-up rough, as the ground had been cut up by a recent rodeo.' Metcalfe won bronze in the broad jump and placed fourth in the high jump. His disappointing performance in the latter, his pet event, was blamed on the damaged feet he'd suffered while hop, step and jump training on the rough track. (Interestingly, the relative lack of success of our track and field competitors at the London Empire Games was widely ascribed to their inexperience on cinder tracks, which were used in England. As events in Berlin two years later would show, the lesson went unheeded by Australia's sporting hierarchy.) Metcalfe erased any doubt that he was a strong medal chance in the hop, step and jump in Berlin when at the NSW Championships in December 1935 he set a new world record of 51ft 9½in (15.78m), beating the existing world record by 6cm. Pushing Metcalfe all the way was the gallant Dickinson, who broke the previous Australian record by nearly 30cm when he notched 51ft 2⅜in (15.62m). *The Referee* hailed the friends' display as 'hop, step and jumping of a brilliance never before seen in Australia . . . Both Metcalfe and Dickinson are capable of winning this event at the Berlin Olympics.' Though disappointed and somewhat shaken that his personal best, and what after all had been the fourth-longest hop, step and jump in athletic history, was only good enough for second place, Dickinson embraced Metcalfe and congratulated him heartily at the event's end. Nick Winter, who had won hop, step and jump gold at the 1924 Paris Olympics, remarked that apart from Metcalfe's magnificent jump, the most pleasing feature of the event was Dickinson's 'ability to rise to the occasion, which is a great asset'.

Barring accident, Metcalfe and Dickinson were on track to go head to head with the Japanese champions Chuhei Nambu and Kenkichi Oshima in Berlin. The hop, step and jump world record looked certain to fall as those competitors would bring out the best in each other. Wrote one excited pundit: 'You'd better lengthen that pit, Mr Hitler!'

On the other side of Australia, Perth Girls School swimmer Evelyn de Lacy was timing her Olympic campaign to perfection. Regularly winning over long or short distances, swimming freestyle and backstroke in the tidal pools of the Swan River and in open water, de Lacy set new Western Australian records in the 100yd and 220yd freestyle at the state championships in December 1933. Under the coaching of prickly taskmaster J.P. Sheedy, de Lacy and fourteen-year-old swimming prodigy Percy Oliver represented Western Australia at state championships in Melbourne, Sydney and Brisbane in January 1934. So impoverished was the WA Swimming Association that had de Lacy and Oliver not been young enough to travel for half fare, they would not have been able to make the trip. The 150 pounds the association did pay all but exhausted its bank account. After de Lacy broke national records in her races, all Australia knew that the tall, slim, freckle-faced redhead with the cheeky smile and graceful style was a swimmer right out of the box. De Lacy's defeat of the British champion Joyce Cooper in the 100yd freestyle in Melbourne was national front-page news. She returned home a celebrity.

There to meet her at Perth railway station were her mother, father and ten siblings, good swimmers all, and a mob of journalists. A reporter for *The West Australian* described how de Lacy, 'a big kid', had disembarked 'hatless and bagless', having left her belongings under the pillow in her Kalgoorlie motel en route. She was 'quite unconcerned as to her appearance when being besieged by cameramen. Whether or not her hair is tidy or her nose powdered doesn't worry her in the least. She is a happy-go-lucky natural schoolgirl, full of enthusiasm and without a trace of false conceit. "I would give anything to go to the Olympic Games in 1936, and the people in the eastern states were talking a lot about Percy's and my chances of going if we keep on improving. We are going to work hard, naturally."' De Lacy's win by a touch over Joyce Cooper had topped off a 'bonzer' time in the east. 'The premier of West Australia was there,' she exulted, 'and I'll never forget how excited he was, especially as Percy won the junior championships . . . He seemed awfully proud of us. He even promised to see that Perth had the best indoor swimming pool in Australia to commemorate the occasion. I hope he keeps his promise!'

In November 1934, de Lacy's fame saw her appear in an advertisement for Sekem swimsuits (for no fee, as payment would have violated her amateur status). Beneath a photograph of the swimmer demurely disporting herself in her Sekem at the beach, the blurb read: 'Miss Evelyn de Lacy . . . wears and recommends a Sekem Swim Suit. "My Sekem beats them all," she declared delightedly. "I've worn other swim suits, but for style, cut and sheer comfort, they can't compare with my Sekem! It has individuality . . . It's thoroughly serviceable . . . It's perfect in every way!" Sekem Swim Suits are West Australian made from the highest grade wool. Ask to be shown the Sekem range at any good store. You'll like their style!'

In a portent of the modern media's obsession with the minutiae of sports stars' private lives, *The Australian Women's Weekly* in 1935 breathlessly revealed that the secret to de Lacy's success was . . . onions. They were her 'favourite delicacy . . . the biggest she can get'. And if that wasn't too much information, readers also learned that she went to bed each night at nine and that when she was swimming interstate, her family and neighbours all clustered around the radio in the lounge room to cheer her on. Her mother told how in her most recent race the group 'went mad. I think we nearly went through the wireless cabinet when she came first!'

When Western Australia's other young champion, Percival Cale Oliver, came to public notice in 1933, he was just fourteen and a student at Perth's prestigious Hale School. The slim, handsome boy was from a sporting family prominent in swimming, sailing and Australian Rules. Oliver was coached by his older sister, Dorothea, who taught him to maintain focus and intensity while

swimming in the often icy and rough Swan River at the Claremont and Crawley baths. Oliver was diligent, and a self-starter.
After his father bought him a sailing boat and told him, 'Here,
it's yours, what you do with it is up to you,' he taught himself to
sail. It was the same with swimming. Once Oliver decided that
he wanted to swim well, he single-mindedly became a champion.
After Dorothea had imparted the basics of backstroke and freestyle
racing, J.P. Sheedy refined Oliver's technique and ordered him to
cease calisthenics, football and athletics because they would dilute
his concentration and develop muscles in places not conducive to
swimming. Oliver reluctantly complied.

On seeing him win with ease the Western Australian 100yd
junior freestyle championship in December 1933, Europe's finest
middle-distance swimmer, Jean Taris of France, praised Oliver's
effortless style and declared, 'That boy might well become a world
champion. He is a swimmer of outstanding quality.' In 1934, 'the
Perth Boy Wonder' won the Australian junior 100yd backstroke
and freestyle titles.

Oliver constantly sought improvement. The genesis of his
bilateral breathing when he swam freestyle was a cricked neck he
suffered when craning to see out of the window on the endless
train trip across the Nullarbor to compete in Sydney. So stiff was
his neck when he trained at Manly baths that he had to learn to
breathe on his less-preferred side. Once he was able to breathe
comfortably on both sides, his times improved.

While still a junior, Oliver boldly entered himself in the senior
backstroke event at one meet and dead-heated with the Australian
champion. 'It took a while for the judges to realise,' he would
chuckle years later, 'because I was so small and in all the clamour
no one saw me touch the wall at the same time as Withers.' Soon
after this he decided to concentrate on backstroke, believing this
would give him his best chance of success if selected for the Berlin

Olympics. In January 1935, aged fifteen, Oliver was narrowly beaten in the senior 100yd backstroke championship of Australia by the Japanese champion Masaji Kiyokawa, who had won the gold medal in the 100m backstroke at the 1932 Los Angeles Games.

The sixteen-year-old schoolboy fulfilled his tremendous promise in February 1936 when, at the Australian Championships in Perth, he won the senior 110yd backstroke in 1 minute, 12.4 seconds, just a fifth of a second outside the Australian record. Olympic selectors took note.

Born in 1911, Dick Garrard was a fire hydrant of a man; 1.5m tall and 66kg, strong-jawed, crinkly haired and pug-nosed, he looked every bit the wrestler he was, though at a pinch he could have passed as a movie gangster. His wrestling career began in his teens, rumbling with mates on the sands of Mordialloc Beach, south of Melbourne, where he was a lifesaver with numerous rescues to his credit. Towards the end of his life, Garrard said: 'Mordialloc Beach, that's where I started, and I found out I could handle a few fellows, and I thought, "Oh, I'd like to learn wrestling," so in 1925 I went to a gymnasium in Melbourne called Weber & Rice [for training] and from there I went to the Railways Institute because that's where most of the wrestlers in Victoria practised.'

Garrard was an aggressive and versatile grappler, as adept at scrapping as wrestling scientifically. Though a lightweight, he happily took on and beat welter- and heavyweights. He lost just five of his first 72 lightweight bouts, and then won 59 in succession. He claimed the Australian Championship in 1930 (he would win the Victorian and Australian championships every year from 1930 to 1956, save for when he was competing overseas) and then the gold medal in the lightweight division at the 1934 London

Empire Games. Garrard's easy self-confidence gave him an air of authority. He was a man of principle to whom others gravitated. Berlin 1936 would be the first of his three Olympic Games.

Tall, slim and toothy, Doris Carter was Australia's finest female high jumper of the early to mid-1930s. She was self-taught, jumping repeatedly over a makeshift bar in her backyard in Melbourne, where she was born in 1912. Carter's resolve to jump ever higher was matched by her questing intelligence which would see her achieve so much in her long life. While employed as a school teacher at Melville Forest in south-western Victoria, she drove a 560km round trip to Melbourne track and field events in her old jalopy. After being transferred to a school in Melbourne, she was able to conserve her energy and concentration for jumping, rather than staying awake, changing tyres and avoiding collisions with kangaroos on her long country treks.

Carter held the Victorian and Australian high-jump titles throughout the 1930s, the only Australian woman of her day to regularly better 5ft (1.52m). She was also one of Australia's best hurdlers and discus throwers, at one time holding the national record in the latter.

As the 1936 Olympics drew closer, Carter's form peaked. In February 1936 she jumped a personal best of 5ft 3in (1.62m), bettering her previous Australian record of 5ft 2in (1.57m), and giving her hope that in Berlin, should she be selected, she might match the strapping American high jumpers who were clearing 5ft 4½in (1.65m).

In the lead-up to Berlin, track and field aficionados often name-checked US runners John Woodruff and Chuck Hornbostel,

Kazimierz Kucharski of Poland and Italian Mario Lanzi as likely medal winners in the 800m, and in the 1500m the American Glenn Cunningham, Englishman Jerry Cornes and, just perhaps, New Zealander Jack Lovelock. Australia's Gerald Ian D'Acres Backhouse rarely entered calculations. Those close to the diminutive, whippet-slim and sandy-haired Backhouse, however—aware of his strength of character, his self-belief and ability to run long distances effortlessly and at speed while merrily waging psychological warfare on opponents—knew better than to write him off. Backhouse, who was born in Terang, Victoria, in 1912, ran for St Stephen's Harriers at Mount Waverley, specialising in the half-mile and the mile. From late 1935 on, no runner challenged him in state and national meets. He spoke of the pleasure he derived from 'annihilating distance'. To Backhouse, running was fun, always fun. 'I run because I enjoy it.'

Even as a child, Backhouse ran and ran. He regularly arrived home long past dinner time and explained to his parents that he'd been playing 'chasey' with pals in games that took the tireless youngsters kilometres from home. No schoolmate ever outran Backhouse. Yet because he was bored by training he didn't involve himself in organised athletics early on, and made no mark in primary school running. It was not until he attended Geelong Grammar School that he began to compete seriously in cross-country events. Even then, he only did as much as was necessary, and no more, on the training track. Where he placed was unimportant to him; all that mattered was legging it at speed over the fields and streets. His first win did not come until his final term at Geelong when, substituting for the Geelong Grammar champion who had withdrawn at the last minute, he came from last place to win the Associated Public Schools mile championship. Backhouse was never able to explain how he went from an also-ran to a champion in a single race. Later, nearing the end of his short and remarkable life, he said that the applause as he crossed the finish line that day was the sweetest he ever received.

After school, in 1931, Backhouse competed for the Harriers with varying success. In 1934, he ran in the club's relay from Adelaide to Melbourne. His fellow runners found him a self-confident young man who was a friendly companion on the road, full of stories and keen to relax over a beer. He played his harmonica to relieve the tedium. When the urge took him, Backhouse would simply limber up and run down any road that took his fancy, stopping after perhaps 30km or more, turning around and running home again. When not burning up the highways of Victoria, Backhouse rode long distances on his 40-year-old bicycle. He once cycled 380km on a single pedal after the other fell off. He also had an unusually high pain threshold. His body never hurt after a gruelling run, and at one stage in the early 1930s, he ran for weeks with a searing ache in his toe, which was later revealed to be a large splinter embedded under his toenail.

On the opening day of the Victorian 1934–35 track season, the 21-year-old broke the benchmark 4 minutes, 30 seconds for the mile, far and away a personal best time. In Australia from then on he was virtually unbeatable.

By early 1936, Backhouse's victories and his idiosyncrasies had made him a sporting name. *The Argus* profiled him in a feature headed 'Unorthodox Methods of Gerald Backhouse—Australian Record Breaker's Rise to Fame'. Sports scribe H.O. Balfe wrote that there was no amateur runner in the land quite like Backhouse: 'If you went through the list of first class amateur runners in Australia, you would not find one more unorthodox in his methods of training than Gerald Backhouse.' Balfe made much of Backhouse's disinclination to train. Backhouse had told him, 'If I make my track work too hard, I get mentally stale and when I am in that condition it is impossible for me to be physically fit.

Therefore I do not allow my training to become drudgery . . . In the fortnight [before an event] I may not do more than jog a quarter of a mile or do a few sharp bursts. I know that some people question my methods, but they suit me and there is no reason why I should change them.' Balfe wrote of Backhouse's steely attitude in races. He cited how repeatedly opponents had 'clung to him to within 50 yards of the tape, and then he has gone ahead with a tremendous burst of speed and left them standing'.

Backhouse was religious, and a forceful preacher when invited to expound on his favourite topic, 'Muscular Christianity'.

Patricia 'Pat' Norton's stellar swimming career really began not in a pool, but on an isolated NSW country road in 1917, two years before she was born, when a young nurse named Bertha Turnbull found herself in a perilous situation. A boy had fallen desperately ill and Turnbull was assigned to collect him at his parents' property and drive him 80km over treacherous potholed tracks back to the hospital where he would undergo an emergency operation to save his life. To protect the patient from being jerked and jolted en route, Turnbull cradled him in her lap as she steered so her legs and knees absorbed the bumps. The hospital was reached safely, the boy survived, and Bertha Turnbull was hailed as a hero. The following year, she married a jeweller named Cecil Norton. Their daughter Patricia was born on 20 March 1919. Serendipitously, Pat Norton later made contact with the lad whom her mother had saved back in 1917. His name was Harry 'Salty' Nightingale and he was a lifesaver at Bondi Beach.

Nightingale felt that the least he could do was teach young Pat Norton to swim. And that wasn't the only blessing bestowed upon her by the Nightingale family. When her parents' marriage foundered, they became her surrogate family while she attended boarding school. She moved into their home, which was close enough to the beach to hear the waves break onto Bondi's silky sand.

In 1930, Pat Norton attended Sydney Girls High and joined Bondi Ladies Amateur Swimming Club. It was there, under the expert tutelage of the dashing Salty Nightingale, that she became one of the finest young freestyle, backstroke and medley swimmers in Australia. A brave performance, which earned her a second place in a 100yd freestyle race against the formidable Briton Joyce Cooper, confirmed Norton's credentials as a promising Olympic contender.

Norton was tiny, with wild russet hair haloing her face. She was a charming and intelligent young woman who did not let a speech impediment caused by a cleft palate dampen her sunny nature. Her heart, say those who knew her, was huge, and during her life many would benefit from her compassion. This generosity of spirit would make the tragedies that dogged her seem even more unfair.

Four decades after the Berlin Olympics, Nightingale, who was one of the few swimming coaches in Australia at the time, reminisced about Norton. Although his stable of swimmers had included 1938 Empire Games swimmers Margaret Dovey (the future Margaret Whitlam) and Russ Bassingthwaite, Pat was 'my best swimmer . . . She was only a slip of a girl. She never had a preparation like the girls have today. In the mid-30s we never dreamed of training eight or nine miles a day . . . the parents would have been down on us with shotguns if we'd suggested it.'

Nightingale, as coach and mentor, would become an integral part of the Australian team in Berlin. In his youth, he was a fan of the American swimming champions Johnny Weissmuller and Buster Crabbe. 'He swam like Weissmuller,' says Nightingale's son, Harry junior. 'If you watch film of Weissmuller you'll see he swims with his head up, like a surf swimmer. When you swim in the surf, if you put your head down you get a gobful of water.

'My father was a king at Bondi,' says his son. 'All he cared about was doing the job and looking after the people. He'd say, "Don't rest on your laurels. You've never done enough. Don't shine yourself, keep working and living hard." He was a real people's person. You won't find many people with a bad word to say about my dad—except maybe a couple of guys who lost girlfriends to him . . . he was a handsome bloke.'

By early 1936, Norton, just sixteen, was national freestyle and backstroke champion, and held the Australian backstroke record. At the end of the February National Games in Adelaide, a glorified selection trial for Berlin, she swam two celebratory laps of the pool: one freestyle and one backstroke, each to rapturous applause.

The Australian Women's Weekly followed up the event with a photo essay on the promising young swimmer: Norton performing calisthenics, Norton eating breakfast, Norton pounding away on a typewriter, Norton giving advice to a young swimmer floating amid chunks of ice in the Bondi Icebergs pool, Norton posing in her racing costume at Bondi. The caption read: 'Pat Norton, Australia's swimming marvel . . . The five special studies above . . . give interesting glimpses of the simple daily life of our Olympic hope . . . Collecting mascots is her chief hobby. Her ability to make new records on nearly every occasion she enters Australian and state championships is earning her the sobriquet of "The Girl Who Makes Records".'

Bertha Norton subsequently held a press conference to assure reporters that success had not gone to her daughter's head—not that anyone had suggested that it had—and that despite her achievements in the pool she remained unspoiled. Part of the reason for this, asserted Bertha, was that she kept Pat on a tight rein, making sure that her swimming did not exhaust her. Bertha made Pat sleep at least eight hours a night and forbade her to swim in the surf, as doing so might alter her racing stroke. Nor was her daughter allowed to ride horses in the swimming season in case she fell and was hurt. Playing and listening to music, she offered, was okay all year round. 'I get far more excited when Pat is racing than she does,' said Bertha. 'Pat is, fortunately, of a very calm disposition and never gets flustered or worried. She takes her successes and defeats in the same philosophical manner. One of the few occasions on which I have seen her excited was when, at a picture show, a newsreel was shown which included her most recent race!'

So certain did Norton's selection in the Australian team seem that long before the squad was named, the logistics of her trip to Berlin were already being publicly discussed. Her mother claimed that she could not afford to accompany her daughter to Berlin, and spoke of her 'deep concern' about whether the seventeen-year-old would need an official chaperone and if so, whether the Olympic Federation would pay for one or take the cheap option and leave her at home. (Days later, although Bertha had said she was too poor to travel to Berlin, she hightailed it to South Africa, claiming the trip was a business opportunity too good to turn down, although according to Basil Dickinson, she had fallen in love with a professional wrestler and followed him to Johannesburg.)

Once more, Nightingale stepped into the breach. He assured the Norton family and the Olympic selectors that he had saved enough money to go to Berlin to coach and watch over his protégée. Bertha Norton was placated. 'Harry will go if Pat is selected . . . With him I am sure Pat would be happy and well cared for.'

Norton's greatest Australian rival—and good friend—was Kitty Mackay, also of Bondi Ladies Amateur Swimming Club. Several years older than Norton, Mackay was born in Melbourne in 1915. Their first race was recorded in *The Referee* on 13 April 1932, under the heading 'Amazing Bondi Mermaid'. It went on: 'Bondi Ladies

Club has unearthed an amazing infant in Patricia Norton, aged 12 [*sic*]. A few weeks ago, Pat was narrowly beaten by the Amazonian Ethel "Kitty" Mackay in the Bondi Club's 100 yards championship in 69 and ⅗ seconds.' 'Amazonian' was an ungracious description, but the beautiful Mackay *was* 182cm tall, statuesque and taut-muscled. She burst into prominence in 1934 when she became the NSW 220yd freestyle champion.

British swim star Joyce Cooper heaped praise on Mackay as well as Norton and de Lacy during one of her Australian swimming campaigns. 'I am astonished at the number of young Australian swimmers who are verging on championship status,' she said. 'In proportion to population and membership of swimming clubs, Australia must have the largest number of first-class swimmers in the world. Australian women generally are definitely ahead of British women swimmers, particularly over sprint distances.' The key factors in becoming a champion, Cooper said, were 'determination, and encouragement from one's family . . . The family is probably the most important factor of all. If it is too keen it can spoil a swimmer by making her too anxious and nerve-wrought, but if it is enthusiastic and encouraging in defeat it can get you a long way.' Mackay's and de Lacy's families fitted the bill, and for Norton the Nightingales gave her all the support she required.

Believing that it would rest her physically and mentally, and so improve her chances of Olympic selection the following year, Mackay withdrew from all but club swimming meets in 1935. When she returned to competition in January 1936, her decision to take a break seemed sound when she defeated Norton in a down-to-the-wire NSW ladies 100yd freestyle championship, and in so doing set a new Australian record. In his report of the race, the correspondent 'Waterman' did not try to conceal his excitement: 'The two outstanding girls provided a large gathering of swimming followers with a thrilling race, the result of which was not certain until the judges had given their verdict. They drew lanes side by side and got away nicely. It was at once apparent that they were in a class of their own.' They battled stroke for stroke up to within three body lengths of the 50yd turn, when Norton spurted and touched in front. Mackay regained the lead in the home stretch, but 'five yards from the finish a remarkable dash was brought to light by Miss Norton, and the two girls touched the finishing board practically together. Hushed silence awaited the judges' decision, and when Miss Mackay was given the verdict in the NSW record time of 63 seconds, the applause was deafening.'

Norton turned the tables at a meet in Adelaide the following month. Then Mackay struck back in the National Championships at Perth's Crawley Baths when, with de Lacy pushing her hard, she won the 100yd freestyle, and then the 110yd backstroke. Both wins set new Australian records. Mackay could have made no stronger claim for Olympic selection.

Bill Kendall's swimming career began in 1926 when he was a ten-year-old student at Sydney Grammar prep school at Edgecliff, in Sydney's east. The headmistress had promised an ice-cream to any boy willing to represent the school in the annual swimming carnival, and although Kendall had never swum in a race before, his mother had been teaching him to swim, so he raised his hand. He won his race at the carnival. Kendall's father, Jim, put Bill in the care of Harry Hay, who had coached many young champions and would lend a hand to Nightingale in his role as unofficial coach of the Australian swimmers at the Berlin Olympics ten years later. After Hay had taught the youngster the basics of competitive swimming, Jim Kendall took over as his son's coach, with, recalled Kendall in 1990, the help of 'a book of Johnny Weissmuller's about swimming, and I did the best I could to follow his style. We were very amateurish!' Australian swimming, it seems, owed much to the Romanian-born American swimming legend Weissmuller. When Kendall and his family were in the United States in 1928, he would recall, 'I was lucky enough to meet Weissmuller and have two days with him at the Chicago Athletic Club.' Kendall's daughter Brooke Ryan has in her safekeeping a photograph of the Olympic champion and future movie star on which he wrote, 'To Billy, I hope you'll be a world champion one day. Best wishes, Johnny Weissmuller.' An inspired Kendall returned to Australia and eventually won the NSW and then the Australian 100yd free-style championships.

'If my father hadn't fallen out of a tree and broken his right elbow when he was eight,' says John Wood, son of four-time Olympian Merv Wood, 'he may never have become a rower.' Nor won three Olympic medals (even though World War II robbed him of the chance to compete in 1940 and 1944) and five Empire Games/Commonwealth Games medals (four of them gold), two Diamond Sculls, a Philadelphia Cup and twelve national championships. Nor carried the flag at two Olympic Games, an honour awarded to no other Australian athlete. Wood himself wrote in his unpublished memoir about the injury and how it shaped his rowing career: 'I've had an Achilles heel all my life . . . I was climbing a tree as a little boy in Randwick, a dead tree, or part of it was dead, and it snapped off and I fell to the ground with my right arm underneath my body. I fractured my right elbow to such an extent that I had no usage of it for some six months, and over the next three or four years constantly attended the hospital in an effort to get it right. Doctors wanted to wire my arm when I was about 11, but my father [Tom, a miner-turned-police sergeant] said, "No, you won't touch his arm," and he had me carrying buckets of water around the yard to strengthen my arm.' The elbow fracture led to the withering of Wood's forearm, and nerve damage impaired the tendons in two fingers. On rough sculling days when he needed to grip his oars tightly, he rowed with his forearm strapped, in tremendous pain. 'I always thought it was the determination to offset this arm trouble that probably gave me the will to do better than I would have, had I been, shall I say, fully fit.'

Tom Wood's unconventional remedy worked. With his arm mended, his son became a rugby player, swimmer and, at age fourteen, a rower, distinguishing himself in all three sports at Sydney Boys High School.

Following his father into the police force when he matriculated aged seventeen in 1934, Wood quit rugby and swimming and devoted himself to rowing. He was invited to join the crack NSW Police rowing club senior eight, as sweep oarsman in seat five. Wood was by some margin the eight's youngest member—most of the other men in the boat were in their mid-twenties—but despite smoking a pipe from age sixteen he more than matched them in strength and stamina. John Wood says that Merv was a born rower, naturally physically and mentally hard. He believes his father 'got his steel from *his* father, who was a real tough old bird. Rowing is one of the most demanding sports.'

Even as a teenager, Wood, who would rise to be NSW police commissioner, displayed the personal idiosyncrasies for which he would be known all his life. In addition to his incessant pipe smoking, he puffed on cigars or cigarettes he rolled himself. No vitamin pills for him; he swore by the strength-giving qualities of molasses, which he scooped from the tin with a dessert spoon. The cakes and sweets he devoured never added weight to his lean frame. He found enjoyment in fishing off the rocks near his home. He always had his hair cut by the same barber, Chipper Young, whose shop was around the corner from the Woods' modest bungalow in

Perouse Road, Randwick. As an athlete and as a policeman, he was a taciturn man, never confiding his feelings to a soul and always keeping his emotions in tight check.

Instead of selecting the best eight rowers in their position from all the competing Australian clubs, the Berlin Olympic squad would comprise the whole crew of eight which was the most successful team over the season. The police crew, wrote Wood, 'was building up so that it could be selected to compete at the Games in 1936'. The eight won race after race, culminating in a victory at the Victorian Henley, which put the policemen in the box seat to be chosen for the Olympics.

Although Australia's 1936 Olympians came from many different walks of life, it would be safe to say that no other had the no-holds-barred background of Wal Mackney, Wood's teammate in the NSW Police rowing eight. 'My father was not of your usual rowing class,' says Wal's son Kim, who himself represented Australia in the men's coxless pairs at the 1972 Munich Olympics. 'Most of the guys who were selected in the eight for Berlin, though policemen, were GPS boys. My old man, on the other hand, was a rough character who had only two years of education, and that was at a tiny public school near Bellingen in northern New South Wales. Dad wasn't dumb, far from it, he just didn't have the opportunities, like many people then.' Wal Mackney's own father fought in World War I, and while he was away, Wal, little more than a child, ran the family farm. 'When my grandfather came home,' says Kim, 'he wanted to manage the farm as before, but my father now regarded the farm as his own. There was a big bust-up, and Dad was out the door.'

Mackney, born in 1905, was thirteen when he found work with his uncle, a bullock driver pulling timber out of Dorrigo. He was so small that to yoke his oxen he had to stand on a kerosene drum.

After that he was employed cutting railway sleepers out of hard wood with a broad axe. He always said this was the most difficult work he ever did. His next job, as a canecutter in north Queensland, couldn't have been much easier. The years of backbreaking toil hardened him, and the muscular 185cm, 82kg Mackney had become, says his son, 'a tough, hard man'.

Mackney's idea of fun was 'to get full of grog and go out street fighting with his canecutter mates. He proved to be ultra-good at brawling,' says Kim. When the circus came to town, Mackney would hasten to the boxing tent, challenge the best-credentialed fighter in the troupe, whom he'd usually knock out in the first round, and then collect his prize money. In the late 1920s, Mackney chanced his arm in the big smoke, and in Sydney he engaged in winner-take-all street fights, as well as sanctioned amateur boxing matches. In the semifinal of one heavyweight tournament, he was knocked out by a young Frank Packer, who outweighed Mackney by 35kg. Mackney later joined the police force, and its rowing team; although never a technically adept stroke, his enormous strength, natural stamina and never-quit attitude made him a valued member of the NSW Police eight. He also played rugby union for Northern Suburbs; a ferocious, relentlessly tackling breakaway and lock, he even made four appearances for the Wallabies, including a test against South Africa in Cape Town in 1933. By then, rugby and fighting had gifted him a broken nose and a magnificent set of cauliflower ears.

So full of promise was young pole vaulter Fred Woodhouse that sometimes when he competed, a banner was strung up outside the sportsground that read: 'Fred Woodhouse: Wizard of the Air Attacking the Australian Pole Vault Record of 12ft 5½ Inches [3.79m]! Seeing is Believing, Woodhouse is our next Olympic Hope!'

As a young teenager in the 1920s, Woodhouse was a promising gymnast, high jumper and diver until he saw Australian champion Max Kroger pole vault and was entranced by the sport. His furniture-dealer father took him to Sassafras where he cut a sapling to craft a makeshift vaulting pole, which Woodhouse used to teach himself vaulting in the backyard of their home in Essendon, Victoria. Soon afterwards, he paid four shillings and sixpence for a book called *How to Pole Vault*, and set about copying the style of the jumpers in the illustrations. He would later recount, 'I'd say, "Dad, look at the picture. Am I doing it right?" and he'd say, "No, you're doing it all wrong." Well I practised and practised and changed my grip from the "hand apart" grip to the "slip up" grip where the bottom hand rises to meet the top when the pole is used, and I got progressively better.'

Then, an epiphany: down at the local river watching kids swinging out over the water on a rope tied to a tree branch, Woodhouse noted similarities between what the children were doing and the sport he had come to believe was an art form. 'I saw that with the correct release of the rope they'd fly out further, and I worked on transferring that horizontal swing into a vertical swing.' Woodhouse's interest in pole vaulting became an obsession. 'I would wake at night and think about how I had vaulted that day and say, "My word, if I'd done so-and-so I'd have jumped higher," so I'd get out of bed and draw little stick sketches . . . and next day I'd take my sapling and execute them. I was always experimenting and striving to improve. Every year I increased the height I was able to jump (in 1938, I cleared 13ft 6in [4.1m] which would have got me into an Olympic final in those years). I won four Australian titles and qualified for the Empire Games in 1934 and 1938 and won the bronze medal in '34.' The Wizard of the Air was set to soar in Berlin.

■　■　■

The Australian team would be announced on 13 March 1936, after lengthy and rancorous debate, but one selection that all members of the Australian Olympic Federation agreed on was that of the flag-bearer at the Opening Ceremony, to be held at Berlin's Reich Sports Field on 1 August.

Ideally and traditionally, the flag-bearer was an athlete in peak form, someone who had performed with distinction at a past Olympic Games, who was respected by officials, teammates and the public, and who could be relied on to be a good sport and a worthy ambassador for Australia. Edgar 'Dunc' Gray had made it known after he won gold medals in the 1000m time trial at both the 1932 Los Angeles Olympics and the Empire Games in London in 1934 that if he qualified for Berlin he would consider it an enormous honour to carry the flag. Once his selection for the Olympic team was formalised, this wish was granted. Gray had the blessing of former Olympian Reg Baker, who enthused, 'Gray is a paragon, is this country rider. He does not drink, he does not smoke, he's a good churchman. He is well spoken. Things intellectual and communal have a deep interest for him and he is very much a man's man.'

When a lad, Gray had piped up to his mother that one day he would cycle in an Olympic Games, and she laughed and said, 'A man's got more chance of flying to the moon!' And of course both things came to pass.

Born in 1906, in Goulburn, New South Wales, Gray was another child who gave no early indication of the champion he would become. He later told Harry Gordon, 'When I started off as a junior I didn't do too well. The first race I ever won was at Goulburn High School and it was the slow bike race . . . that was a race [in which] the winner is the last to cross the finish line!' When Gray began racing, his peculiar sprawled riding style, in which he seemed to slouch in the saddle and drape himself over the handlebars, counted against him, and it was not until he rectified that and began riding in a conventional racing manner that his times improved. 'I got the shock of my life when I started to do alright . . .' Gray contested the Australian championships in 1928, and his form in the 1000m sprint and the 1000m time trial saw him selected in Australia's 1928 Olympic team. At those Amsterdam Games he won a bronze medal in the 1000m time trial.

Gray improved on that in 1932 in Los Angeles when he won gold in the 1000m time trial. He was fortunate to even make it onto the track, having been stricken with a high fever soon after arriving. 'I was hallucinating, seeing snakes and devils, and I lost weight,' he recalled. His recovery was aided by hot lemon drinks generously spiked with brandy acquired by resourceful team manager Jim Eve, quite a feat in Prohibition-era America. The Los Angeles Olympics was the first to house athletes together on site, and Gray remembered cruising around the Olympic Village on his bike, and seeing 'cowboys' on horseback patrolling to prevent the public getting in.

Gray was often asked how he came to be called Dunc when he had been christened Edgar Laurence: 'I was twelve or thirteen, we lived at Kingsdale . . . Everybody had a nickname and one bloke said to me, "I think I'll call you Dunny-Can . . . that's the name for you." So Dunny-Can was condensed to Dunc and the name stuck.'

Gray was an outspoken man who said exactly what he thought when he thought it and who cared nothing for the consequences. In Berlin, his vociferous criticism of Adolf Hitler and his Nazis would unsettle teammates.

CHAPTER 4
DARKNESS DESCENDING

To the alarm of most of the world, Germany had become a different, darker place since the heady day in 1931 when Berlin was awarded the Games of the XIth Olympiad.

On 30 January 1933, just days after the inaugural meeting of the Olympic Organising Committee at Berlin Town Hall, President Hindenburg, who was desperate to keep the ambitious and increasingly popular National Socialist leader Adolf Hitler under his control, made the fateful mistake of appointing him chancellor of Germany, a powerful political role but one that was traditionally subservient to that of the president. Tradition meant nothing to Hitler. As the ailing Hindenburg looked on horrified and helpless, Hitler trampled the German constitution. First, he ordered the police and army, which fell under his aegis, to terrorise and so neuter his political opponents. Jews would also be targeted. This was Hitler's first step towards realising his obsession of expelling from Germany any race—particularly Jews—that did not fit his Aryan ideal, and rearming the Wehrmacht (the combined armed forces) to achieve lebensraum ('living space'): snatching territory in which the German population could grow, in Poland, Czechoslovakia, Russia and Austria. Avenging the punishment meted out by signatories to the humiliating Treaty of Versailles—Jews and the French especially—was also high on his agenda.

In February 1933, a fire destroyed the chamber of deputies in the Reichstag, Germany's seat of parliament in central Berlin. When police arrested Marinus van der Lubbe, a Dutch communist and convicted arsonist, Hitler took the opportunity to assert that the Dutchman had been acting under the orders of his communist masters who were bent on snatching power. Hitler browbeat Hindenburg into suspending civil liberties so that Hitler could quell the communist 'insurrection'. Then he rammed through parliament a raft of legislation that gave him control over the executive and legislative branches of government, meaning that he was no longer answerable to the president or parliament and could arrest and jail citizens without explanation. Hitler now had unprecedented power to do exactly as he pleased. And that was to escalate his persecution of 'enemies of the state'—anybody not Aryan or a National Socialist.

Although Hitler was still sufficiently intimidated by Hindenburg not yet to dare proclaim himself Führer, by April 1933 he was dictator of Germany in all except title. Under his command were Prime Minister and Interior Minister for Prussia Hermann Göring, and the police force, under the control of the Reich Minister of the Interior Wilhelm Frick, and the Nazis' own elite guard, the black-shirted SS (Schutzstaffel) and the brown-shirted SA (Sturmabteilungen).

Hitler's opponents were terrorised, disenfranchised and dispersed. In defiance of the Treaty of Versailles, Hitler ordered a stop to all reparation payments and made plans, which he fulfilled the following year, to withdraw from the League of Nations. By July 1933, the National Socialist Party was the only legal political party in Germany. 'We enter the Reichstag,' noted Dr Joseph Goebbels, Hitler's confidant and Reich Minister of Propaganda and Enlightenment, 'like wolves into the sheep pen.'

Hitler ended free speech and freedom of assembly. His head-cracking storm troopers ran wild on the streets. Jews were discriminated against in every area of life. For the purposes of definition, a Jew was someone with one or more Jewish grandparents, although the Nazis force-fitted the definition to whomsoever they chose. Hitler ordered 'loyal' Germans to ostracise Jewish people, boycott their businesses, and exclude them from clubs and associations. Some Jews were murdered, and many more received savage beatings, or were imprisoned in the detention camps that were sprouting up all over Germany, administered by the secret state police, the Gestapo. (The compounds would later be run solely by the SS and be known as concentration camps.)

Harassed along with Jews and those ideologically opposed to the regime were writers, filmmakers and artists who refused Goebbels' demand that they use their talent in the service of National Socialism. Many of these creative people fled to Britain or the United States.

Hitler now brazenly escalated the manufacture and purchase of planes, tanks, warships and weapons, and troops were openly trained. The chancellor also suppressed his own paramilitary groups that he considered a potential threat, notably the SA, led by Hitler's old friend the sabre-scarred Ernst Röhm, who had been at his side in 1923 at the Beer Hall Putsch. On the so-called Night of the Long Knives, from 30 June to 2 July 1934, SA leaders and foot soldiers were arrested—Röhm reportedly by Hitler himself—and up to 200 of them, including Röhm, were shot. The declawed SA now did Hitler's bidding as a civil goon squad, typically smashing the windows of shops run by Jews and daubing crude anti-Semitic caricatures and slogans on walls.

On 1 August 1934, with President Hindenburg on his deathbed, Hitler abolished the office of president and merged its responsibilities and powers, including supreme command of the armed forces, with those of chancellor. He was now, in actuality and name, Führer of Germany.

The 1935 Nuremberg Rally of the Nazi party was staged in the beautiful medieval city that was one of Nazism's spiritual capitals. The rally, an orgy of swastika-festooned torch-lit parades, military pomp and spittle-spraying harangues by Hitler, Göring, Goebbels and SS chief Heinrich Himmler, was filmed by the Nazis' film-maker of choice, the brilliant Leni Riefenstahl, who would also, beautifully and chillingly, chronicle the Berlin Olympics.

The first item on the agenda at Nuremberg was to sanction a new German flag: the existing standard—comprising horizontal black, red and gold bars—was replaced by a black swastika in a white circle on a blood-red background. Hitler then formalised the persecution of non-Aryans. The Reich Citizenship Law ordained that anyone not of 'German or kindred blood' was now an inferior 'state subject' and, as such, was forbidden to vote and liable to have their property and bank accounts seized by the state. The Law for the Protection of German Blood and German Honour outlawed the marriage of Jews and non-Jews and nullified any such existing marriages. It banned extramarital sex between Jews and non-Jews. Jews could not employ non-Jewish women under 45 in their homes, and—hard as it may be to believe that they would want to—Jews were forbidden to fly the new national flag.

The Nuremberg Laws drove Jews out of German society. They prevented Jews from being employed in the civil service or as lawyers, doctors, journalists, teachers or business leaders, from attending school after the age of fourteen or from being treated in state hospitals. Jews could not claim state-run lottery winnings: the money was funnelled into Nazi coffers. Jewish names were chiselled off war memorials. Jews' passports, which were now stamped with a large 'J,' entitled them to leave but not re-enter Germany. Jews were barred from libraries, beaches, swimming pools and public parks.

Jews could not compete in any form of organised athletic activity or belong to a sporting club, which of course made Olympic selection impossible. The Olympic dreams of a host of well-credentialed German Jewish athletes were dashed. Some of these were medal hopefuls, such as middle- and light-heavyweight amateur boxing champion Erich Seelig, sprinter Werner Schattman, middle-distance runner Franz Orgler and the high jumper Gretel Bergmann. As far as is known, the only person of Jewish extraction to represent Germany at the Berlin Olympics was individual fencer Helene Mayer, for whom a most reluctant exception was made, simply and cynically because as world champion she seemed certain to win a gold medal.

The Nuremberg Laws would guarantee 'racial purity' by preserving Aryan domination of 'sub-human Jews, Negroes and Gypsies or their bastard offspring'. Should the laws fail, Göring told the adoring crowds at Nuremberg, 'it will be necessary to transfer the Jewish problem to the National Socialist party for a final solution'. This was the first recorded instance of the term 'final solution' in this context; today, of course, it is a euphemism for the Nazi slaughter of six million Jews.

The Nuremberg Laws of 1935 also enshrined in law the targeting of Slavs, blacks and Asians, liberals, socialists and communists, homosexuals and the disabled. The Law for the Prevention of Hereditarily Diseased Offspring saw German gypsies—or Romanis—sterilised, and the Law against Dangerous Habitual Criminals gave the Nazis carte blanche to imprison alcoholics, prostitutes and the unemployed, petty lawbreakers, beggars and the homeless.

■ ■ ■

It would be difficult to find a more unlikely person than Hitler to champion an Olympic Games. In 1932, the pro-Nazi newspaper *Völkischer Beobachter*, affronted by the Olympic principle that the Games should be open to all athletes of the world, proposed instead a 'National Olympiad' for Aryans only. 'Blacks have no place at the Olympics. Unfortunately these days one sees the free white man having to compete with blacks for the victory palm. This is a disgrace and a degradation of the Olympic ideal without parallel, and the ancient Greeks would turn over in their graves if they knew what modern men were doing with their sacred Games,' the paper brayed. With the Berlin Games due to take place in just four years' time, *Völkischer Beobachter* prayed that 'the men in control will do their duty' and exclude blacks and Jews: 'We demand it.' As late as 1933, Hitler seemed likely to cancel the Olympics that he had inherited, disparaging them as 'a Jewish nigger-fest', 'a plot of Freemasons and Jews' which 'cannot possibly be put on in a Reich ruled by National Socialists'. Hitler had also sneeeringly turned down Lewald's invitation to become honorary chairman of the Olympic Organising Committee.

Although the Führer required Germans, as befitted a master race, to be fit and healthy—'the German boy must be slim, with long limbs, as rapid as a hare, tough as leather and solid as steel'—Hitler himself took almost no interest in sport. He could not swim, was never seen to run and rarely rode a horse. He even refused to dance. Hitler restricted his exercise to gentle hiking in the Alps and, curiously, holding his right arm aloft for lengthy periods. Partly his refusal to participate in physical games was because he feared losing and therefore being exposed as mortal.

To transform Hitler from an opponent to a supporter of the Berlin Olympics took Machiavellian cajoling by Lewald, who suggested that it would be a clever idea to welcome inferior races to Berlin because when German athletes inevitably trounced them, it would prove beyond doubt that Aryans were indeed superior beings. Then the wily Goebbels convinced his leader of the propaganda benefits. With the world watching, and more than a thousand international journalists in town, he argued, presenting Germany as a peace-loving, cultured, racially tolerant, highly efficient nation of good sports would silence the Reich's foreign critics and lower their guard, buying time and making Hitler's agenda of persecution and territorial expansion easier to pursue. The spin doctor also reminded Hitler of the core ideological belief of Nazism—that the modern-day Aryan descended from the ancient Greeks. The Berlin Olympics would reinforce the link between the civilisations. Goebbels persuaded Hitler that the Olympics would 'strengthen the character of the German people, imbuing it with the fighting spirit and steadfast camaraderie necessary in the struggle for its existence'. With all their patriotic pageantry, the Olympics would raise national morale, distracting Germans from everyday woes and making them feel positive about themselves and, more importantly, National Socialism. Architect Albert Speer also persuaded the Führer that the Olympics would present an opportunity to rebuild Berlin into a city of grandiose buildings, iconic statuary and sweeping swastika-bedecked boulevards, all reflecting the glory of National Socialism.

If for all the wrong reasons, Hitler came to embrace the Games. Espousing Olympic values, in words penned by Goebbels, he now declared: 'Sporting and chivalrous competition awakens the best human qualities. It does not sever, but on the contrary, unites the opponents in mutual understanding and reciprocal respect. It also helps strengthen the bonds of peace between the nations. May the Olympic Flame therefore never be extinguished.' Then a backflip worthy of an Olympic gymnast: although he had at first turned down the honour, he now accepted 'with great gratitude' the

Organising Committee's invitation to succeed the fallen Hindenburg as patron of the Berlin Games.

To his followers, Hitler vowed to make the German Olympics the greatest the world had seen, as befitting a revived Germany peopled by Aryans who had overcome the humiliation of Versailles, the ravages of the Great Depression, the lurking communist and Jewish plotters, every obstacle the outside world had thrown at them, and who yet had emerged a master race. Every nation would envy the sporting prowess, organisational ability and cultural achievements of the Third Reich.

For all his flowery pronouncements, to Hitler the Berlin Games were nothing more than a means to achieve National Socialist ends. To ensure that all would go precisely as he wished, he parachuted hardline Nazis into the Organising Committee, rendering impotent Lewald and Diem who, while arch-conservatives, were both genuinely sports-minded and were not Nazi party members. Foremost among the new guard was the man Hitler had appointed to run all sport in Germany, Reichssportführer ('Reich Sport Leader') Hans von Tschammer und Osten, a former SA colonel known to flay subordinates with his riding crop, and Hitler acolyte Karl Ritter von Halt, a 1912 Olympic decathlete, Great War hero and banker. Von Halt had another strategic value: he was a close friend of Avery Brundage, president of the US Olympic Association and Committee, and as such he was expected to keep Brundage onside to ensure that the Games proceeded despite inevitable criticism. Also on the Organising Committee were Joseph Goebbels and staunch Nazis Lieutenant Colonel von Reichenau (who would order the slaughter of thousands of Jews on the Russian front), Lieutenant General Wilhelm Keitel (who would be hanged as a war criminal at Nuremberg in 1946), Major General Busch, future foreign minister Joachim von Ribbentrop's chief of staff Wilhelm Rodde, the murderous SS chief and director of the Gestapo Reinhard Heydrich, and General Kurt Daluege (who would succeed Heydrich as protector of Bohemia and Moravia after Heydrich was assassinated by Czech freedom fighters in 1942).

Any of Hitler's appointees could, with his blessing, veto any decision of Lewald and Diem, thus giving the Nazis control over the staging of the Games. Hitler had been determined to dismiss Lewald and Diem from the committee because the former had Jewish blood and the latter's wife was Jewish, but had reluctantly buckled to pressure from IOC president Baillet-Latour, who had heard of his scheme and in an uncharacteristic show of fortitude made it clear that if the two administrators were ousted, he would consider overturning the delegates' vote and awarding the event to Barcelona. Hitler allowed Lewald and Diem to remain as promi-nent faces of the Organising Committee, but replaced Lewald as chairman with Tschammer und Osten (Lewald was made an 'adviser', though later reinstated as a figurehead chief) and had Diem sacked from his job at the sports college he had established. Even though their paths crossed the Führer's throughout the Games, sometimes sitting together at functions and during Olympic events, the Führer's glacial demeanour left Lewald and Diem in no doubt that they were in the official party under sufferance and that their future in sports administration was not guaranteed.

Tschammer und Osten concocted an Olympic pledge that was read aloud by 100 young athletes at a ceremony and broadcast nationally. The oath, bristling with martial references, presumed to speak for all those who would be tapped to try out for the Olympic team. 'I will voluntarily follow the call of the Reich Sport Leader to enter into the ranks of a German youth cohort determined to commit itself to the German cause, which is also my cause,' chanted the athletes. 'I swear to conduct myself in accordance with the requirements of a German Olympic combatant. During the period of training I will forswear all of life's pleasures, keeping as my sole goal the task of schooling and hardening my body, so that I may be worthy of fighting nobly for my Fatherland. I subordinate myself fully to the Reich Sport Leader and to his cadre of trainers, who are my helpers on the way to this goal. I will follow their teachings and training guidelines exclusively. I promise to remain silent regarding the measures that have been taken and will be taken in the future.' It's probable that the vow of silence was to prevent word leaking of the regime's violations of Olympic amateurism—including compensation for athletes' lost wages while training, tax breaks for their companies, and food, travel and accommodation expenses.

German officials could not resist expressing themselves with crude and inappropriate analogies of war. Of his hopes for the Olympics, even the comparatively moderate Carl Diem exclaimed, 'The Berlin Games will lead a victory charge for a better Europe!' Another Reich publication referred to winning the Olympics as 'fighting the battle' and preparing for the Games as 'decisive warfare'. The Games themselves were often called in Germany 'war without weapons'. Athletes must display 'fighting spirit'. As early as the 1932 Los Angeles Olympics, the *Völkischer Beobachter* newspaper had declaimed that there was no room in German sport for milksop 'poets and thinkers' or 'fine gentlemen' and only those who had a 'taste for blood' and were prepared to 'struggle' need bother trying out.

A devious method was devised to get around the IOC and international critics of National Socialism and successfully eliminate German Jewish athletes from Olympic contention. First, Jewish athletic clubs were deregistered, leaving only Nazi-sanctioned clubs to nominate Olympians from their ranks, and with membership of these clubs denied to Jews, they had no way of training and competing in official competition and therefore qualifying. George Messersmith, the US chief consul to Germany, saw through the ploy and alerted the US State Department. He wrote in a report that the Germans, through 'deft manipulation and sheer terror', were ensuring that no Jews would represent Germany at the Olympics. 'Many Jews who were potential competitors had left Germany because they knew they would not be able to train in the manner demanded of an Olympic contender.'

At the behest of his members, Baillet-Latour sought a written guarantee from the German government that Germany would honour the Olympic charter in every regard, which included allowing athletes of every race and creed to compete and not be mistreated in Berlin. Hitler, who had already put in place measures ensuring that no German Jew was eligible for selection, ordered the beleaguered Lewald to give Baillet-Latour his pledge.

At the behest of Hitler and Goebbels, and with a little help from Tschammer und Osten, Lewald drew up and circulated these hollow assurances:

1. Neither the Reich Government nor I have issued any order excluding Jewish members from athletic clubs.
2. Neither the Reich Government nor I have issued any order barring Jewish clubs from training facilities.
3. Neither the Reich Government nor I have issued any order prohibiting Jews from competitions.
4. If I should learn of any local authorities having issued any order contrary to the above statements I should investigate them and make them conform.

And in a further attempt to head off calls to halt what were even then being called the Nazi Games, Lewald guaranteed the safety of both German Jews and Jews from other countries. Under instructions from his masters, he also assured the Americans that the regime 'had no objections to blacks coming to Germany to compete'.

Many were deceived. One *New York Times* journalist wrote that Lewald's assurances represented a complete backing down by the Hitler government. The promise made by the German government proved that 'a real blow has been struck in the cause of racial freedom'.

Behind all the Olympic window-dressing and lies, the victimisation of Jews and rearmament continued. Even while Lewald was uttering his honeyed assurances, Tschammer und Osten was reassuring fellow Nazis that the pledges were bogus: 'We shall see to it that both in our national life and in our relations and competitions with foreign nations only such Germans shall be allowed to represent the nation against whom no objection can be raised.'

CHAPTER 5
AMATEUR HOUR

In early March 1936, Perth swimming prodigy Percy Oliver was enjoying a night out at the open-air cinema in Claremont. 'I was with two girlfriends, Dorothy Green, who was a very good swimmer, and Dorothy Christie. I was sitting in the middle, with an arm around each girl.' As he recalled to his granddaughter, 'the film was interrupted halfway through and a message flashed onto the screen: "Percy Oliver has been selected in the Australian Olympic team for Berlin." I knew a fair few of the people in the audience, and a cheer went up, and afterwards they all congratulated me. I was thrilled. I honestly thought I was too young to be chosen for Germany, even though I'd swum very well over the past two years. I don't remember how the Dorothys got home, and I've no idea how the projectionist knew I was in the team.' Oliver's daughter Anita Hutchinson knows, however. 'Dad's father heard the news on the radio,' she says, 'and telephoned the proprietor of the local picture show, who scrawled the news on a cellophane slide, which he projected onto the screen!'

For Oliver, as for other Australians in 1936, going to the sixpenny movies was a special event. So, with most budgets permitting only one night out a week, families invested a few pounds in wireless sets that Olympic year. Many bought a radio because of the Olympic reports they'd hear in August. Till then, they could tune in to serials and sing along to the hit songs of the era or popular home-grown ditties, such as 'Our Don Bradman', 'The Bridge We've Been Waiting For', 'The Aeroplane Jelly Song', 'Phar Lap Farewell to You' and 'Let's Take a Trip to Melbourne'. (Back then, families and friends also made their own music, gathered around a piano or playing an accordion, guitar, ukulele or mouth organ. Percy Oliver played ukulele and harmonica, and fellow champions Evelyn de Lacy and Gerald Backhouse were dab hands on the mouth organ.) The wireless also allowed Australians to follow—via simulated broadcasts from Australia or in the dead of night on the BBC from England—the run-scoring exploits of Don Bradman. The other news preoccupying Australians in early 1936 was the death of King George V and the succession to the throne of Edward VIII, a series of disquieting reports from Europe on the activities of the bellicose Adolf Hitler, and, considered totally unrelated by most, the soap opera that was the selection of the Australian Olympic team.

Picking the likely Games squad was a popular pastime among the sporting public. So Australians avidly followed the Australian National Games being held at Adelaide Oval in early 1936 as an Olympic selection trial. (Profits from ticket sales were to help send the team to Berlin.) The organisers trumpeted that their games would be as spectacular as any Olympics, so the Australians would not be overawed when competing in the real event. According to publicity, 'the most notable gathering ever assembled in Adelaide' would be there to honour the athletes, including Prime Minister Joseph Lyons and AOF chairman and IOC delegate James Taylor. Officially opening the National Games was Governor of South Australia Sir Winston Dugan, in front of whom the athletes paraded in state or territory groups. There were brass bands, an orchestra and a 1000-voice choir. On opening day, a fanfare of trumpets was followed by the Australian Field Artillery firing three volleys. To ape the Olympic Torch Relay, a succession of Australian runners had carried a torch from Melbourne to Adelaide Oval, where it was used to light the National Games urn. One thousand doves were released.

Despite the pageantry, comparing the National Games to the Olympics was to compare a backyard barbecue to a banquet. The Australian National Games was a microcosm of what ailed Australian athletics. In many respects, the Games were of little use to selectors. Most times set were below those that would be required to win a medal in Berlin. And as preparation for international competition, the event was of little use. The swimmers swam in a freezing tidal saltwater pool, the runners and jumpers ran on grass, and the cyclists cycled on concrete, bitumen and dirt surfaces. In Berlin, swimming events would be contested in fresh water, track and field on cinder tracks, and cycling events on timber surfaces. Again, at the Australian Games, boxers and wrestlers fought under local, not international, rules. Mocking the event's claim to being an Olympic selection trial, genuine medal hopes including Jack Metcalfe cried off competing; and selectors' bias led to swimmer Clare Dennis and Clarice Kennedy, the best-performing athlete at the National Games (winning the hurdles and javelin), missing Berlin selection. As well, imperial, not metric, measurements of distance were used. With 100yd equalling 91.44m, the longer distances Australians would have to run, swim, dive and cycle in Berlin would adversely affect their preparation and performance.

Hard to believe nowadays when coaches, physiotherapists, masseurs, sports psychologists, strategists and nutritionists are almost as integral to an elite sporting team as the athletes, but in the financially strapped and technologically unenlightened Australian sporting world of the 1930s, such support was considered super-fluous. Nick Winter, the 1924 Olympic hop, step and jump gold medallist, wrote that our lack of coaches and support staff, such as masseurs, especially in track and field, put Australia at an enor-mous disadvantage against athletes from countries where coaches were valued, and doomed Australia to failure in Berlin. 'Without a doubt, the first man to be selected [for the Olympics] should be the [head coach] and he should be on the job now, studying all prospective representatives and supervising their training.' He continued, 'Australia has not taken to heart the lessons she should have absorbed deeply from previous Olympiads. When will it be realised that the preparation of a team for contests of the Olympic type is a vital necessity and essential to success? Other nations for some time have been preparing for Berlin.'

Dennis, who had won 200m breaststroke gold in Los Angeles and at the 1934 London Empire Games, unfavourably compared Australian swimmers' preparation to that of German, American and Japanese swimmers. She wrote in February 1936 that the Japanese women 'have been housed together at the YWCA in Tokyo where they have their own [heated freshwater] pool and the best coaches Japan can find for them. From now until the team leaves for Berlin they will remain together and carry on with their training at the expense of the authorities. If Japan can do these things, why can't Australia?' Dennis said that Australia had a number of women swimmers who could reach Olympic standard if they were encouraged and given correct training. Swimming in saltwater tidal and ocean pools—freshwater pools being a rarity—was not good enough. 'A tepid freshwater pool in each state in which to train during the winter months would greatly facilitate matters . . . The times recorded at the Australian National Games are far from Olympic times and until conditions for swimming and swimmers improve in Australia they will probably remain so.'

The man likely to manage the Australian team in Berlin, veteran official Harry Alderson, put on a brave face about Australia's chances at the Games, but was under no illusions as to how disadvantaged elite athletes in Australia were compared to overseas counterparts. He realised that his charges were not used to freshwater pools, the harder cinder athletics tracks and timber bike circuits, and that acclimatising them to the different facilities once they arrived in Berlin was a priority, so he begged the AOF to allow the Australians to arrive in Berlin five weeks before the Olympics began to practise in Berlin's heated freshwater pools and on the cinder running tracks. As it was, five weeks was not nearly long enough. New Zealand 1500m runner Jack Lovelock had said it took him twelve months to become used to running on cinders after grass tracks, and Australian 1934 Empire Games representative Jack Horsfall said two years was needed. There was also the problem that rather than competing over their usual imperial 100yd, 200yd or 1000yd distances, the Berlin Olympic events would be contested in metres, so, for example, our 100yd runners and swimmers in their 100m events would be racing over a 109yd course. This, too, took getting used to.

Despite the German regime's attempts to keep it quiet because it was contrary to Olympism's amateur ethos, Alderson knew the Nazis were bankrolling their athletes to give them a winning edge. The regime had ordered companies to allow employees earmarked to compete at the Games time off work at full pay to attend magnificently equipped training camps. The government reimbursed the companies with income tax concessions. German Olympians in training received the prestigious German Sports Medal and an 'Olympic Passport' entitling them to be compensated for lost wages, as well as free travel, housing, food, and medical care, which included physiotherapy and dietary supplements, such as the phosphate additive Recresal, and Dallkolat, comprising kola nut powder and cocaine; both, while legal, were almost unheard of in Australian sporting circles. German athletes were also encouraged to inhale oxygen and take ultraviolet radiation baths. Alderson believed that a large proportion of German athletes had not done a day's work since the end of 1935. There were similar hushed-up schemes in the United States and Japan, where government and corporate financial support made some athletes, by any standard, professionals. Australia's chances of success, argued Alderson, would improve if the federal and state governments at least supported amateur sport and didn't treat it as a necessary evil to be subsidised only when an Olympic Games forced them kicking and screaming to contribute.

As well as a chronic lack of government inclination and funds to support sport, Australia's location was an impediment. Being so far from Europe, America and Asia consigned Australians to competing in a vacuum, denying athletes the chance to regularly test themselves against elite sports people from other countries, and to see and learn from the sporting advances that were being made.

It was estimated that the AOF would need to provide every athlete sent to Berlin basic spending money of 200 pounds, and pay travel fares (120 pounds per athlete), plus pay for food and beverages while the competitors were not in the Olympic Village (where Germany picked up the tab). The source of these funds would be the profits of the National Games, and whatever money could be raised by affiliated amateur sporting associations. These proceeds would be met pound for pound (up to a total of 2000 pounds) by the Australian government. (By contrast, the Japanese government funded its Olympic campaign to the tune of 60,000 pounds, and the US and German governments contributed much more.) The AOF was also counting on financial assistance from the public and the athletes themselves. Help also came from an unexpected source. Club Tivoli, comprising Victoria-based Germans, raised 200 pounds for the Australian team by holding a dance at its clubroom.

Despite such generosity, with contributions from sporting associations falling far below expectations, the AOF announced that it could afford to send only a token team to the Olympics. It seemed that just twelve athletes and a manager would be going to Berlin.

All the more essential then that the twelve chosen should have a genuine chance of success. Unfortunately, the home-state bias of the selectors meant that impartial decisions were not made. When the list was released on 13 March, the names of some of Australia's best athletes were not on it, while some with little chance of success were. It worked this way: the state and national unions representing the various Olympic sports chose in order of preference those they thought worthy of selection and forwarded that list to the AOF's final selection committee of five. Their job was then to sift through the suggested names and determine the composition of the team for Berlin. The problem was that four of the five selectors in that final committee were from Victoria: Hugh Weir (who chose all the track and field athletes), H.A. Bennett (the swimmers), H.G. Wakeling (the boxers and wrestlers) and E.E. Kenny (the rowers). New South Wales had just one selector, H.K. Maxwell, whose brief was to decide which cyclists would go to Germany. The other Australian states and territories had no representation on the final selection committee. Had certain of these selectors not put their state interest above the national interest there would have been no problem and the best dozen athletes would have been selected. This was not the case. The atmosphere throughout the selection meetings was poisonous, as the selectors bickered and horse-traded to arrive at the final twelve.

As well as fears of state partisanship, the Women's Athletic Union (WAU) worried that male athletes had the inside track to

Games selection. Their qualms were justified. The WAU wanted to ensure that women swimmers and track and field athletes (for these were the only sports in which women at this time were allowed to compete at the Olympics) had as much chance as men of being chosen. The WAU had been ordered by the AOF in late 1935 to affiliate with the Men's Athletic Union, and was then informed that the final selection of the team would be made by an all-male committee. The WAU accepted that with a men-only panel their hope of equal male–female representation would not be realised. Privately they were confident of four women being selected. They would be sorely disappointed.

Taylor's announcement of the Olympic team on 13 March was met with accusations of state and gender bias. Of the athletes named, five were from Victoria: distance runner Gerald Backhouse, hurdler Alf Watson, wrestler Dick Garrard, and cyclists Chris Wheeler and Tasman 'Tassie' Johnson. The balance of the squad were swimmers Percy Oliver (WA) and Pat Norton (NSW), hop, step and jumper and broad jumper Jack Metcalfe (NSW), wrestler Eddie Scarf (NSW), welterweight boxer Leonard 'Rusty' Cook (Qld), cyclist Dunc Gray (NSW) and sculler Cecil Pearce (NSW). Of the twelve, only Backhouse, Garrard, Metcalfe, Norton and Gray were considered by pundits to be possible medal hopes. The rest were chosen for their future Olympic potential or owed their place in the team to a friendly selector. NSW sporting officials were adamant that a number of the Victorians chosen 'were not up to Olympic standard' and that they were in the squad in the place of more deserving athletes from New South Wales.

The team's sole woman was Pat Norton. The paucity of women in the team prompted Mary Chambers of the NSW Amateur Swimming Association to despair, 'The girls have been sacrificed.'

There was outrage over the snubbing of Clarice Kennedy, who as reigning Australian hurdles and javelin champion was flummoxed by her non-selection. Her case was argued in the newspapers and in federal parliament. 'My name was in *Hansard*. Questions were asked in parliament,' she said. '*The Truth* newspaper offered to pay my expenses, but [the selectors] said I couldn't go. The Women's Athletic Union said they sent my name and Doris Carter's to the men's selectors and the men said they only received Carter's. I was never bitter. I just didn't understand it.'

The honorary team manager was selected at the same time as the squad. The job description had called for a sports official who was respected and inspirational, calm in a crisis, and intimately conversant with Olympic history and sentiment. The successful aspirant would have to meet foreign sportsmen in a spirit of give and take, and be as much diplomat and educator as sporting official. Alderson was a popular winner. A genial but no-nonsense man, a proponent of Olympism and critic of Australia's slapdash Olympic preparation, he was vice-chairman of the AOF, chairman of the NSW Olympic Council, and since 1918 had been executive officer of the NSW Rowing Association, and president since 1921.

There was an addendum to the selection sheet. The NSW Police rowing eight, its cox, two reserves and a double sculls team would be able to compete at Berlin, providing they paid their own costs. The police—Wal Mackney, Bill Cross, Don Fergusson, Len Einsaar, Clyde Elias, Wal Jordan, Joe Gould, Norm Ella (the cox) and Merv Wood—set to work raising funds, and with just weeks to go before departure had raised the necessary money. They would be accompanied by their coach George Mackenzie, Fergusson's mother Mary and police inspector father George, and NSW Police Commissioner William MacKay and Mrs MacKay. The NSW taxpayer ended up subsidising the police rowers' expenses when MacKay wangled a fact-finding tour of London police stations for them at the end of the Games.

Some of the athletes omitted from the team—in particular Basil Dickinson, Kitty Mackay, Evelyn de Lacy, Doris Carter, diver Ron Masters and Clare Dennis—were considered more likely to hold their own in Olympic competition than at least seven who gained selection. Hugh Weir's choice of the 30-year-old Alf Watson, who had been found wanting at past Games, in place of the world-class youngster Dickinson raised particular ire. Said Dickinson years later, 'Alf competed in the hurdles in the 1928 Games at Amsterdam. His times were not good and he didn't get out of the heats. He missed the '32 Games, and when the '36 Games came up he was selected even though his times were no better than in Amsterdam. He was favoured because he was a Victorian.' Later it was revealed that Dickinson had polled more votes than Watson or Backhouse, yet Weir had bypassed him for the two Victorians. Carped *The Referee*: 'Watson will have to show greater form than he was ever able to reveal in his years of athletic prime if he is to justify his selection. There is nothing personal in this criticism. It merely seeks to emphasise that in this matter the selectors have been not rigidly guided by what everyone regards as a principle of selection in such a team, *viz*, that the chosen should be capable of going close to the world's record.'

The excluded champions' associations, the sporting media and the public angrily demanded to know the reason for their omission and demanded that a way be found for them to be added to the squad. Taylor cited a clause that had been added to the AOF constitution in 1932 stating that once an Olympic team was selected it could not be altered. Dickinson's St George Athletic Club countered by moving that 'the Amateur Athletic Union Association of Australia be requested to take steps to have B.C. Dickinson included in the Olympic team for Berlin, provided that his expenses be raised from outside sources . . . [and] that in the event of there being a rule preventing such an addition to the team, the Union be requested to move to have such restrictions rescinded.' The influential *Referee* backed the motion by the club and the NSW Amateur Athletic Association to have Dickinson and other worthy athletes included if the money to send them could be raised. It editorialised, 'The NSW Amateur Athletic Association has the hearty good wishes of sportsmen in its efforts to get B.C. Dickinson included in the Olympic team. There is nothing parochial or factious about this move. Dickinson has the athletic credentials. If there is no rigid rule to prevent an addition to the Olympic team (Olympic officials say there is), Dickinson ought to be there.'

Alarmed at the groundswell of support for the overlooked athletes, the AOF back-pedalled and said that the clause banning additions applied only to 1932. It then dramatically announced that the names of four athletes who had narrowly missed selection had been placed in a sealed envelope, and now the envelope would be opened and they would be included in the team after all, with their expenses paid. Incredibly, given the rancour, the first three of the four names drawn from the envelope were those of Victorians: high jumper Doris Carter, diver Ron Masters and light heavyweight boxer Les Harley. The last name read out was that of NSW sculler Herb Turner. Although few denied that the four deserved inclusion, rather than placating critics, the announcement brought more accusations of favouritism from the non-Victorian sporting organisations and press. If four could be added to the squad—and three of them Victorians—then why not more?

Taylor blinked a second time, saying that so long as they could meet their own expenses within five days, then *nine* more athletes could join the team. They were Dickinson, Mackay, Kendall, Dennis, de Lacy and Woodhouse, as well as boxers Harry Cohen and Harry Cooper of New South Wales and Victoria respectively, and the Victorian wrestler Jack 'Spud' O'Hara. A frantic race to raise the required 200 pounds expenses money for each of the newly named nine began. Incredibly, there was still no place for Clarice Kennedy.

(The AOF misstepped again when the official letters notifying selection in the team were sent to the wrong athletes. High jumper Doris Carter received a letter requesting her to include in her wardrobe for Berlin boxing boots, trunks and a singlet, while boxer Les Harley was ordered to pack a white frock.)

Taylor announced that the AOF executive committee took responsibility for overruling the final selection committee and pleaded for an end to the rancour. He called the selection controversy 'distasteful' and hoped that now 'all criticism and recriminations [would] cease and be forgotten. Send this team away with our united good wishes feeling sure that whether they win or lose they are ambassadors of goodwill [which is] so necessary an attribute in this troubled world of ours.'

One who could not forget the brouhaha was federal opposition leader and future prime minister John Curtin, who, although born in Victoria, accused the selection panel of having made 'mistakes because of internal jealousies and personal prejudices'. Another sporting official was even more succinct: 'Most of the Olympic selectors know no more about athletics than cows.' A humiliated and angry Weir resigned from the selection panel, and fellow Victorian Wakeling did likewise. Weir claimed that the move to increase the team was a weak-kneed response to pressure from the press and politicians.

Boxer Harry Cohen almost immediately withdrew from the team, citing his fear of what might befall a Jewish man such as himself in Hitler's Germany and, perhaps more to the point, his recent signing of a contract to turn professional. Clare Dennis, possibly miffed that she had not been an original selection, also withdrew, saying that an infected toe had prevented her from training. When the pair pulled out, an invitation was extended to New South Wales sculler Bill Dixon. This brought the number in the team to 33: 29 men and four women. The stern Mary Fergusson's offer to chaperone the women athletes was readily accepted, by Alderson if not by the athletes themselves. The older woman's brief was to teach the women enough German to make themselves understood in Germany (how fluent Fergusson herself was in the language is not known), to ensure that they exercised well and were in bed by 9 p.m., and to guard them from European Lotharios.

Seventy-seven years later, Dickinson could still bridle at the selection chicanery. Recalling those messy and unedifying times when his Olympic hopes were dashed and redeemed, he said, 'There was such a shortage of money. Remember there was no sponsorship then. Jim Eve, a fine man, was the secretary and treasurer of the AOF. He had no office, and had to organise everything. There was not enough money in the coffers to send more than a few athletes to Berlin, but then the federal government kicked in with 2000 pounds, which, with some other fundraising, would allow eleven or twelve to be sent to Berlin. Hanky-panky and gerrymandering went on, definitely. The Victorian Athletics Association wanted all five track and field athletes to come from their state, regardless of Jack Metcalfe and myself being the best-performed such athletes in Australia. They couldn't put Jack out, though Hugh Weir might have tried. His claims were too hard to ignore, but the selectors found no room for me. Weir saw to it that four Victorians were chosen ahead of me, with his friend Alf Watson at the head of the list . . . I was rated the sixth best track and field athlete, and Weir said they couldn't send two from the one event, which in my case and Jack Metcalfe's was hop, step and jump. This didn't stop more than one swimmer, more than one cyclist, more than one wrestler, more than one boxer being selected. It was ridiculous. Weir had a bee in his bonnet about me.

'When the extra athletes were added I found myself in the team, but I had no money, and thankfully people from all over, including Victoria, went in to bat for me.' The public was asked to donate any sum from sixpence to a guinea to help send Dickinson to Berlin, and the people responded. 'My parents gave me all they could afford, 34 pounds,' Dickinson recalled. 'The money came rolling in and I was humbled. The whole selection fiasco took two months to resolve, and by the time the team was finalised there was just three weeks to get us fit and ready to compete, to have our uniforms made, say our farewells and board the boat for the long voyage to Europe. It wasn't an easy start for those who were brought into the team late. Jack Metcalfe wrote me a letter just before he died, and he said, "You know, Basil, we were so unfit when we got to Berlin."'

Many athletes relied on public support to fund their Olympic journeys. Dickinson and Metcalfe spoke at a function at the Sydney YMCA to raise money. Evelyn de Lacy's expenses were paid by Perth's *Daily News*. The Lebanon Society contributed to the expenses of Eddie Scarf and Clyde Elias, who vowed to his supporters that he would summon 'the strength of a miniature Samson on the day of the eight oar race'. The makers of Speedwell bicycles staged a glittering event to support Dunc Gray. The German consul-general hosted a farewell fundraiser for the NSW Olympians at the Hotel Australia, Sydney's finest, on 8 May.

Overcoming parochial selections in the team wasn't the only issue athletes faced, and the difficulties Dickinson confronted at work were shared by many amateur athletes who received no sponsorship, scholarships or other subsidies, and relied on the wages of a nine-to-five, six-day-a-week job to survive. This forced many a fine athlete to turn their back on sport. 'When my selection was announced,' Dickinson remembered, 'a journo from the Sydney *Sun* came to interview me at the Royal Insurance Company, but my boss refused to let him onto the premises. We ended up going elsewhere for the interview and to have my photo taken, and when I returned to the office my superior said, "Dickinson, I understand you've been selected for the Olympic Games." I said, "I have, sir." "Well," he said, "I hope you'll not be so foolish as to give up your job with us and all the wonderful things we have planned for your future career. You'll not be a junior clerk forever." I said, "Sir?" He said, "I'm telling you straight. If you go to Berlin we'll have no choice but to replace you, and you'll never be welcomed back. I'll have no choice but to ask for your resignation. Now, go home and talk to your parents and I'm certain they'll put you straight." I went home and had a powwow with Mum and Dad, who until then had shown no great interest in my athletics. But they were adamant that Berlin would be the experience of a lifetime and I could worry about finding a new job on my return. Next morning I knocked on my boss's door. He gave me a big smile and put his arm around my shoulders. "Now, Dickinson, I hope you're going to tell me the good news that you'll be forgetting this Olympics nonsense." I said, "Well, sir, I've talked to my family, and they support my decision to go to Berlin. I'm sorry. The opportunity to represent Australia at an Olympics may not come again."' The fellow's avuncular demeanour changed in a snap. 'He asked when the boat was leaving and when I told him, "In three weeks," he said, "Then I want your resignation on my desk the day before you go." I had no second thoughts, even though I'd got that job in 1932 when employment was scarce.'

At the last minute, the AOF buckled to the pleas of Alderson and respected sportsman and politician Sir Joynton Smith that masseurs be sent to Berlin to treat the athletes. Two, Neil Morrison and Fred McKay, were assigned. 'Someone told me they gave their services free, and I hope they did and that they didn't take the spots that two athletes could have occupied,' said Dickinson. 'McKay fell ill and played no part, which left Morrison running like a crazy man from the Olympic Village where the men were to the women's headquarters and then to another location to treat the rowers. He was spread much too thinly and did nobody much good, and besides he didn't seem to know much about massage. If we had no capable masseurs in Australia, it would have been better to appoint qualified masseurs from Europe.'

Apart from Mackenzie the rowing coach, there would be another coach in Berlin, Harry Hay, who would join Norton's chaperone Nightingale advising the athletes in an unofficial and unpaid capacity. Hay was a Sydney-based swimming and diving coach who had competed as a swimmer at the 1920 Antwerp Olympics, and mentored Andrew Charlton, Kitty Mackay, Bill Kendall and other elite swimmers. Before leaving for Berlin, Hay offered reporters a somewhat optimistic opinion of the Australians' chances. 'Pearce, the sculler, should win, and Garrard the wrestler, who I consider a champion, will, I think, win an event. Of the cyclists, Gray and Wheeler have as good a chance as anybody and jumpers Metcalfe and Dickinson have to their credit performances which show that they are at least as good as any man they are likely to meet. Ron Masters has a very hard task ahead, particularly in view of the difficult dives overseas competitors are likely to perform. Of the swimmers, Kitty Mackay, Evelyn de Lacy, Bill Kendall and Percy Oliver are all young, keen, and brilliant in Australia but will need to improve on their times. That is by no means beyond them. In fact, it is almost certain that they will do considerably better once they get to Berlin and are able to concentrate for some weeks on their particular races.'

No surprise, given the months of compromise, that many pundits did not share Hay's optimism. On 6 May, a week before the team sailed for Germany on SS *Mongolia*, Alderson tried to quell qualms and rally support. 'Despite criticism which has been levelled at the selected team in certain quarters, I feel certain that all will co-operate with the one object in view—to worthily uphold the good name of Australia on and off the sporting fields, to carry out the great traditions set by previous Olympic teams. The followers of amateur sport in Australia can rest assured that no effort will be spared in the endeavour to hoist this country's flag at the top of the Olympic mast to signify a victory in the many events in which Australia will compete.'

A poem, 'Olympic Athlete', was composed and read aloud at the farewells:

Olympic Athlete! Stand by your Country Flag.
When breath is short and you can hardly drag
Each lending step, then for your Country's sake
Fight on until the last, until you make
One final spurt, and stagger 'cross the line
And think, 'I did this for that land of mine.'
If you lose, Olympic Athlete, though you try
With straining heart and lungs and eye,
If you have done your best, fall not ashamed,
For you were honest and will not be blamed.
But if you win, and make inglorious boast,
Then the flag you fought for indeed has lost.

Every Australian newspaper ran an editorial wishing the team well. One editor wrote: 'Australia has a small population, with but few populous and wealthy cities to be the localities of centralised sport; and for this and parallel reasons, the professionalism (open or veiled) in Australian athletics is on the whole genuinely and spontaneously amateur.' In such rich and populous countries as

Germany and the United States there was a 'professional devotion to training and practice' which produced champions who would usually beat 'the naturally gifted performer who is less assiduously engaged . . . With a minimum of wealthy assistance and only a modicum of allowance to meet expenses, Australian athletics have therefore a spontaneity beyond that of the countries we most frequently challenge. It might be said, with some pride, that we breed our young Olympians from the health and strength of our people; we do not manufacture them from our patronage and our purse . . . Circumstances and conditions, such as have been detailed above, cannot promise for an Australian team that it will win premier Olympic honors in the total of victories. All the same, we send away a fine troupe of hearty, muscular young men and women who are athletes because of the energy of Australian life; and not from the constant application of money from clubs and patrons to provide virtually professional coaching.'

All true. What Olympic success Australia had enjoyed in the past was achieved on heart and raw talent alone. Athletes, all needing full-time employment to survive, did their best in whatever time they could snatch in the early morning, lunch hour and weekends in antiquated facilities without coaches, conditioners, physiotherapists and dietitians. To them, training was running or swimming lap after lap. They were also held back by officialdom. Australian sporting organisations' devotion to the principles of amateurism was admirable, but too often amateurism was a euphemism for ineptitude, penny-pinching and blatant self-interest. In 1936, this was no longer good enough. The world had moved on.

CHAPTER 6
BOYCOTT BERLIN!

From 1933, when Hitler seized power, until the final days of 1935, seven months before the planned Opening Ceremony, there was a chance that Berlin would be stripped of the Olympics—both the Winter Games in February and the Summer Games in August—as organisations particularly in America viewed with dismay events in Nazi Germany.

Although Hitler had no intention of altering course, the regime conducted a charade to allay the world's fears. Realising that the Olympic festival was a crucial propaganda component of his plan to re-establish Germany as a world power, Hitler unleashed a massive public relations campaign to mask those aspects of the Third Reich that were outraging international opinion. To distract attention from his agenda, he set about dazzling outsiders by brazenly presenting an image of the Reich as a peace-loving paragon of international decency and tolerance wanting nothing more than to treat the world to a grand and friendly Olympic Games and become again a respected member of the world community. Reichssportführer Tschammer und Osten claimed to have no idea where lies about German Jewish athletes being excluded originated. Why, even now, he insisted, 25 Jews were taking part in Germany's Olympic training programs. Hitler and Goebbels trumpeted genuine domestic achievements such as the construction of infrastructure, spectacular buildings and autobahns, rescuing the economy and reducing unemployment. (Never mind that conscription of young German men into the illegal army, navy and air force, and the internment of thousands of the regime's perceived enemies in concentration camps significantly reduced the length of dole queues.)

That was the myth. The reality was different. In the lead-up to the Games, the Reich's activities belied Hitler's posturing. By the beginning of 1936, the Hitler Youth numbered four million (including the *Jung Volk* division of ten- to fourteen-year-olds), and the parks and fields of Germany were filled with children and teen-agers thrusting bayonets, throwing hand grenades, shooting pistols and rifles, burrowing under barbed wire, digging trenches, reading maps and practising the goosestep. Tschammer und Osten denied that the Hitler Youth and Strength Through Joy movements were quasi-military organisations: despite their banners proclaiming that members' duty was to die for Germany, these organisations, he insisted, were nothing but good, clean fun and physical fitness.

On 7 March 1936, Hitler despatched 32,000 soldiers and police to reoccupy the Rhineland, a region of Germany alongside the Rhine River demilitarised by the Treaty of Versailles. In June, Hitler ordered manufacturers of munitions, tanks and aircraft to increase production so Germany could wage war in 1938. Early in July, the month before the Olympics, Sachsenhausen concentration camp was opened just 35km north of Berlin, and interned there alongside convicted criminals were Jews, communists, Jehovah's Witnesses and homosexuals. Germany's army, navy and air force were becoming frighteningly formidable forces, and were paraded before the populace in vast displays of militaristic pageantry. On

17 July, less than two weeks before the Opening Ceremony, Hitler despatched German troops to Spain to bolster the fascist Nationalist forces of General Francisco Franco at the beginning of the Spanish Civil War.

In Germany, classical, jazz and popular music not composed and performed by Aryans was banned, and plays, books and paintings written and painted by non-Aryans or by those deemed corrupting influences were taken from public view and destroyed. The books of Thomas and Heinrich Mann, Ernest Hemingway, Erich Maria Remarque, Karl Marx and Helen Keller (because her work championed the disabled) were banned. Even as the Games commenced, Hitler was putting the finishing touches to plans to introduce compulsory two-year military service, and to redouble arrests of Jehovah's Witnesses, who were outspoken in their opposition to Nazism; the plans were enforced seven and eleven days, respectively, after the Olympics finished.

Some overseas observers refused to be hoodwinked. In the United States, the Jewish community and organisations representing it, such as the Jewish Labor Committee and the Jewish Congress, warned the IOC that National Socialist Germany hosting the 1936 Games would be a desecration of Olympism and that any nation that competed in Berlin would be complicit in Hitler's barbarism.

Argument ensued across the United States in newspaper think pieces, on radio broadcasts and at public meetings. The American public was split on the issue, with 43 per cent of participants in a Gallup poll saying that the United States should not go to Berlin and 57 voting to attend. (It was a hypocrisy, and one certainly not lost on Germans, that the main thrust to boycott the Berlin Olympic Games came from the United States, a nation whose advocacy of sporting equality did not extend to its own black athletes. Jesse Owens, for one, even while the premier athlete in

America, was shunned and insulted by whites and not allowed to reside on campus at Ohio State University.)

The move to boycott the Games never gained traction in Australia—so far from Europe, so obsessed with sport—where the faint pleas from the Jewish community and a sprinkling of students and leftists that Australia not compete in Berlin went unheeded by the general public, sporting bodies and governments. Australians knew enough to consider Hitler a threat to world peace, but refused to countenance a connection between international politics and sport. Most who *were* aware of an Olympic boycott movement damned it as a spoilsport crusade. 'I was a well-informed young man and had an idea of what Hitler was up to,' recalled Dickinson, 'but I was at the peak of my form at age 21 in 1936 and could never have supported a boycott and missed the Games, because I didn't know if my opportunity to represent my country at the Olympics would ever come again. Germany was rearming and threatening all kinds of mayhem . . . The world was getting darker and if there was to be a war, I wanted to compete now, before the chance was taken from me. I thought there was a chance there would be no Games in 1940, which is exactly what happened. I put my blinkers on. I opposed a boycott and hoped that the Berlin Games would be a success, Hitler would be somehow voted out of office, and all would be well. I suppose I was being self-centred, but that's how I felt. With hindsight my teammates and I allowed ourselves to be used as Nazi propaganda pawns. Did I, do I, worry? No. There were hundreds of other athletes from more than 50 countries competing too.'

In the early 2000s, Dickinson's teammate Percy Oliver said, 'I was sixteen when I was selected for Berlin and it was the most wonderful thing that had ever happened to me. Of course I knew Hitler was the dictator of Germany and he was a dangerous man—I picked that up in the playground at school—but he wasn't going to stop me from competing at Berlin. All my Olympic teammates felt the same, and if any of us was put under pressure not to compete I don't know about it. I still believe sport should be above politics. The 1936 Games should definitely have gone ahead.'

The only Australian athlete to refuse to compete was the boxer Harry Cohen. At different times he gave different reasons for pulling out. First he said he could not represent Australia at the Olympics because he had committed to turning professional. Then, right afterwards and for the rest of his life, he claimed that he had pulled out of the team because as a Jew he feared for his life in Hitler's Berlin. Whatever the reason for it, Cohen's withdrawal barely raised a ripple. There is no record of any discussions held by the AOF about the desirability or otherwise of boycotting Berlin.

An article ran in *The Referee* on 30 January 1936, contributed by J.M. Dunningham, president of the NSW Amateur Athletic Association, who had just visited Berlin to inspect Olympic facilities. Fresh off the boat from Europe, Dunningham enthused about his experiences: 'The organisation in Germany, which has striven for years to make these Games a world class event, features in all its publicity the quotation which appears on the invitation to attend the Games: "May the Olympic flame light the way for all mankind to a more aspiring, courageous and pure conception of life." What greater ideal could be placed before the world than this? . . . The possibilities arising from this great gathering must appeal to all who desire a welding together of the nations for the preservation of peace.'

The only known protest from any Australian political party against the Berlin Olympics came from a handful of members of the Victorian central executive of the Australian Labor Party, who moved 'that the party should protest against teams of athletes attending the Olympic Games in Germany in view of the fascist regime'. The motion was never aired, either at local, state or federal level.

Despite the federal government increasing the strength of Australia's armed forces in direct response to Germany's and Italy's aggression in Europe, the 1936 Berlin Olympics was only ever officially discussed in any Australian parliament when the government agreed to donate 2000 pounds to the Australian team, and when state governments defended their own sports administrators and selectors against charges of parochialism.

Australian memories of the Great War remained raw. People, including opinion-forming politicians and newspaper proprietors on both sides of politics, feared another world conflict and so wanted to believe that Hitler was not as bad as portrayed. He was, they assured themselves, only trying to resurrect Germany from the ashes and keep communism at bay, and while his methods may have been unpalatable, his aims were surely worthy. So why antagonise him by boycotting his Olympics? Australian political criticism of National Socialism was perhaps also muted by the belief that when compared to the other great bogey of that time, communism, Nazism was the lesser of two evils. Those who wanted to believe the best of the Berlin Games reminded themselves that the Olympics would be under the ultimate control of the IOC, with the Nazis simply hosts.

Australian church groups were conspicuously non-committal about the boycott issue. Not even the German Evangelical Church's brave, some said foolhardy, denunciation of Hitler—'Anti-Semitism is a crime against God . . . Honour is being accorded to Herr Hitler which is due only to God'—on the very eve of the Games elicited a peep of support.

Of the few newspaper reports that advocated opposition to the Berlin Games, one was published in *The Referee* on 12 March 1936, and another in the Melbourne *Argus* two days later. The former quoted the Oxford University publication *Isis*, which said that participation in the Berlin Olympics 'cannot be otherwise construed than as acquiescence in the breaking of the Olympic charter, and the perversion of sport to political ends by Dr Goebbels and the movement whose doctrine he spreads . . . Quite a lot of people in countries other than our own are now beginning to realise that it might have been a colossal blunder to have agreed to the holding of the Games in Germany. It might conceivably do international sport a lot of harm.'

In its article 'Nazism on Parade: What Germany Expects from the Olympic Games', *The Argus*'s Berlin correspondent observed that the 'earnestness' with which the Games were being 'hurried on' denoted 'some motive infinitely stronger than an enthusiasm for sport . . . Germany intends to make a supreme effort through these Olympic Games.' If the Government succeeded, Adolf Hitler would go down in history as a statesman comparable with Bismarck and Frederick the Great. If not, the peace of Europe would be jeopardised. 'When the million guests that pass through Germany this year leave the country they must go home as converts, eager to spread the gospel of National Socialism.' Great care, he wrote, was being taken to create a convivial atmosphere and provide visitors with interpreters and translators and to billet them with carefully chosen families steeped in National Socialism. 'There is no chance of the traveller finding out what things are like below the surface . . . Guests will judge by what they see and everything they are intended to see will be kept under the searchlights. And it goes without saying that everyone will praise German hospitality, because it has always deserved honest praise . . . What the German Government is hoping, desperately, without making any secret of the fact, is that the Olympic Games will generate so much goodwill in favour of Germany that a new atmosphere will be created, making German commercial expansion again possible.' And yet, despite all the effort, it was by no means certain that the result would be all that was hoped for. 'There seems to be a kind of twist in the German mentality that prevents it from understanding how the Anglo-Saxon mind works. Sport stands, first and foremost, for fair play—fair play for everyone, even Jews. Nazi Germany cannot swallow that, but it has at least been forced by facts to realise that the world will not stand for anti-Semitism either. So for the duration of the Winter Games at Garmisch-Partenkirchen all notice boards in Bavaria intimating that "Jews Are Not Allowed Here" were taken down. Not a trace of anti-Semitism could be found anywhere. Some foreign journalists were so surprised that they cabled home saying that allegations as to anti-Jewish feeling in Germany were "lies". If they had come to Berlin they would have found notices everywhere saying, "Those who buy at Jewish shops are traitors" etc. etc. And that is what is likely to upset German calculations about the Anglo-Saxon world.'

Of course, by the time the Summer Games began, those signs in Berlin had been stowed away too.

While the boycott movement was a non-event in Australia, groups in other countries, first and foremost the United States, but also France, Spain, the Netherlands, Sweden, Czechoslovakia and Great Britain, at least debated the issue. In Britain, support for a Berlin boycott came from the Jewish community, and from sections of the Labour Party, trade unions, universities, communists and socialists. The *Manchester Guardian* was, however, the only mainstream newspaper to oppose Berlin, on the grounds that a Nazi Games would violate Olympic principles, 'which provide that amateurs of all nations shall assemble on an equal footing, and that only natives or naturalised subjects of a country shall participate . . . German Jews would not be capable of competing on an equal footing with other athletes . . . because Germany has decreed that they are no longer natives or naturalised subjects.'

Britain's Conservative government, led by Neville Chamberlain, would not hear of a boycott, despite being well aware that

Nazi assurances that Jewish athletes would be considered for selection were bunkum. Chamberlain was prepared to do anything to appease Hitler in the hope of avoiding another war and stemming communism. On 23 March 1936, the House of Commons swiftly concluded that government had no business preventing British athletes from competing.

The British Olympic Committee's Lord Aberdare wrote to Baillet-Latour to assure him of his organisation's full support for the Berlin Olympics, but asked the Olympic chief to approach Hitler and ask him to consider including Jewish athletes, coaches and officials and then, as international window-dressing, to publicise the fact. Baillet-Latour summoned the courage to put the proposition to the Führer, who told him to tell Aberdare to mind his own business.

Lewald and Diem continued to globe-trot, spreading the word about the wonderful new Germany and how the Berlin Games could not fail to be the most efficient, inclusive and joyous Games in history. Lewald had his work cut out in New York City and Boston, where 1500 boycott proponents demonstrated in the streets.

The US boycott movement might have had a chance of success had not Avery Brundage, president of the all-powerful American Olympic Committee (AOC), been one of Germany's staunchest supporters. Brundage, who had grown up in poverty in Chicago, had competed with moderate success in the decathlon and pentathlon at the 1912 Stockholm Olympics. He went on to become a millionaire civil engineer in Chicago, attributing the canny investments that saw him prosper in the Depression to the calm thinking and hard-headedness that sport had taught him. In 1928, Brundage was appointed president of the AOC. As well as being an effective administrator, Brundage was an autocratic arch-conservative with, it was said, a discus where his heart should have been. He genuinely believed that sport and politics were church and state. He was ideologically sympathetic to right-wing National Socialism and saw Nazism as a safeguard against world domination by communism. He admired the Hitler Youth movement, which he said had transformed German youngsters from sickly, pale weaklings into strong and sporty men and women. In one address he stressed that America had much to learn from Germany. 'We, too, if we wish to preserve our institutions, must stamp out communism. We, too, must take steps to arrest the decline of patriotism.' Earlier in his career, Brundage had said that the very foundation of the modern Olympic revival would be undermined if individual countries were allowed to restrict participation 'by reason of class, creed or race'. Now he, whose own gentlemen's club in New York banned Jews, was abandoning those principles to ensure that his cherished Olympics went ahead.

Knowing that if the influential Americans backed Berlin, other countries opposing his Games would likely fall into line, Hitler had invited Brundage to Berlin in September 1934 to charm him, and to let him see the preparations and meet key officials. At their meeting, Hitler exuded bonhomie and passed himself off as a sports fan. He gave Brundage his word that 23 Jewish athletes would be chosen in the German Olympic team. The Germans introduced Brundage to a group of Jewish athletes who assured him that life for them in the Reich had never been better. This was not surprising, for sitting in on these discussions was the much-feared deputy Reichssportführer Arno Breitmeyer, decked out in his SS uniform.

The courting of Brundage had the desired effect, for he returned to America saying that the Berlin Olympics would be an enormous success and the Germans ideal hosts. He was in no doubt that German Jews had every chance to be selected to represent Germany. 'I accept the German Government's unqualified assurances of non-discrimination,' said Brundage. He said that there were no reports in existence, 'official or otherwise', that Germany had 'failed to give Jewish athletes a fair opportunity'. Therefore the AOC had no right to 'interfere in [Germany's] internal, political, religious or racial affairs . . . The Olympic Games belong to athletes, not politicians.' Moreover, 'Certain Jews must understand that they cannot use these Games as a weapon in their boycott against the Nazis.' Any problems the Jews were experiencing were of their own making, and those who would boycott Berlin were 'un-American alien agitators'.

Days after Brundage's return, the AOC officially accepted the German Olympic Organising Committee's invitation to compete at the Berlin Olympic Games. AOC secretary Frederick Rubien stated that if Jews were not being selected, this was simply because they were not good enough athletes: 'Why, there are not a dozen Jews in the world of Olympic calibre.' Charles Sherrill, an American member of the IOC, said that the United States had no more right telling Germans who they should select in their team than Germans should have to give America advice on dealing with the 'Negro situation' in the south.

In Nazi headquarters in Berlin there was rejoicing. The Americans' acceptance of the Olympic invitation was interpreted as a victory for National Socialism and 'a defeat for the Jews', and the exclusion of Jews from society, as well as from the Olympics, was intensified.

In the United States, anti-Nazi groups stepped up their protests. Pro-boycotters petitioned President Franklin D. Roosevelt to overrule the AOC. Although Roosevelt personally abhorred Nazism, he knew that popularity lay in isolationism, and refused to involve himself.

The Nazi regime backed its propaganda crusade by publishing 32 million pamphlets in 27 languages detailing Olympic events and rules, and how to make the most of Berlin. They sent them to all parts of the world and flooded international wire services with progress updates.

Countering the pro-Games propaganda, New York governor Al Smith, mayor Fiorello La Guardia and Boston mayor James Curley lobbied for a boycott. The US chief consul to Germany, George Messersmith, and the US ambassador there, William E. Dodd, who both saw Nazi anti-Semitism at close hand every day, reported to the US State Office that 'all German sport is today directly controlled by the Government and is professedly an instrument of the Party for the shaping of youth into National Socialist ideology . . . To the Party and to the youth of Germany, the holding of the Olympic Games in Berlin in 1936 has become the symbol of the conquest of the world by National Socialist doctrine. Should the Games not be held in Berlin, it would be one of the most serious blows which National Socialist prestige could suffer within an awakening Germany and one of the most effective ways which the world outside has of showing to the youth of Germany its opinion of National Socialist doctrine. [It is] inconceivable that the AOC should continue its stand that sport in Germany is non-political, that there is no discrimination. Other nations are looking to the United States before they act, hoping for leadership; the Germans are holding back on increased economic oppression against the Jews until the Games are over. America should prevent its athletes from being used by another government as a political instrument.'

The debate in America was finally resolved on 8 December 1935 when, at a meeting of the Amateur Athletic Union in New York, a proposal to boycott was narrowly defeated. Once the Americans opted to go to Berlin, what clamour there was elsewhere in the world to boycott the Nazi Games dwindled. Some Jewish American competitors declared themselves unavailable, but most athletes in America and in other countries opposed any boycott.

In all, 4783 athletes from 49 nations—including the United States, whose 312-strong team numbered five Jews and nineteen African Americans—would contest 129 events in Berlin.

On 13 March 1936, the day that the Australian Olympic team was named, Baillet-Latour declared: 'Nothing short of a war will stop the Summer Olympic Games being held in Berlin in August.'

CHAPTER 7
ALL AT SEA

On the morning of 13 May 1936, SS *Mongolia* lay at anchor in Sydney Harbour awaiting precious cargo. The P&O vessel was a fourteen-year-old passenger, mail and cargo one-class steamer which normally plied the Australia to United Kingdom route. This voyage would be different. *Mongolia* was carrying the Australian Olympians to Europe. The Queensland and NSW contingent would embark in Sydney, then the vessel would steam to Melbourne via Hobart to collect the Victorians, and then to Fremantle for the young Western Australians de Lacy and Oliver. The ship's itinerary included Colombo in Ceylon, Bombay, Aden in Yemen, Port Said in the Suez Canal, and Malta's Valletta. The 37-day voyage would end in Marseilles in the south of France, from where the Australians would travel by trains to Paris and Cologne and, nearly six weeks after leaving home, disembark in Berlin.

Excitement ran high as the athletes gathered at Circular Quay in drizzling rain. By late morning, a crowd of 5000 well-wishers had crammed onto the quay, bursting through a barricade erected around a police band. The male athletes preened in their new green and gold blazers with an emu and kangaroo emblem on the breast pocket, green ties and caps, cream jumpers and slacks, all ceremoniously presented to them the day before at the official state government farewell. The two women team members promenaded in wide-brimmed white hats, green blazers and cream frocks.

The athletes greeted each other and farewelled loved ones amid coloured streamers and Australian flags. Boarding in Sydney were team members Norton, Mackay, Metcalfe, Dickinson, Gray, Cook, Scarf, Pearce, Dixon, Turner and the rowing eight. (Bill Kendall was already travelling in Europe and would unite with his team-mates in Berlin.) There, too, were the support staff—Alderson, Nightingale, Mackenzie, masseur Fred McKay, and Inspector Fergusson and his wife, Mary. NSW Police Commissioner William MacKay and Mrs MacKay were also on *Mongolia*'s passenger list. Bidding the squad bon voyage were AOF chairman James Taylor and secretary Jim Eve, who would sail to Europe on the more salubrious liner SS *Ormonde* the following week.

Joining *Mongolia* in Sydney, too, was a six-strong New Zealand Olympic team minus that country's finest athlete, Jack Lovelock, who was studying medicine at Oxford University on a Rhodes Scholarship and would meet his fellow Kiwis in Berlin. The New Zealanders were greeted as antipodean brothers by the Australians.

As haul-anchor time neared, the police band honked out 'Auld Lang Syne', 'Advance Australia Fair' and 'Waltzing Matilda', the large crowd waved their flags more frantically than before, 'hip-hip-hurrayed' and cried 'Godspeed!' Hats were thrown high and happy tears shed. At 1 p.m. *Mongolia* steamed through grey harbour waters past the four-year-old Harbour Bridge and on out of the Heads.

After deciding that there was a 'jolly fine crowd of people in our team', Dickinson 'chatted with Kitty [Mackay] and Pat [Norton] who are quite nice and it was a pleasure', then took off his shoes and socks and ran fifteen times around the wooden deck.

Early on 15 May, *Mongolia* docked in Hobart. The two days in Tasmania were busy. The rowers trained and Gray cycled along the Hobart shore. Track and field athletes were bussed to an Australian Rules match where they entertained the crowd by running up and down the field. To the particular delight of Wal Mackney and his police rowing mates, a visit was squeezed in to Cascade Brewery. The mayor of Hobart presented the team with two cases of apples, and Harry Alderson bought a further twelve large cases of the fruit to be stowed in the *Mongolia*'s freezer and consumed on the voyage. It was the athletes' job to load the apples.

Two days later, when the ship docked at Port Melbourne, Prime Minister Lyons made a speech and toasted the health of the team. He presented Olympic blazers to the departing Victorians: Carter, Watson, Backhouse, Woodhouse, Masters, Wheeler, Johnson, Harley, Cooper, Garrard and O'Hara, and the masseur Morrison. Lyons used his oration to take a pot shot at Hitler (who had infamously declared that 'German athletics are in the complete sense of the word political'). Said Lyons, 'With the spirit of cheerfulness and concord which it will take to Berlin, the Australian Olympic team should be able to do that which the statesmen of the world are finding most difficult. The team should do much to foster the peace and friendship of which this old world is sadly in need . . . In amateur athletics I see the real spirit of sport. Success brings no reward other than the knowledge that you have done your best. When the Olympic torch is finally extinguished at the great stadium in Berlin, the Australian team will have lighted another torch which will burn brightly—the torch of peace and mutual friendship.'

That evening, the male athletes were guests at the men-only Victorian Amateur Sports Club 'smoke concert'. While puffing on cigars, pipes and cigarettes they were again toasted by Prime Minister Lyons. Meanwhile, the club treated Mackay, Norton,

Carter and chaperone Fergusson to a theatre party. Descending the gangway for their night on the town, Mackay and Norton were interviewed by a reporter from *The Argus*. 'Two pretty girls in evening frocks and wraps, coming down the gangway of *Mongolia* last night, did not suggest prowess at sport; yet they were none other than Kitty Mackay and Kathleen [*sic*] Norton, NSW swimming representatives, who are on their way with the chaperone, Mrs Fergusson, to the Olympic Games . . . In their luggage they carry green silk bathing gowns for practice and black silk ones for race days; all are high-necked to conform to Olympic regulations.'

Basil Dickinson's nemesis Hugh Weir joined *Mongolia* in Melbourne. The athlete was too polite to tell the official what he thought of him and was civil when their paths crossed. In his diary, Dickinson opined, 'I must declare myself a hypocrite!'

When *Mongolia* docked in Adelaide, there was yet another civic reception, at which Adelaide's Lord Mayor aired his hopes that the team 'would comport themselves as true Australians and bring honour to Australia'. In response, Alderson trumpeted that eight gold medals was a realistic target, before backtracking: 'If only we had the facilities overseas athletes enjoyed, Australia would equal any other country.'

One Adelaide newspaper reported breathlessly on Doris Carter's sartorial style: 'Miss Carter has an all-white outfit of athletic singlet and shoes. Even the spikes of her jumping shoes are white. For wear on the ship she has a number of crisp linen and silk blouses, tweed suits, white divided linen skirt with shirt blouse to match and a number of light frocks for the tropics. For evening wear she has two floral gowns and heavy velvet wraps.'

Mongolia reached Fremantle early on 25 May, after a rough voyage across the Bight that had made half the team seasick. Dickinson, who wasn't afflicted, quipped in his diary: 'We are having difficulty restraining some of the affected members of the team from jumping overboard but I doubt if they have that much energy at present. Fred McKay was so bad we discussed what we should do with his body. It was a big storm. We stood on the for'ard section of A deck to see the waves smashing against the boat sending up huge sprays, and hear the wind whistling through the wires.' Pat Norton developed a painful ear infection, likely contracted in the ship's tiny canvas swimming pool.

To the bemusement of the other passengers, makeshift training facilities were set up on board. An eight-man rowing machine was installed on the emergency bridge deck aft, and rubber mats were strewn on the deck for calisthenics and wrestling. Athletes ran laps around the deck and swam as best they could but, to avoid collisions, only at times when regular voyagers were dining or sleeping. Training was strictly voluntary. Looking back years later, Dick Garrard told Harry Gordon, 'They sewed ship mattresses together and put a canvas cover over them and I wrestled with Eddie Scarf, but I couldn't wrestle on a rocking ship. *Mongolia* was not the *Queen Mary*.' Sculler Cec Pearce reminisced to Gordon about manager Alderson erecting 'a machine sort of thing that somebody had made, it wasn't very good, but the eight used it on the boat deck. It was no good for me because I was on two sculls, not one oar. I tried to maintain fitness by wrestling with Eddie Scarf and sparring with Rusty Cook, but it was not ideal.' Gray rigged up a makeshift bike treadmill by attaching to the deck a pair of metal cylinders on which he set up his cycle and pedalled. 'It was unsatisfactory. We were fit when we boarded the boat but we were blown out when we got off. I felt sorry for the runners and the swimmers. The swimmers dived into the pool and hit their head on the other end. And the runners, they had it rough trying to avoid bumping into passengers and negotiating corners on the deck. The wrestlers and boxers weren't too badly off. They could work out on their mattresses.'

'They had a makeshift saltwater pool, a canvas tarpaulin stretched over a wooden frame, barely one metre deep,' recalled Dickinson. 'The swimmers tried to train by attaching a rope to a fixed object at the poolside, tying the other end around their waist and swimming on the spot. It was hopeless, and funny to watch. Apart from being shallow, the blazing sun turned the water into hot soup. Poor Ron Masters, the diver, had no chance! Dive into that pool and you'd end up with a spinal injury.' In what Dickinson considered a 'wonder of wonders', Harry Nightingale taught him to swim in that sorry pool.

In Fremantle, swimmers Evelyn de Lacy and Percy Oliver boarded. They weren't the only distinguished Australians to join *Mongolia* at the port. Team supporter A.V. Sundercombe stepped forward to present the team with a mascot, a live grey kangaroo, which they christened 'Aussie'.

Metcalfe whiled away the time at Fremantle by schooling a group of well-wishers in the arcane arts of high and broad jumping. Doris Carter told admirers that she was confident of doing well in Berlin because she was regularly jumping 2in (5cm) higher than the Empire Games record of 5ft 1in (1.54m). Although opportunities for high jumping on *Mongolia* would be few, she would practise by leaping over a stick resting across two crates. She also had every intention of skipping, she announced, if she could find a suitable piece of rope. To be at her best in Berlin, she was even considering special training and a special diet. 'To date, I'm afraid I've never bothered about it.'

A reporter from Perth's *The Mirror* gave snapshots of the team. His editor had clearly despatched him to Fremantle with the brief to offer insights into the personalities of the Olympians. He described Dunc Gray as 'good-looking', which was true, and 'modest and inclined to be shy', which was news to those who knew the outspoken cyclist well. Tassie Johnson and Chris Wheeler were 'happy personalities', while Jack Metcalfe possessed a 'studious nature' befitting a 'medical student' (in fact he was studying law) who enjoyed lecturing youngsters about the character-building qualities of athletics (at least that was true). Alf Watson's claim to fame was that he was 'the only member with a mo'. Dickinson had 'a boyish but pleasant personality' and looked to be 'a bundle of energy possessing plenty of confidence'. Gerald Backhouse 'like all blonds . . . has a cheery disposition and looks as though he is satisfied with the world in general'. Pole vaulter Fred Woodhouse had 'shed all excess weight so as to make himself light as he flies over the bar'. Doris Carter was blessed with 'a pleasant face and prominent teeth'. Pat Norton commanded much interest: she did not look her seventeen years, observed the journalist, and her complexion was 'very fair'. The reporter was also much taken with Kitty Mackay, '6ft in height, she has a cheerful disposition and is good looking [and her] first words on arrival was the enquiry where she could have a swim'. 'Short and squat' diver Ron Masters was having trouble making his hat fit on his head. Oliver and de Lacy were too well known to readers of *The Mirror* to even warrant describing. Boxers Rusty Cook, Harry Cooper and Les Harley were all masters of the ring who 'packed TNT in each hand and had remarkably few battle scars'. Eddie Scarf the wrestler was a 'big, bad man' who nevertheless managed to be a natural comedian. 'We have not tested his wrestling ability, but are certain that he is the goods.' Nor had the reporter grappled with Dick Garrard, and considering the size of the wrestler's hands and feet, he was thankful for that! The other wrestler, Spud O'Hara, had 'rippling muscles and a magnificent chest topped by a rather good-looking face with an expression of serious thought'. The rowers were all husky and it was surprising that alterations did not have to be made to their boats to accommodate their bulk. By the time he reached rower Bill Dixon, the intrepid reporter was running out of inspiration. Dixon, it was reputed, 'has a weakness for cheese and biscuits'. The scribe summed up: 'Altogether, the team members are a bright and happy crowd of young Australians who are out to do their best for their country, and above all to advance still higher the good name of Australia.'

In a still, blue twilight, *Mongolia* departed Fremantle for the next port of call, Colombo. On the harbour quay, around 500 supporters cheered and whistled, throwing streamers that clung to the ship's side. Local heroes de Lacy and Oliver had their own cheer squads, who gave them three hurrahs as they waved back from the deck, clutching streamers. *Mongolia* gathered speed and was gone.

Once they were steaming north-west through the Indian Ocean, Alderson formed a sports committee, and games and activities were organised. The weather was fine, the sea calm, and those team members so inclined trained as best they could. Cook's eyebrow was split in a sparring mishap and his wound was stitched by the ship's doctor. To make the hours fly, a makeshift picture show was erected, with films projected onto a sheet. The team also performed handstands, and put on skipping, boxing and wrestling demonstrations for the other passengers, who apparently appreciated these displays. The musicians among them—Oliver strummed a ukulele, Backhouse and de Lacy blew harmonica, and Masters played the fiddle—held impromptu concerts. Flyweight boxer Harry Cooper was a dervish at the Irish jig. In those days, too, everyone sang, and reeled off, in varying degrees of tuneful-ness, popular songs of the day.

Alderson and Mrs Fergusson told reporters that the Australian team was 'one big happy family'. Generally that was true, although according to Dickinson, early on some of the Victorians remained aloof from athletes of other states. Dickinson got along well with Victorians Carter—'a lovely young woman with qualities that saw her have a distinguished life after athletics'—and Cooper:

'delightful little man, quick on the uptake, a fast tongue, amusing, lovely fellow, the world was an apple for him'. Victorian boxer Harley 'was a rough diamond but easygoing, a working class boy who could handle himself'. Victorian runners Backhouse and Watson and Dickinson's cabin-mate Woodhouse 'were decent enough, but a bit distant', found Dickinson. 'It was a class thing . . . It seemed the Victorians who attended Geelong Grammar or Scotch College looked down a little on anyone who didn't. Backhouse was a Geelong Grammar School boy and had that manner. He and Watson stuck together. Woodhouse went to Scotch College. It was he who stole the drinks off the waiters' trays at the big British Embassy party in Berlin. That's why we locked him in the bus.'

Gray was another athlete around whom Dickinson never felt completely at ease. 'Dunc was opinionated. He didn't like the Germans and didn't like being out of Australia.'

Dickinson also felt that the police rowers, while quick to join the partying and last to leave, preferred each other's company— 'perhaps this was because they'd been a tight team for years, while, mostly, the rest of us were strangers and had to get to know each other . . . In the beginning, the track and field athletes stuck together, and the swimmers and the others hung around with their fellows. Inevitably as we became familiar, natural friendships formed that transcended our particular sports.'

Dickinson bonded with Scarf after a rocky start. 'Eddie, who was a butcher . . . pulled me up at one point of the voyage and gave me a stern talking-to, and he had every right. I came from a family that never socialised, and I was naïve. With my sheltered upbringing I was, I'm afraid, a very judgemental little bugger. I was shocked by some of the things that went on during the trip, what I considered to be loose behaviour and some people's tendency to use the trip to play up and change cabins and drink too much. I made a critical remark in an offended tone of voice and Eddie overheard. He said to me, "Look, young fella. The others are not bothering you. Everyone's different and you have to respect that. What they do is their own business. You should mind yours." He put me in my place and taught me to be tolerant. I've always valued Eddie's advice. We all learned about each other's foibles on that ship, and became a team united.'

There was excitement when, as recorded in Dickinson's diary, Alderson informed the athletes that 'there was a notorious adventuress on board in the person of Jessie Kidd and we have been advised to steer clear'. Dickinson was of the opinion that some of the police rowers took the warning as an invitation. However, no scandal ensued.

One of the most valuable, and enjoyable, documents surviving from the 1936 Australian Olympic campaign is the diary of Evelyn de Lacy, containing the thoughts and impressions of an intelligent and vivacious young woman as she travelled overseas for the first time, to compete against the world's best swimmers: 'May 25: Boarded the *Mongolia* at quarter to six. Left Fremantle at 6 after wonderful send-off. Established myself in cabin 297.

'May 26: Awake about quarter to eight, up and out on deck . . . About 10.30 everyone started training. Mats put down for wrestlers and boxers. Athletes skipping, everyone hard at work. Swim at 11. Pool very small, only six yards square, can't do much work, only leg action . . . Played bucket quoits and bull board and deck tennis. Feeling a bit light-headed so went and had some sleep. Awoke about half past six feeling rotten. Oh! Sea sick. Tried to eat an apple, not very successful so went to bed in disgust, while the others went to the pictures and saw *Popeye*. Took medicine.

'May 27: Feeling much better today and able to enjoy myself. Even Aussie the kangaroo keeping fit.

'May 28: Went up to the bow of the ship and watched the flying fish. Really remarkable the way they dip like swallows over the waves.

'May 29: The day was cloudy and then we got the rain. Too wet for games so I wrote letters. Gave Aussie some lettuce. Too wet for boat drill so went into the music room and sang till dinner.

'May 30: Eleven o'clock went for a swim but Percy and Pat were there first practising their turns. Then Kitty and I. Then the four of us had it for leg work before the crowd were allowed in.'

Dickinson had begun the voyage as the sole occupant of a tiny—1.8m by 2.4m—three-bunk steerage cabin. Gradually the cabin filled. In Hobart, he was joined by a large crate of apples that would not fit in the hold, and then by Cooper and Woodhouse after they boarded in Melbourne. 'Harry, Fred and I were on top of each other. There was no air conditioning. Going through the tropics, the heat in our cabin was unbearable. The apples rotted. We took our mattresses and slept on the deck overnight. Sailors swabbed the decks and drenched us. There was little respite from the heat in the small, sea water pool, and the showers too were tepid salt water. We couldn't train properly, so grew unfit and gained weight . . .

'There was lots of alcohol on the boat if you were so inclined,' noted Dickinson. 'And you could buy six cigarettes for three pence! Many of the male athletes smoked and a few of the women too. I didn't smoke until I bought a pipe in Berlin. Then I puffed away for the next 50 years, pipe and cigarettes. Life was different then.'

At 6 a.m. on 3 June, the *Mongolia* arrived in Colombo. At the dock, wrote Dickinson, 'Dozens and dozens of rickshaw drivers clamoured for our patronage.' The Olympians were collected in cars, except for the police rowers, who were taken in an open-topped charabanc donated by the Colombo police force, and all were escorted to the country estate of Sir Solomon Dias

Bandaranaike, Ceylon's aide-de-camp to the British governor. 'My eyes were wide open,' said Dickinson. 'Remember, this was my first time out of Australia, and I could not believe that such things as we experienced existed. We enjoyed a morning tea of tropical fruit that none of us had ever seen before. We were entertained by acrobats and magicians and devil dancers wearing grotesque costumes. Sir Solomon owned ten elephants and after they did tricks for us, we rode them throughout his lush gardens. We thanked him with a boomerang, and taught him how to throw it.' Back then to the YMCA for a spicy curry lunch, after which the boxers and wrestlers had exhibition bouts against local fighters, and the swimmers and runners took on Colombo's best, trying not to abuse their hosts' hospitality by winning too easily. The party made its weary way back to *Mongolia* in the late afternoon for a 6 p.m. departure.

The outing gave de Lacy much diary fodder: 'June 3: [The locals] have a marvellous sense of balance as all the women carry loads on their heads. Most wear bright colours and some sit in the gutter and play dice . . . In the outlying districts the children wear no clothes and the men work wearing a loin cloth . . . [They] eat betel nut which makes their gums bright red. The locals were trading black elephant [statuettes] of all sizes and descriptions . . . They had tobacco jars and ship and bullock wagon models, walking sticks, mats and sun hats and they shouted and shrieked . . . We left the boat at about half past eight and were taken ashore in a big tug. We noticed old-fashioned galleons and black crows. We found people begging till they nearly drove you cracked . . . We were shown two deadly snakes, a green viper and a coconut flower crite [krait] . . .'

A few hours out of Colombo, boxer Harry Cooper was not ready to turn in. He strung up a sheet in his cabin, shone a torch through it and engaged in a spot of vigorous shadow-boxing.

Unfortunately, the sheet concealed a steel post. After a few minutes' jabbing and hooking, Cooper's right hand hit the stanchion. 'Poor blighter,' recalled Dickinson, who witnessed his cabin-mate's mishap. 'Imagine the little bloke dancing around and *bang bang . . . Ow!*' The ship's doctor set Cooper's broken hand, and at the next port of call, Bombay, his swollen, throbbing fist was X-rayed. *Mongolia's* medico had done a good job and Cooper was told there was a reasonable chance he would be able to lace on a glove for the boxing heats in Berlin. There could, however, be no training in the meantime.

Approaching Bombay on 5 June, the squad gathered for a grand feast to honour Kitty Mackay on her 21st birthday. On the heels of the birthday party was a fancy dress ball. Team members strived to look the most outlandish, but the police rowing crew stole the show when, emboldened by beer, they arrived as ballerinas in frilly paper tutus, ballet shoes and with bows in their hair. Wal Mackney, with his broken nose and cauliflower ears, looked a picture. They had learned some ballet steps, and a couple even managed to perform them without falling down. Normally serious Jack Metcalfe, with his tree trunk legs, starred as the prima ballerina.

Dickinson's memories of *Mongolia's* stopover in Bombay were soured by the boarding of 350 British civil servants and army personnel returning home for annual leave. 'The ship was too crowded before they joined us, but that wasn't the main problem. These representatives of the Raj were a nasty type. They seemed to *hate* us.'

Dickinson was similarly affronted by the poverty of Bombay when he and three teammates spent a few hours in the markets while *Mongolia* was being loaded. 'The Indians carrying all the boxes and crates on board were poor skinny wretches dressed in rags. The dock was stained red with betel juice. When we explored the city we saw diabolical living conditions . . . rats everywhere . . . meat hanging in shops crusted with flies, people sleeping in filth, the heat . . . I have read avidly about India ever since. Before we returned to the ship, we enjoyed a lemonade at the Taj Mahal Palace hotel.'

On to Aden in the Red Sea, where Basil Dickinson purchased a copy of the *Rubaiyat of Omar Khayyam* in a stall, and then Port Said. In her diary, de Lacy wrote: 'June 8: Today we had a cool breeze off the ocean but it has been very rough since we left Bombay, with 450 more passengers now on board. We are overcrowded, we can't get near the pool and when you can you nearly get knocked out because the boat rolls so much. I have given up swimming. Eddie Scarf has got a touch of the sun, Mrs Fergusson is seasick. I feel a ball of muscle but caged up like a lion . . .

'June 10: Awoke to a beautiful day. Not a ripple disturbed the surface of the ocean. About half past nine we saw from the bow of the boat shoals of fish being chased by sharks . . . About one we saw the towering cliffs of Arabia in the distance, and from then land all the way. We saw 50 dolphins having a great game. The Arabian sunset was thoroughly disappointing, but twilight was wonderful and the evening cool and delightful.'

At Port Said, Ron Masters at last had a chance to dive. When he saw local children on the dock diving for coins thrown by the ship's passengers, he donned his togs, climbed up onto the ship's railing and plunged into the water. Percy Oliver and Les Harley, the latter inconvenienced by an outbreak of boils on his arm, dived in too.

The time spent at the port of Valletta in Malta was too short for sightseeing, which was fine by the Australians, who, after their long voyage, were now desperately keen to reach Marseilles.

They arrived at 6 p.m. on 19 June. 'It was so hot, and we were sick of life at sea and wanted only to be on dry land,' remembered Dickinson. 'Our cabins being so small, we were only allowed to have hand luggage with us, and our suitcases were stowed in the hold. We had to go down and find our cases among all the cargo and carry them up on deck ourselves for disembarking. Just our luck, there was a general strike in Marseilles and there were police with rifles everywhere.'

Pat Norton and de Lacy slipped into a newsreel theatre to escape the heat. Norton was one of the few Australian Olympians who was politically aware—having attended the fiery political rallies of NSW Labor premier Jack Lang in Sydney's Hyde Park—yet nothing prepared her for what she saw on the screen. In the tiny theatre, she 'watched a short on Herr Hitler—interesting and threatening. It showed a white map of Europe with boundaries in black. Then a section of Europe was blacked out—it looked like Poland—then came Hitler's photo and another section was blacked out. And so it went on until the whole of Europe disappeared into black, except a section of France. The reality of Hitler and the situation rising in Germany hit home. The irony of this, an Olympic team on its way to Germany, watching their host making threatening [overtures] to another community.'

De Lacy wasn't much impressed by her hour at the flicks in Marseilles, or by the French port itself: 'Soldiers and police were walking in the streets armed with guns and truncheons. The whole place was dirty and smelly. The back streets were like rubbish dumps and the houses half falling down. The people are slovenly and even wash their clothes in the gutter, when they do wash. All the French men wear ridiculous berets. We went into a 60-minute Around the World Gazette [a newsreel cinema] and saw Charlie Chaplin and a Mickey Mouse cartoon, but couldn't understand either because they were in French. The most peculiar thing is that the people here eat and drink in the streets.'

Because of the strike, the train to Paris was eight hours late, and it was 11.15 p.m. before the Australians boarded. Despite the green, rolling fields blanketed by vivid red poppies through which the train passed, the journey to Lyon was an uncomfortable and stifling experience—six passengers stuffed into each tiny third-class compartment. Alderson later reported that the team took the hellish train trip 'in good part, knowing that sleepers were out of all reason, as the cost in Australian money on the French trains was about 5 pounds each'. At 12.30 p.m. on 20 June the train wheezed into Paris, where the group was greeted by the Australian trade commissioner.

'We arrived in Paris too exhausted to be excited about finally being in Europe,' said Dickinson. 'It didn't help that like most of the team all I knew about France was the Eiffel Tower, and that they'd had a revolution a couple of hundred years before. We had an overnight stay at the very cheap Louvre Hotel, just across the road from the Louvre museum. After a nap, Harry Alderson dragged us out of our cots to go to the Folies Bergère. The Folies had a reputation of being racy, with naked dancers, and we thought "Ooh-la-la!" All we saw were some fully clad singers and comedy skits in French. It was no more shocking than a Sunday school picnic. Only the men attended, because Mary Fergusson would not allow the women to attend such a scandalous show and she organised a bus tour of Paris and Versailles. The next day we were left to our own resources until we boarded the train for Germany about 11 p.m. We all split up. I spent all day at the Louvre and saw our special girl, the Mona Lisa. No one wanted to join me. Some of the team didn't leave the hotel. Can you believe that? They were grumbling that Paris, where they'd been for a few hours and of which they'd seen virtually nothing, wasn't half as good as Sydney or Melbourne.' There was even a kerfuffle when the Australians were served breakfast in the hotel dining room. 'They brought us coffee and rolls. Well, didn't that put on a rodeo!' recalled Cec Pearce. 'We said, "This is no good to us. We want bacon and eggs!"'

A few of the team did venture into the wilds of Paris, which was enduring a heatwave. The Australians were all taken aback by Paris's high prices. Mackay quipped that she would definitely return but bring a few million francs with her next time.

Although they'd been in town just a day, the Australians felt qualified to pontificate about Paris and Parisians. After interviewing the police rowers, a reporter for *The Sydney Morning Herald* told how 'Inspector Fergusson and his men did not appreciate Paris's traffic laws [because] their efficiency was not equal to those in force in Australia, a view confirmed by the series of accidents seen. They say the main trouble is due to the selfishness of motorists who refuse to give way whether they are right or wrong.' Another team member was confident that 'despite the beauties of the art and architecture of Paris and the charm of strange customs, there is infinitely greater happiness in Australia with its immeasurably greater potentialities'.

At 3 a.m. on 22 June, six hours into the train journey from Paris to Cologne and just across the German border, those Olympians who'd been able to sleep in their stuffy and jammed compartments were startled awake by shouting, doors slamming and the grinding of brakes. 'German soldiers came on board, making a lot of noise, passing from compartment to compartment, demanding to see our passports, visas and tickets and wanting to know how much money each of us was carrying,' remembered Dickinson. 'It was very intimidating and we wondered what on earth we were getting ourselves into in Germany. These blokes with their swastikas and eagle insignia seemed so angry and self-important. Had we been more aware of what was happening in Germany with Hitler, we may not have been so surprised by their attitude . . . as soon as they realised we were Olympians, the soldiers were courteous. I learned later that they were under instructions from Joseph Goebbels to treat Olympic visitors well, and if word reached him that we'd been bullied they'd have had hell to pay.'

The bedraggled, tired troupe disembarked at Cologne at 7.30 a.m. and were met by an underling from the German Olympic Committee—in brown uniform with swastika armbands and gleaming black leather boots—and, maybe even more ominously for some of the weary athletes, directors of the Bayer Aspirin Works. At this stage of their journey a factory tour would not have been a high priority, but they were whisked in buses to Bayer headquarters to be treated to a mind-numbing demonstration of how the white pills were manufactured. According to Dickinson, only Alderson and Mrs Fergusson bothered feigning interest, although there were hoots of laughter when a Bayer doctor lanced Harley's boils.

'At the factory, more speeches were made; we were quickly learning how Germans love speeches!' said Dickinson. 'We also saw staff doing experiments with synthetic materials to produce uniforms and gear. None of us realised it then, but they were getting ready for war.' Indeed, there were strong links between Bayer's parent company IG Farben and the Nazis. In World War II, Farben would use concentration camp inmates as slave labour in its factories, and owned 42.5 per cent of the corporation that produced Zyklon B hydrogen cyanide, produced for the gas chambers of Auschwitz and other death camps.

On a less sinister note, De Lacy was entranced by what she saw as the team journeyed by coach through the Rhine Valley to neo-Gothic Berg Castle on Lake Starnberg. The day elicited a rapturous diary entry: 'Ah! Let me take you from this modern world back to olden days when beauty was beauty . . . let me take you to a fairyland, along highways where tall trees arch overhead, such a drive to the ivy-covered castle of Berg that I shall ever remember. I cannot express such wonder in words. On the drive back, winding in and out of hills and scenery so wonderful that my eyes ached through opening them so wide at the beauty and the picturesque countryside. Little towns were situated in the heart of these hills and it seemed we were trespassing from the modern age into Fairyland. At the sports stadium, second only in size in Germany to the Olympic stadium in Berlin, we were given bathers and went for a swim. It was 8.30 p.m. and still very light. Afterwards we travelled back to dinner at a hotel where Mr Alderson gave the mayor of Cologne and other high guests a boomerang and a souvenir card with the team's autographs on it. Now we are leaving Cologne, my wonderful Fairyland, with cheers and Australian coo-ees to the people who wave farewell to us. I hope someday I might revisit this wonderful town.'

On the night of 31 May 1942, less than six years after de Lacy and her teammates visited Cologne, 1046 bombers of the Royal Air Force attacked the city with 1320 tonnes of explosives. The raid, which lasted 75 minutes, killed 486 civilians, made 60,000 people homeless and destroyed 243 hectares of homes, shops, office buildings and factories. During World War II, Cologne would suffer more than 260 Allied air raids which killed as many as 20,000 civilians and left the glorious medieval city in ruins. De Lacy's despair when she learned of the destruction of her 'wonderful town' can only be imagined.

CHAPTER 8
INTO THE LAIR

The Australians' train rattled into Berlin's Friedrichstrasse station at 7.55 a.m. on 23 June, five weeks before the Games began. Alderson had convinced the AOF that as the Australians had the longest, most arduous journey to Berlin of any national team, they would need time to regain fitness and lose the excess weight many would inevitably gain.

Even before they stepped onto the platform in the cavernous station, they could hear the assembled Berliners chanting, *'Willkommen in Deutschland!'* ('Welcome to Germany!') and a military brass band belting out 'God Save the King', 'Deutschland Über Alles' ('Germany Above All') and the National Socialist anthem 'Horst-Wessel-Lied' ('Horst Wessel Song'). At the playing of the latter two, the locals flung the Nazi salute and the train's dining car attendants, porters and ticket collectors stuck outstretched arms through compartment windows.

As the first foreign team to gather in Berlin, the Australians were feted. Dickinson remembered 'swastika flags everywhere, and flowers and of course many speeches'. Wrote de Lacy: 'Oh, what a welcome! The band played the national anthem three times . . . and they greeted us with open arms, exclamations of delight and we were photographed a million times.'

Lewald was there to welcome Alderson and his squad to Berlin. Captain Wolfgang Fürstner, who had been awarded the Iron Cross for bravery in the Great War and was now commandant of the Olympic Village, where the men would be staying, wished the Australians a happy and successful campaign and placed himself at their service. Also on the platform was Captain von Benda, the Australians' designated attaché, who would accompany the athletes everywhere and attend to their needs. A close friend of Nazi chieftain Göring, von Benda's affability and command of English compensated for his lack of knowledge of Australia.

Joining his teammates at Friedrichstrasse station was Sydney swimmer Bill Kendall, who had been travelling in Europe. There too were AOF president James Taylor, secretary Jim Eve, and supporter and volunteer swimming coach Harry Hay. After collecting their baggage, the team was bussed to Berlin Town Hall, where the mayor presented Alderson with an outsized gold key denoting that the Australians had the run—within reason—of the city. At the civic reception afterwards, they sat through a propaganda film about Hitler. Each athlete was presented with an 'Olympic Passport', providing access to those areas in Berlin that the regime deemed suitable.

The group was then taken on a tour of Hitler's Berlin. Traffic in all directions halted for them and the public formed lines on both sides of the streets to cheer and wave. The delighted team cheered and waved right back. What they saw as their vehicle made its way through the magnificent and historic city made a profound impression on the wide-eyed Australians.

With a population of four million, Berlin was the third-largest city on earth, and had been as sophisticated and creative as Paris and New York. But after the National Socialists seized power, the sound of laughter and erudite chatter in the streets was replaced by angry harangues, the goosestepping of storm troopers, the rumble of armoured vehicles and the din of breaking glass. National Socialism had turned Berlin into a bleak and threatening metropolis where philistinism and xenophobic order were brutally enforced by the government and its guardians. For those whom the Nazi regime considered enemies, Berlin was a dangerous place.

Now, as impressionable visitors flocked to Berlin for the Olympic Games, the challenge that faced the Nazis was to present their Berlin as something it wasn't: a cultured, well-ordered, technologically advanced, sport-obsessed, and socially and politically tolerant city. In July and August 1936, Berlin would be a place where illusion was passed off as reality and reality was hidden from view. The Führer and his Olympics brains trust of Goebbels, Göring, Tschammer und Osten and Frick all subscribed to the idea that if those who came to Berlin departed with a favourable impression, they would spread the word that there was nothing to fear from National Socialism, and this would lessen international resistance and buy time for the Führer to put into operation his aggressive plans.

The relentless national and international promotion of the Games ensured that the beds designated for visitors in hotels, inns, pensions, private homes and tent camps were booked out months in advance. In July and August, Berlin's population officially swelled by 385,211. This does not count the many tens of thousands who stayed with friends or arranged their own accommodation. While most visitors to Berlin came from elsewhere in Germany, 14,408 arrived from the United States, 8546 from Great Britain and Ireland, 5018 from France and 344 from Australia. Visitors could reserve their Games tickets before leaving home, or take their chances once in Berlin. Lengthy queues formed outside the Deutsche Bank and Disconto Gesellschaft in Mauerstrasse when tickets went on sale on 15 June, and within a month the 2.7 million-plus tickets for the various events and the Opening and Closing Ceremonies had been snapped up. Some 400,000 applied for a ticket to the Opening Ceremony, a lucky 100,000 of whom were drawn from a ballot.

In June, the newspaper *Der Angriff*, on the instigation of Goebbels, lectured Berliners on the role they were expected to play in the Reich's Olympics. 'We are not only going to show off the most beautiful sports arena, the fastest transportation, and the cheapest currency: we are also going to be more charming than the Parisians, more easy-going than the Viennese, more vivacious than the Romans, more cosmopolitan than London, and more practical than New York.' Berliners should never miss the opportunity to tell visitors how wonderful was their Führer and his regime. A sunny day must be referred to as 'Hitler weather' and the period from 17 to 24 July was earmarked as a 'Week of Laughter' during which Berliners were required to be jolly. Taxi drivers, shopkeepers, hoteliers, restaurateurs and others in contact with visitors must be friendly and helpful. Marshals had been assigned to punish those who were rude or dared to frown. Citizens needed to be servants of Olympic guests, inviting them into their homes, answering their questions . . . although if a visitor was overly curious about the fate of Jews, gypsies, political opponents of the Reich, the disabled or other 'undesirables', that visitor must be reported to the Gestapo.

To further impress outsiders, Goebbels' Ministry of Propaganda and Enlightenment announced a raft of edicts to be enforced in July and August. Littering was banned, and street rubbish (including wagon horse droppings) must be picked up immediately; shabby houses had to be painted or whitewashed and front gardens kept in good order; homeowners must fly state-supplied swastika and Olympic flags and plant red geraniums in window boxes, and should they be damaged by the elements they must be immediately replaced. Decrepit cars needed to be removed from visitors' view; conversely, shiny new vehicles should be parked in the street outside homes to give the impression of prosperity. Convict labourers and concentration camp inmates could not work where they might be seen.

In her 'Berlin Letter' to the *New Yorker* magazine, American expat writer Janet Flanner noted that 'Germany profoundly wants visitors to feel at home'. This meant pretending that it wasn't what it had become since Hitler's ascension to power in 1933. 'The brown-shirted men of the SA and the black-shirted men of the SS have been ordered to keep their uniforms in the closet as much as possible for the duration of the summer games, and . . . ordered not to discuss racial problems in public, and to give a foreign lady, no matter what her profile, their seat in a tramcar.'

During the Olympic festival, Jews from overseas were not to be insulted, excluded, denied service or attacked; Jew-baiting signs ('No dogs or Jews allowed', 'Jews enter at own risk', 'Drive carefully! Sharp curve! Jews 75 miles an hour!') were taken down and stowed away to be re-posted when the eyes of the world were no longer on Germany, and any other traces of institutionalised discrimination against German Jews were hidden. Brown-shirts who routinely prowled Berlin's streets and beer gardens demanding donations for their cause were told to put their money tins away for a bit. Nazi newspapers such as the anti-Semitic *Der Stürmer* and *Der Judenkenner* were ordered to temporarily muzzle their daily diatribes. (*Der Stürmer* had only recently ranted, 'Jews are Jews . . . and there is no place for them in German sport . . . Germany is the Fatherland of Germans, not Jews.' And another rag had echoed the Führer's oft-stated hope that soon Berlin would become the permanent home of the Olympics, and the only eligible competitors would be those who 'master the

Nazi ideology and make known not only in athletics contests but also in national life that they stand up for that ideology'.)

Hitler and Goebbels stressed to Nazi officials that there must be no chest-beating about territorial expansion or rearmament, at least not where visitors might overhear. It must have rankled, but during the Olympic festival even Hitler toned down his furious rants, sprinkling his speeches with expressions of his love of peace and tolerance.

To keep pickpockets and muggers from targeting foreigners and leaving a negative impression, the regime locked up known criminals. A handbook containing the names and photographs of more than 1000 international crooks was distributed to guards at border entry points, and to the Reich Sports Field special police in case they slipped by the border guards. Special squads were assigned to arrest ticket scalpers and beggars.

The regime was determined that language would not be a barrier to visitors' enjoyment or, more importantly, prevent them from tuning in to the Nazi message. The Olympic Organising Committee's official report on the Games stated: 'In order to enable the Olympic visitors to gain some conception of the developments in the Third Reich and to place them in a position for acquainting themselves with actual life in Germany, an attempt had to be made to eliminate the language difficulty, since this is always an obstacle to the proper appreciation of foreign customs and activities.' Responsible for providing language assistance for foreign guests was the Olympic Transportation and Lodgings Bureau (OB), with its staff of trained interpreters and guides who had the necessary 'understanding of the psychology of foreign travellers'. If travellers from abroad wished to utilise their short stay in Berlin 'to become acquainted with German life and customs, a telephone call to the special headquarters established by the OB [is] sufficient for obtaining an expert guide and interpreter. Or if foreign visitors wish to meet their countrymen for a social hour or the exchange of impressions, they merely need to pay a call at one of the 10 centres provided for this purpose.'

The regime allowed around 7000 former prostitutes back on the streets for the benefit of the international visitors, having first examined them for venereal disease. Strip clubs, gay bars and racy cabarets that had been shuttered by the Nazis were suddenly back in business. 'Everything was free and the dance halls were reopened,' wrote one commentator on the return of licentiousness to Berlin. 'They played American music . . . Everybody thought, "Well, Hitler can't be so bad."' (Two weeks after the Olympics, the prostitutes, absinthe sellers and pornography purveyors were again banished to the underground—or to the private Nazi clubs, such as Salon Kitty in Charlottenburg, a favourite haunt of Goebbels and Reinhard Heydrich.)

Railway and bus stations were cleaned, repainted and modernised. Beer gardens were tarted up, with bands playing and strings of electric lights for alfresco imbibing, and publicans were ordered to serve cut-price beer and bratwurst to foreign patrons.

Virtually all German Jews had been driven from the streets, and so could no longer embarrass the Reich by telling visitors how intolerable their lives had become, but there were still gypsies in Berlin who were distinctly non-Aryan and therefore enemies of the state. Arrests, ordered by Frick's Ministry of the Interior, began at 6 a.m. on 16 July. Nearly 600 Sinti and Roma men, women and children were interned in a 'collection camp' in the suburb of Marzahn. Most never again knew freedom.

A building boom unprecedented in German history had begun in 1934 when work began on the Reich Sports Field, railway lines and autobahns, all of which Hitler demanded be completed well before the Games. Running over deadline, he made clear to contractors, would mean international humiliation for National Socialism.

In July 1936, at the end of that manic construction program, Berlin was a city that mixed the graceful and ornate palaces and mansions of past centuries with 'neo-classical' or 'severe deco' National Socialist buildings designed to intimidate, impress, and typify the power and purpose of National Socialism. Hitler had ordered his architects, notably Albert Speer, to create monumental stone, steel and glass edifices whose enormous front porticos looked like gaping maws set to devour all who entered. These utilitarian monoliths, even when prettified with banners and red velvet bunting, garlands of flowers and gold ribbons, struck many visitors to Berlin as scary and grim.

The imposing yet romantic Brandenburg Gate, smothered in banners and flowers, was reduced to a mere prop for totalitarianism. The leafy linden trees that gave Unter den Linden its name had been uprooted for the new north–south railway that would carry Olympic hordes and to create space for 94 silver-and-gold-garlanded flagpoles spaced a couple of metres apart, from which hung 14m Nazi and Olympic standards. The flags flew on major roads and side streets, beside railway lines, and in Berlin's squares, on its palaces, offices, shops and municipal buildings, Nazi administration blocks, museums, sumptuous hotels and budget fleapits alike, on its fabulous statues and monuments, along the banks of the River Spree and in the parklands of the Tiergarten. Loud-speakers were installed in the branches of trees and on flagpoles to broadcast Olympic news and results, and to blast out martial music between events and at night.

The upgraded and widened Via Triumphalis, the 10km parade route west from the Brandenburg Gate in central Berlin to the Reich Sports Field, was also highly decorated. Each day during the Games, Hitler would be driven along the road beaming broadly and stiff-arm saluting as hundreds of thousands stood twenty-deep to applaud him and hurl flowers at his car. Many, to get a closer look at the Führer, brought cardboard periscopes. As with much else at this Olympic festival, Hitler had an ulterior motive. He had decided that after he took Germany to war, Via Triumphalis would be an ideal ceremonial route along which his armies could return to Berlin from overseas conquests.

The government was heartened by visitors' reactions to the amusement park Berlin they had conjured. Visitors, including the Australian athletes, raved about the friendly locals and officials, the cheap beer and the efficiency. Even American journalist William L. Shirer, who had been trying to warn the world of the Nazi menace for three years, credited Goebbels' propaganda machine. 'The good Aryan people struck most visitors from abroad as happy, content and united under the swastika dictatorship.' Which was precisely what the regime hoped visitors would feel.

Not all fell under the Nazi spell. American novelist Thomas Wolfe was simultaneously overwhelmed and troubled by the Olympic city. His protagonist George Webber's impressions of Berlin in 1936 in *You Can't Go Home Again* were Wolfe's own. 'The daily spectacle was breathtaking in its beauty and magnificence . . . a tournament of color that caught the throat.' Wolfe wrote that the massed splendour of the banners made the gaudy decorations of America's great parades, presidential inaugurations and world fairs seem like shoddy carnivals in comparison. 'The whole town was a thrilling pageantry of royal banners . . . banners 50ft in height, such as might have graced the battle tent of some great emperor.' Yet while Wolfe was thrilled by the organisational genius of the Germans, he was also oppressed by it, finding the pageantry 'ominous' and sensing that behind all the hoopla lurked a regime bent on war. 'It was as if the Games had been chosen as a symbol of the new collective might, a means of showing to the world in concrete terms what this new power had come to be.'

British diplomat Sir Robert Vansittart was impressed by the friendliness and efficiency he encountered in Berlin in July and August 1936, but this critic of National Socialism was not tricked. He was repelled by the naked nationalism on display in Berlin. Although Hitler, publicly at least, maintained a genial disposition, occasionally his guard slipped, as Vansittart noted in *A Busman's Holiday*. His report to the British government on the Berlin Olympics remarked on the Fuhrer's 'harder, more violent, mystically ambitious, hotly and coldly explosive traits which flare capriciously and keep everyone in such a state of nervous tension'. After the Games, Vansittart's wife said that Hitler had had a conversation with her in which he denied having aggressive aims, praised the athletes and asked, 'Do you think I would let them die in battle?'

The Berlin diarist Victor Klemperer in *I Shall Bear Witness* found the Olympics hoopla 'repugnant' and an 'absurd over-estimation of sport; the honour of a nation depends on whether a fellow citizen can jump 4 inches higher than all the rest'. Klemperer railed that while in England and America sport had always been 'uncommonly and perhaps excessively valued, but probably never so one-sidedly, and at the same time with such a disparaging of the intellectual aspect as in this country now . . . I find the Olympics so odious because they are not about sport . . . but are an entirely political enterprise. "German renaissance through Hitler" I read recently.'

A few doubters aside, however, Hitler and Goebbels seemed to have pulled off their grand illusion. 'National Socialism as an idea has cast a spell upon the whole world,' exulted Goebbels, 'but for a foreigner to become truly acquainted with the Germany of National Socialism without seeing Berlin is an impossibility . . . may all foreign visitors to this city, in the rhythm of her life, in the tempo of her work, and in the enthusiasm with which she devotes herself to Adolf Hitler and his idea, catch a breath of the spirit with which the new Germany is inspired.'

CHAPTER 9
BELLS, WHISTLES AND A GRAND ARENA

On their second day in Berlin, a humid and rainy 24 June, the Australian athletes and manager Alderson visited the centrepiece of the Berlin Olympics, the Reich Sports Field with its swimming and diving complex. While exploring, the group saw filmmaker Leni Riefenstahl and her cameramen in the grandstands and down on the field, rehearsing how they would film for *Olympia*, her documentary of the Games.

The Australian squad stood in the centre of the arena, admiring the awesome stadium with its manicured grounds, cinder tracks and pits, and the high grandstands which in little more than a month would accommodate 110,000 spectators. Gasped de Lacy, 'The place is a marvel!' And it was. Dickinson always spoke of the Reich Sports Field in hushed tones. 'Oh, it was unbelievable. None of us had seen anything like it. The stadium was a grey granite structure, open at the top, a magnificent building but built in that austere German architectural style. Around the top of the stadium were supposed to be the flags of the competing nations, but when we visited every flag was a German swastika flag. There were swastikas on the towers and swastikas on the Olympic bell. There were swastikas everywhere.' (Two weeks later when IOC president Baillet-Latour learned of the surfeit of German flags, he reminded Hitler that the IOC was running the Olympics, and that it was not a promotional showpiece for National Socialism. 'Hitler wasn't very happy about that,' said Dickinson. 'Baillet-Latour stood up to him and protected Olympic ideals and ordered that the flags of *all* nations be flown.' Hitler reluctantly complied, but punished Baillet-Latour by barely speaking to him from then on.)

In 1931 when Berlin was awarded the Games, the German Olympic Committee and the then government assumed that the stadium that had been built by architect Otto March for the aborted 1916 Olympics in the Grunewald Forest, just west of the capital, would suffice as a venue. However, on 5 October 1933, when new chancellor Adolf Hitler inspected the site, he found that although it had undergone modernisation, it fell far short of his grand vision, and he demanded changes. The Reich Sports Field must be nothing less than the most stupendous arena in history. 'The stadium must be erected by the Reich; it will be the task of the nation,' he said. 'If Germany is to stand host to the entire world, her preparations must be complete and magnificent. The exterior of the stadium must not be of concrete, but of natural stone. When a nation has four million unemployed, it must seek ways and means of creating work for them.' He ordered construction of a new arena to commence at once.

Hitler summoned Goebbels, Frick, Tschammer und Osten, Lewald and Diem, and architects Werner and Walter March, who had renovated their father's stadium. Germany, he told them, was in a 'difficult and unfavourable foreign-political situation' and the Reich Sports Field had to be among National Socialism's 'great cultural accomplishments' that would help redress the world's adverse opinion of the regime. He ordered Werner March to make his dream a reality, and then ominously stipulated that March would no longer answer to the Organising Committee but directly to Interior Minister Frick, who in turn would report to Hitler. March's brief was to demolish the old stadium and design and build a mammoth circular athletics arena and swimming and diving complex redolent of the colosseums of ancient Greece and Rome. It must be not only the largest sporting complex in the world, but the largest in history. Cost was no object. Hitler pledged 20 million reichsmarks from the government, and the Krupp steel and munitions works and other companies sympathetic to National Socialism would contribute. The 2000-plus labourers would be recruited from the unemployed, whose existing welfare payments would be slashed, thereby saving the state money. Of course, only loyal Aryans would be given jobs. Hitler's lackeys suggested that the sporting complex be called Adolf Hitler Field, but the Führer concluded that as political as these Games were going to be, perhaps naming the complex after himself was a step too far, and Reichssportfeld remained its name.

Astoundingly, March, a devotee of modern architecture, defied the Führer. He drew up plans for an arena of modern materials: glass, cement and steel. Hitler inevitably exploded and a chastened March hastily came up with a new blueprint, this time faithfully fulfilling Hitler's orders. Too little, too late—March had lost Hitler's confidence, and Albert Speer was assigned to oversee the wayward architect. With the Führer's blessing, Speer came up with a series of spectacular additions, including mighty cornices and towers.

From the moment Frick and Speer wrested control of the Reich Sports Field, work stepped up. And it needed to, for the Olympics were just two years away and Hitler wanted the project completed by 1 April 1936.

The finished arena that the Australians traipsed through in June had an eight-lane 400m cinder track (composed of a blend of coarse and finely crushed cinders, crushed brick, crushed clay and powdered tile) with eight-lane 100m sprint and 110m hurdles tracks. The tracks bounded an immense field of lush grass (a mix of meadow, fescue, German pasture, cockscomb grasses and white clover) for soccer and hockey, and for the jumping, javelin, discus and hammer throwing. The grandstand had 71 tiers.

High in the grandstand was an 'honour platform' for Hitler and his guests, pointedly located directly above the area assigned to Baillet-Latour and other Olympic dignitaries. There would be no mistaking who was running this show. The Führer's enclosure was accessed via the subterranean Marathon Tunnel, and then the Marathon Steps, and was the best seat in the house. It opened at the back onto a 'hall of honour', Hitler's private apartments, his personal dining room and a kitchen where his meals were prepared.

The blue-green tiled eight-lane pool was heated at a constant temperature of 20 degrees Celsius. The diving tower, with one 10m platform, two 5m and two 3m springboards, was hailed as 'an elegant framework of reinforced concrete, of dazzling whiteness'. The swimming and diving grandstand accommodated 18,000.

Outside the stadium was a flag-bedecked red and white flagstone square. Visitors approaching the Olympic Gate walked between two 47.5m towers festooned with swastikas and the Olympic rings. Two more similarly decorated sets of towers were at the rear of the stadium. Directly opposite the stadium was the May Field parade ground, where the equestrian events and polo would be contested and the athletes mustered for the Opening and Closing Ceremonies.

One of Frick's tasks had been to commission 'suitable' works of art for the Reich Sports Field. In February 1935 he formed the Committee for the Artistic Adornment of the Reichssportfeld.

This committee, comprising artist and administrator friends of the regime, organised a competition whereby sculptors and artists submitted designs of proposed works, and funding was given to those which best embodied the ideals and strength of National Socialism while harking back to Greek and Roman antiquity. Among the winning entries were Josef Thorak's bust of Adolf Hitler, Georg Kolbe's two pillars topped by eagles positioned at the entrance to the arena, and Adolf Wamper's two massive entrance columns at the Dietrich-Eckart Theatre, the open-air auditorium for concerts and plays. There were works by Arno Breker, aka 'Hitler's Michelangelo'. Although the craftsmanship was at times stunning, the prevailing aesthetic was, rather than awe-inspiring and beautiful, bloated and bogus like papier-mache props in a 1960s sword and sandals movie.

Each nation had its own cabin at the stadium with showers and toilets. There were food kiosks and gleaming amenity blocks for the spectators. And the media had never had it so good. Reporters were ensconced in a covered area with seating for 1000, the most advanced telecommunications available, 46 telephone boxes and writing desks with stationery and typewriter, and a post office. There were twenty 'transmitting cells' for radio broadcasters. Again, there was method behind the largesse. Goebbels believed that if the media was happy, its reports would be favourable to the regime.

There were two clocks on the towers at the Marathon Gate. Each had a dial large enough to be seen from every seat. One told the current time, the other was an electric stop-clock, the largest ever made, activated when the starter fired his pistol, and synchronised to the stopwatches of the starters and judges, so spectators could note the athletes' times.

Hitler underestimated the final cost of his showpiece. The price tag was 47 million reichsmarks. Along with extra government funding and public and corporate donations, money needed to be diverted from other building programs to foot the bill. To the German Organising Committee it was worth every mark, because the project had 'the dignity and harmony which were demanded of anything so representative of the Third Reich'.

The other great symbols of the Games of the XIth Olympiad were the Olympic bell and the Torch Relay. Even the most virulent opponent of National Socialism conceded that these innovations provided rich theatre and were apt additions to the existing Olympic iconography of the five rings and the flaming urn.

The Olympic bell was rung each day at the Games. One side of the 9614kg, 2.43m high, 3m diameter Olympia-Glocke was emblazoned with a Reich eagle clutching the Olympic rings in its claws, and on the reverse was the Brandenburg Gate. Circling the rim of the bell was the inscription *Ich rufe die Jugend der Welt* ('I summon the youth of the world'). The official report of the German Organising Committee noted that the bell 'was pitched in E of the minor octave, and the first overtone in the interval of the minor third of the main tone was pitched in G so that the total effect was a minor tone. The plainly audible overtones resulting from the strokes of the clapper combined with the mighty undertone to produce a rich, full sound.'

The bell was the brainchild of Theodor Lewald and was sculpted by Walter E. Lemcke. Setting out from its foundry in Bochum, north of Cologne, on 16 January 1936, the bell and its ringing equipment of clapper, yoke and cogged winding wheel were slowly transported by truck on a ten-day, 540km, Goebbels-choreographed triumphal procession to Berlin. Escorting it along the way, providing the pomp and ensuring no harm befell the bell, were the army, the SS and SA, the National Socialist Motor Corps, the Reich

Association of Physical Training and Hitler Youth, as well as an assortment of runners, musicians, choirs and local dignitaries. There were parties, grandiloquent speeches and political rallies to welcome the bell to each town and village. Hundreds of thousands of citizens lined the streets to pay homage. Hymns to the bell were composed and sung. Its progress was excitedly reported by newspapers, radio stations and cinema newsreels. As it rumbled by, factory sirens sounded and smaller, far less grand church bells pealed.

So heavy was the bell that a wooden bridge near Potsdam needed to be reinforced to bear its weight. After passing the Reichstag, under the Brandenburg Gate and down Unter den Linden, the great bell was presented to the Organising Committee at Kaiser Franz Josef Square.

Reichssportführer Tschammer und Osten's oration was nothing less than a war cry. For Germans, he declared, the Olympic Games were less about winning medals than elevating physical fitness to become a lifelong habit, one of the benefits of which was to prepare Germans to carry on the age-old tradition of being warriors. 'The bell, ringing from its tower [at the Reich Sports Field], below which the hall of honour commemorating the sacrifice of those who fell at [the World War I battle of] Langemarck is situated, shall not merely summon the youth of the world but shall remind us constantly of those who gave their lives for the Fatherland. Its tones shall not only herald the beginning of an international festival, but shall announce to the German nation the revival of national vitality . . .' He invited those present to look to the future, where he saw 'generation upon generation of German men and women approaching, magnificently resolute in their physical strength and in their staunch loyalty to the sacred soil of the Fatherland, and brought up in undeviating, unshakeable faith in the mission of National Socialism. And all of these, as they come and go, experience a festive hour at the foot of the Bell Tower.'

The bell was displayed in five Berlin squares over the next months, then was transported to the May Field. On 11 May it was hoisted to the top of the bell tower.

The Torch Relay's 3331 runners, every one a fit, lithe young man, each held aloft a flaming torch for around 1km in a procession from Olympus in Greece to the Reich Sports Field. There on 1 August, before a vast crowd, the final runner, German athlete and Nazi role model Fritz Schilgen, would touch his flame to the fire bowl in the 2.3m high altar mounted on a tripod, to commence the Opening Ceremony. The cauldron would burn until the Closing Ceremony on 16 August. Slim, blond 29-year-old Schilgen was not chosen to be the final, and most iconic, partici-pant in the Torch Relay because he was a champion athlete—he did not compete at any Olympics—but for his gazelle-like running style and stereotypical Aryan good looks.

The logistics of the Torch Relay had been smoothed out in September 1935 by organisers who drove the 3187km route together, arranged details with the locals and distributed the stainless-steel torches. The torches contained two magnesium wicks, one a reserve should the first fail, and were made to burn through all weather conditions for around ten minutes, sufficient to complete a kilometre. The names of the route's major cities and 'In gratitude to the bearer' were carved into each torch's wooden grip.

The pageantry of the relay had been painstakingly planned to identify National Socialism with the Olympics, and to link the rites and rituals, and the warrior, artistic and sporting values of ancient Greece and Rome with those of modern Germany. At midday on 20 July, twelve days before the Games began, amid the broken columns and scattered stone blocks of an arena in Olympus, site of the first Olympics in 776 BC, one of a group of young women dressed in serge tunics focused the rays of the sun through a German-made Zeiss magnifying glass and set alight a small pile of sticks. As the sticks smouldered and sparked, Pindar's 'Olympic Hymn' was chanted and Baron de Coubertin blessed the event. Germany's ambassador to Greece voiced his joy that the Olympic Torch would soon be bound for 'my Führer Adolf Hitler and his entire German people'. Naturally, a German band struck up 'Deutschland Über Alles' and 'Horst-Wessel-Lied'. The first Olympic Torch was then lit and presented to a youth, who began running towards Athens, 260km to the east.

While the Olympic bell was dreamed up by Lewald, the Torch Relay was proposed by Diem. The flaming cauldron had been introduced at the 1928 Olympics, but a Torch Relay from Olympus to light it was a novel concept that the Nazi hierarchy regarded as a dramatic symbol of the new regime that would surely impress the people of Greece, Bulgaria, Yugoslavia, Hungary, Austria and Czechoslovakia, the countries through which it would travel on its odyssey to Berlin; lands which Hitler eyed hungrily as suitable locations for lebensraum. By 1942, Germany had invaded every one.

The relay passed through Athens, Delphi and Saloniki, up through Sofia and Belgrade and on to Budapest and Vienna, where National Socialist thugs celebrated the occasion by attacking supporters of Austria's anti-Nazi President Miklas. The Torch Relay lit up Prague and then progressed across the German border to Dresden and thence to Berlin. All the way it was filmed by the Department of Propaganda and Enlightenment's newsreel cameras and by Leni Riefenstahl for her film *Olympia*. The onlookers dressed in German folk costume and the storm troopers who yelled '*Heil* Hitler!' were bit players in Riefenstahl's film. What ended up on the cutting room floor was the footage of one relay runner being all but washed away by flooding near Thessalonika and the moment when the flame went out near Jagodina, 136km south of Belgrade (the torch carrier was driven to the next point, where he was handed a new torch and ordered to continue running as if there had been no glitch).

The official 1936 Olympics publicity poster was the result of a national quest in which artists were invited to submit designs. It remains a striking piece of poster art today. In the foreground is a dramatic blue-grey illustration of the majestic bronze sculpture *Quadriga*—a chariot drawn by four steeds and driven by Victoria, the winged Roman Goddess of Victory, who holds the German Eagle standard—atop the Brandenburg Gate. Hovering above is an illustration of an antique bronze bust of an ancient olive-wreathed victor with his right arm raised in the Olympic greeting—its similarity to the Nazi salute was no accident. Behind the warrior-athlete's head are the Olympic rings. The poster was distributed to every country in every language.

Some 960 victory medals were created, as well as 14,000 badges and 20,000 commemoration medals to be presented to every athlete and official and indeed anyone who contributed to the Games, including the pigeon breeders who offered their birds for the Opening Ceremony. On one side was engraved the Olympic bell and on the other the figure of an athlete tugging on the bell rope. When I visited Percy Oliver's daughter Brenda Oliver-Harry 78 years later, I was invited to hold her father's commemoration medal. It was heavy and handsome.

13 May 1936: To the cheers of the well-wishers lining Circular Quay, the cramped, no-frills SS *Mongolia* with its precious cargo of Olympians steams past the four-year-old Sydney Harbour Bridge, bound for Marseilles. (NLA)

On SS *Mongolia* in Fremantle. The four women (in white hats, from left) are Evelyn de Lacy, Kitty Mackay, Mary Fergusson (the chaperone) and Pat Norton. Gerald Backhouse is to Norton's left. To his left are Alf Watson, Norman Ella and Percy Oliver. Standing with cap in hand is Basil Dickinson, with Dunc Gray at his feet. Harry Alderson and Jack Metcalfe are at the far right. Dick Garrard kneels second from left. (NLA)

As Percy Oliver's Box Brownie photos show, the Australians made the best of SS *Mongolia*'s poor training facilities. They ran laps of the crowded wooden decks, tried to swim in the tiny canvas pool and wrestled on makeshift mats. All disembarked heavier and less fit. (Courtesy of Brenda Oliver-Harry)

The official Berlin Olympics poster featured the *Quadriga* atop the Brandenburg Gate and a classical warrior–athlete, presumably giving the Nazi salute.

The Australians' neat appearance and relaxed manner hid exhaustion and frayed nerves when, after their exhausting journey, they were welcomed at the Berlin Town Hall.

Australian boxer Harry Cooper dances a lively jig in the Olympic Village, to the accompaniment of a German officer's accordion and diver Ron Masters' fiddle. Among the athletes of many lands in the audience are Basil Dickinson (seated centre front) and Percy Oliver (at Masters' right).

The laidback Australians were amazed by the intensive regimes of the super-fit and focused athletes of Germany, the United States and Japan (here doing calisthenics in the Village).

To impress visitors and the watching world, Hitler and propaganda minister Goebbels ensured that Nazi flags outnumbered Olympic standards on the streets of Berlin.

The grand thoroughfare Unter den Linden was the first sector of a ceremonial route leading from central Berlin to the Olympic Stadium. Each day, Hitler led the procession of dignitaries and senior Nazis to the stadium in his black open-topped Mercedes-Benz.

The 110,000 crowd at the Opening Ceremony roared when Hitler strode down the Marathon Steps onto the Olympic field. He was flanked by IOC president Henri de Baillet-Latour (at left, with top hat) and president of the German Olympic Committee Theodor Lewald (on right). Hermann Göring dismissively referred to them as 'flea circus directors'. (Getty)

From Olympia to the heart of the Third Reich. The penultimate torch bearer, flanked by young German athletes, carries the flame beneath the Brandenburg Gate en route to the stadium. (Getty)

The Olympic torch arrives in the stadium. The final torch bearer, archetypal Aryan Fritz Schilgen, runs past storm troopers and Hitler Youth to approach Nazi heavyweights and Olympic dignitaries on the official rostrum.

CHAPTER 10
SETTLING IN

After being welcomed to Berlin, the male athletes and officials were driven to the Olympic Village at Doeberitz, 14km from the Reich Sports Field and 32km west of central Berlin. The women were escorted to a central Berlin pension where they would remain for a fortnight until their dormitory accommodation at the three-storey Friedrich Friesen Haus (Friesian House) near the entrance to the Reich Sports Field was ready.

That night near their pension, Evelyn de Lacy, Kitty Mackay, Doris Carter and Pat Norton witnessed the German army and air force stage a mock bombing raid. Aeroplanes 'bombed' a hotel and soldiers stormed in and stretchered out the 'injured'. The women tried to move closer for a better view but were turned back by storm troopers, so they trudged off to bed.

On 5 July, the four athletes and their chaperone Mary Fergusson went to the Reich Sports Field to watch the military band rehearse for the Opening Ceremony. They were among 30,000 ferried in to gauge whether the stadium could cope with large crowds. 'We had seats in Hitler's box,' recalled de Lacy. 'Unfortunately he wasn't there . . . After dinner we had a sing-song in the music room [of their accommodation] until it got too hot and we took rugs and went out on the lawns . . . A full moon came up over the stadium and shed its soft light on the playing fields [the May Field]. It was a marvellous night.'

On 8 July, the women moved to their austere rooms—the furniture was worn and the mattresses rock hard—at Friesian House. They, and after their arrival the other 400 female athletes, fell under the control of the formidable über-chaperone—or Frei-frau—Baroness Johanna von Wangenheim, a tall woman with grey plaits and a sharp tongue, widely reputed to have eyes in the back of her head. Norton told the authors of *A Proper Spectacle: Women Olympians 1900–1936*: 'It was probably the longest four weeks of Freifrau Von Wangenheim's life . . . Our dorm housed about 20; we shared with the South Americans and the Japanese girls. We couldn't understand each other but had fun trying.'

Despite the no-frills accommodation and plain meals (unlike those enjoyed by the men at the Village), starry-eyed de Lacy found Friesian House 'gorgeous': 'Oh boy! What a place to live in! It is surrounded by lawns and on one side a deep gully. There is a tennis court and from our window we can see the Olympic Bell and the arena . . . also the swimming pool. Oh, it's simply heaven. Just after we had dinner we walked up to the open air theatre . . . Gee, it was wonderful. Returning, we saw little rabbits running all over the place . . . Oh boy! What a place, too wonderful for words!'

'Everybody is so kind to us,' enthused Mackay. 'I only wish we could take our three girl attachés, Irmgard, Elga and Inga, back to Australia with us. They are marvellous, but I'm afraid they are spoiling us. We never have to ask for anything. They anticipate all our wishes.'

Music rang through the halls of Friesian House. The athletes needed no excuse to sing and perform on their instruments. The American and British girls played their Billie Holiday, Louis

Armstrong, Bing Crosby and Fred Astaire 78 rpm records, and the French the joyous jazz of Django Reinhardt and the Quintet of the Hot Club of Paris. Those who could play piano, such as Mackay, tinkled out George Gershwin and Noël Coward. The Japanese women dressed in their kimonos and danced to their gramophone records. Mackay noted that the Mexican women 'dress and look like movie stars. They are always singing and full of life.'

Norton, who at seventeen was the baby of the Australian squad, made friends with her American counterpart, thirteen-year-old diver Marjorie Gestring. 'We think the American girls awfully attractive,' said Norton. 'The German girls might think they use overmuch makeup but they admit the Americans have splendid figures, and dress more fashionably than the other competitors. We find the Americans just as friendly as Australians. They are always joking and having fun, and they have given us lots of training tips. That's what I like about them. They don't mind answering our questions.' Norton was nicknamed 'the student' because she, like Percy Oliver, studied the techniques of the international swimmers, especially the Japanese and Americans, and adapted her own style accordingly.

The Australian men were the first team to move into the Olympic Village. 'When we reached the town of Doeberitz on the way to the Village,' recalled Basil Dickinson, 'we looked across to Spandau Prison. This was where Rudolf Hess, one of the main Nazis who we often saw at Hitler's side at the Olympics, was imprisoned after the war. He fared better than a lot of his mates who paid for their crimes with their lives.'

The 55ha Olympic Village was laid out in the shape of a map of Germany. It had been constructed as army and air force barracks, and was ceded for the period of the Games. The Village, which was bounded by high cyclone fencing to keep the athletes in and the public and media out, comprised 140 single-storey houses, each accommodating up to 26 athletes. Built in gently curving rows, the cottages had whitewashed walls and red tile roofs. They were picturesque against the summer growth of the neighbouring forest. There was a 400m cinder practice running track with 100m straights, high jump, broad jump and hop, step and jump pits, and a 25m indoor heated swimming pool. The well-fitted-out gymnasium had separate auditoriums with boxing and wrestling rings. Incorporated into the Village were a shopping mall, post office, dentists' and doctors' surgeries, a barber shop, dining halls and auditoriums. All of this was set among parks, a lake and forests through which roamed imported animals.

At the entrance to the Village was a large sign which proclaimed in the language of every team: 'Welcome to the Olympic Village! This is your home during the weeks to come. Here you will dwell together with your friends and fellow participants, a community of comrades serving the same ideal, who are overjoyed to greet you, live with you and pass pleasant hours in your company. Everything that has been provided here is for your comfort and convenience, and the regulations have been considered and drawn up in your interest so that you may be assured undisturbed enjoyment of your new home. Over this Village waves the Olympic flag and the national banner of your native land. Each morning the chimes play the Olympic Hymn. May the Olympic spirit and Olympic peace reign here from the first to the last day . . . The German army erected this Village for the Olympic guests. It performed its task gladly in the interest of sport and because it reveres the Olympic ideals. Thus the army, as well as the German people, extends to you, its guests, a hearty welcome.' The first signature on this message of peace was that of Minister of War Werner von Blomberg.

'As we pulled up at the front gate,' said Dickinson, 'there was a large group of German dignitaries and two seamen from the German navy at the flagpole and up went the flags. Another ceremony, more speeches. They welcomed us again and again, mixing in a little propaganda about how Germany desired only peace and telling us what the Führer was doing for the nation's youth. A band played "God Save the King". The Village was immaculate and guarded by many, many soldiers. No females were allowed. When the ceremony at the gate was over, they took us to our house where there were yet *more* speeches and another band. The houses bore names of German cities, towns and villages . . . ours was named Worms, after a city in a wine-growing region by the Rhine. *Worms!* We had a good old chuckle over that. It was beautiful to have a rest and a shower and put on clean clothes after our journey. Never in our wildest dreams did we think we would have quarters so terrific. The sleeping arrangements, the training and dining facilities, the entertainment at [the Village's] Hindenburg House, were all first class.' The rooms for the 3300 male competitors were comfortable though sparsely furnished: two single beds, a large curtained window, two stools, a table and chair and two wardrobes.

The Village was alcohol-free unless you were French, Italian, Belgian or Dutch. The French and Italians were permitted wine with meals and the Belgians and Dutch beer because it was their culture. While alcohol was undoubtedly smuggled into the Village by the Australians, Dickinson recalled 'a small beer garden outside the Village that we frequented. I liked one or two glasses of beer. A couple of the other boys were not quite so abstemious.'

Worms was in the midst of a League of Nations cluster of cottages including those of Haiti, Uruguay, Chile, England, New Zealand, Egypt and Greece. Dunc Gray and Eddie Scarf, who had stayed at the Olympic Village in Los Angeles in 1932, thought the

German lodgings superior. One Norwegian athlete told a reporter, 'It is so lovely here that we dread the return of everyday life. We are living in the midst of paradise.'

Wrestler Dick Garrard years later told Harry Gordon how his own naïveté earned him some good-humoured ribbing from teammates. 'We moved in before the Village was completed. This was my first Olympics and the first time I'd been to a European country. [The accommodation] was a big housing allotment and there were no trees around the houses. In the night we [heard] a commotion but didn't know what it was. Next morning we had half a forest surrounding us. What had happened was fully grown trees were planted overnight, but I concluded that European trees just grew very quickly and were just more examples of the strange things that happened in Europe.'

Jack Metcalfe shared his room with Harry Alderson who, he said, was 'liked by every member of the team . . . he did his utmost for us. I suppose some would say that he should have been more of a disciplinarian but that wasn't his attitude towards the Olympics.' (Alderson himself explained his laissez-faire attitude to his athletes by saying that he trusted them implicitly, and besides, 'the boys are not in prison'.)

The 250 male Japanese athletes arrived at the Village on 27 June, and shocked the acclimatising Australians by immediately hurling themselves into hard training, taking over the athletic field and pool at the Village. In practice, Shunpei Uto swam 400m in 4 minutes, 42 seconds, which was *four seconds* inside the world record. Harry Nightingale attributed the Japanese swimmers' superiority to 'physique, clean living and physical culture training. The competitors had been carefully selected and their bodies scientifically developed.'

Nightingale conceded that it simply wasn't the Australian way to be as intense as the Japanese swimmers, whom the Australians called 'human motorboats'. Said the coach, 'We'll have to work much harder to catch up with them, because of the independent spirit of the average Australian who would simply refuse to submit himself to the Japanese regime of slavery. I doubt whether our swimmers have the stamina and physique to stand up to the Japanese methods which are positively ferocious. Young swimmers are required to swim all distances from 200m to 1000m daily, regardless of the race for which they are training. The day's work begins with a fast 200m for relaxation. In addition, an almost unbelievable self-discipline is imposed, resulting in the Japanese leading the world.'

The Japanese performance in training was a reality check for anyone thinking Australia would bring home a swag of medals. 'It is impossible to view the methods of the teams of other nations without contrasting the intensity of their training with the Australians' rather casual methods,' fretted an AAP journalist. 'The Australians could not be expected to tolerate being barked at all day by coaches like the Japanese, but there should be some happy medium between this and the leisurely Australian conception of Olympic swimming and other preparations, which seems to give too important a place to relaxation and the sanctity of weekends. For instance, the Japanese and American divers worked through a wet Saturday afternoon while the Australians were resting.'

There was much else about the exotic Japanese that captivated the Australian women swimmers. As Norton related, 'The Japanese uniforms were grey and made the girls look drab, but when we met them at a concert one night we saw the ugly duckling turn into a swan. They came dressed in beautiful kimonos complete with obis [sashes] around their waist . . . They looked delightful.' The Japanese men had also made an impression for something other than swimming. 'One day we were at the training pool and they arrived to train. They immediately began to undress at poolside which made us three modest Australian girls let out a yelp and dive for cover! We were only just used to men wearing topless costumes. When this was explained to the Japanese trainers [the men] undressed in the rooms provided.'

Accompanying the Japanese team was a delegation of Tokyo city councillors seeking German support for a Tokyo Olympics in 1940. To ingratiate themselves with Hitler, the councillors presented him with a ceremonial sword and a silk kimono embroidered with swastikas. The Japanese bid would succeed but, thanks in no small part to the man they were trying to impress, the 1940 Tokyo Olympics would never be staged.

There was high excitement when the Bulgarians moved in, led by none other than King Boris of Bulgaria. He would die in August 1943, possibly poisoned by the Nazis following his refusal to join Germany in waging war on Russia or deport Bulgarian Jews. The Argentines struck the Australians as 'cheery chappies', while the South Africans looked like giants—five of their squad exceeded 1.8m and one was 2m tall. The Australians were quite relieved to discover that the Canadian athletes had a similar relaxed view of life to themselves, the English and the Kiwis.

Dickinson bumped into Hitler in the Village. 'It was soon after we arrived,' he recalled. 'He came to inspect the German army and air force personnel, the Hitler Youth and the others whose job it was to look after the athletes. The boys ran to Hitler and he patted them on the head. I was twenty yards away. Hitler came over and spoke to me. I couldn't understand what he was saying, but I will never forget his cold blue eyes.' Swimmer Bill Kendall encountered Göring near the Australian quarters. The Reich minister was also spotted by the Australian women swimmers when he visited the training pool. 'Through the entrance came the storm troopers in their black uniforms forming a laneway. In swept . . . Herr Göring! Big, fat, rotund Hermann Göring,' recalled Norton. 'He looked beautiful! Not in the garb of a Nazi officer, but for all the world like a country squire, immaculately tailored, jauntily hatted, and carrying a walking stick and bestowing a broad smile for all and sundry.'

The Australians were content in their Olympic home away from home. The only bugbear for many was homesickness. In a radio message to Australia, Alderson updated listeners with news from the Village, and added that what would make the athletes even happier was 'more letters from sweethearts and wives'.

Leni Riefenstahl spent days shooting lyrical footage of the Village. And there in *Olympia: Part 2: Festival of Beauty* is Aussie the kangaroo bounding through a Hans Christian Andersen–like dell. 'When Aussie saw the parks and the forest and the lake, he was in seventh heaven,' said Dickinson. 'Having been on tight rations on *Mongolia* he was delighted with all the foliage he found to nibble in the parkland. He put on quite a bit of weight.'

The Olympic Village was officially opened on 1 July at 1 p.m. on a sweltering summer day. War Minister Blomberg resorted once more to martial metaphor. 'This Europe of ours is too small for a war, but it is large enough to contain a field of combat, *sporting* combat, upon which the youth of the world will win a decisive battle for the cause of peace. To cooperate in the solution of this task is the sincere and sacred wish of the entire German nation.' In a portent of stormy times to come, following the singing of 'Deutschland Über Alles' there was a deafening clap of thunder, forks of lightning split the sky and the heavens opened, sending everyone scurrying for shelter. The rain pelted down for the next few days, flooding some of the Village houses, and when the clouds cleared the weather was unseasonably cool.

That afternoon, the Australian rowers moved to new quarters at Köpenick, near the Olympic rowing course on the Langer See at Grünau. They expected to stay at the grand Castle Köpenick, and had been teasing the Village athletes about their good fortune. Instead they unpacked at, of all places, Köpenick police barracks. Wal Mackney entered the barracks with a disgruntled expression, carrying his prized aspidistra in one hand and the rudder of a boat in the other. After a week the rowers decided their digs were not so bad. The food was excellent, even too plentiful. The only thing marring the idyll was that their vessels—the single and double sculls and the eight-oar craft—had been held up in London and they were training in borrowed boats. The Australians, reported coach Mackenzie, had seen the German crew rowing 'and they worked well, but that does not scare us. The Japanese crews are arriving on Friday morning. The real fun will start when the Henley [British] crews turn up. The Grünau course is the finest I have ever seen—such a beautiful setting, charming surroundings, a magnificent straight stretch of water, and excellent boat sheds . . . We shall give a good account of ourselves . . . If only our boats were here.'

When the boats were finally delivered, on 6 July, the Australians' joy was 'boundless'. So glad were they to see them at last, they refused to let them be taken to the barracks on the back of a truck for fear they'd be damaged; the rowers carried the boats themselves all the way from the train station to their barracks, to the amusement of bystanders. Mackenzie's relief may have temporarily affected his thinking, because that day he boasted to a group of journalists that he expected the Australian eight would win the gold medal. All that was capable of stopping them was breaking their oars.

Like their female counterparts at Friesian House, the Australian men made friends with many of the athletes at the Village. 'My general experience in those days of international competition was that individuals were individuals, not members of a team,' said Dickinson. 'Smoking was not allowed, so some of the Japanese would creep from their house to behind where we were staying to have a cigarette. We had a bit to do with the Argentine fellows. We'd go across to their tent and sit around in a group and drink their special tea, called *mate* [brewed from the herb *yerba mate*], which they passed around in gourds. The African Americans gave jazz sessions, dance steps and so on . . .' Metcalfe, Ron Masters and Inspector Fergusson staged a boomerang-throwing demonstration for the athletes of other countries that created a 'sensation'. So much so that some Australians were sure that it was only a matter of time before boomerang throwing became an Olympic sport.

Hearty as the Australians' welcome was, it was a tea party in comparison with the rapturous welcome extended by Berliners to the US team. On 24 July, the Australians were at Friedrichstrasse station with thousands of Germans who had jammed in to catch sight of the celebrated Americans. When the US team alit from their train from Hamburg after sailing to Europe on ocean liner *Manhattan*, bands played 'The Star-Spangled Banner' and 'Stars and Stripes Forever'. Before Jesse Owens stepped out, the spectators chanted, '*Wo ist Yess-say? Wo ist Yess-say?*' ('Where is Jesse?'). (The cry '*Yess-say O-vens! Yess-say O-vens!*' would be heard again and again at the Reich Sports Field in the weeks to come as African American Owens, one of ten children of a near-destitute northern Alabama sharecropper, made a mockery of Hitler's claims of Aryan superiority by winning every race he entered. Some fans came at Owens with scissors, hoping to snip a piece of his clothing as a souvenir.) In open-topped army buses the Americans proceeded to Unter den Linden, where tens of thousands screamed themselves hoarse and waved Nazi and American flags. US Olympic chief Avery Brundage declared at the team's town hall reception, 'No nation since ancient Greece has captured the true Olympic spirit as has Germany.'

The Australian women were formally introduced to their US rivals that night at dinner at Friesian House, and showed the 'nice and friendly' newcomers around the Reich Sports Field.

The Americans brought with them a scandal. De Lacy diarised that much of their conversation at dinner that evening concerned Brundage sacking from their team the glamorous and headstrong swimmer Eleanor Holm. On board *Manhattan*, the 23-year-old reigning Olympic 100m backstroke champion broke a 9 p.m. curfew to get roaring drunk with actress Helen Hayes and her husband playwright Charles MacArthur. When the women's team chaperone tried to drag her away from the revelry, Holm pulled free and gloriously demanded, 'Did *you* make the Olympic team, or did *I*?' She received an official warning from Brundage but Holm was having too much fun on board and partied on regardless. When she was discovered shooting craps with reporters, it was too much for Brundage and he expelled her from the squad. Instead of competing at the Berlin Games, she—or, rather, her ghostwriter—reported on them for a US newspaper.

Dickinson bumped into Jesse Owens in the Village. 'He was relaxing outside the Americans' quarters in a white tracksuit. Jesse impressed me as a most modest and likeable individual. We chatted for quite a while and at no stage did I get the impression he believed he was a mighty man. On the contrary, he was rather humble. Jesse was so popular with the Berliners. Wherever he went in Berlin or at the stadium, even among his fellow athletes at the Village, people called out his name and he happily obliged with a few words and an autograph. I saw all of his races at the Olympics and he was a beautiful athlete to watch. Almost perfection. In any race he was in, the other runners seemed to be struggling in comparison. He enjoyed glory on the track but I don't think he enjoyed those Olympics, with all the militarism and the puffed-up officials who looked down on him because of his colour. Afterwards, he said to me, "I think the Olympic Games have lost their purpose."'

Dickinson's most enduring friendship in Berlin was with German press attaché Heinz Schweibold. 'Heinz was the resident journo in the village, because the regime didn't want foreign reporters chasing the athletes and distracting them from training, and maybe, too, reporting what they thought of National Socialism. I learned about Germany from Heinz. He had lived in Kent in England for three years and spoke good English. He was a charming, decent bloke, and he knew better than to spin me Nazi propaganda. Thanks to him and my own observations, a few weeks into my time in Germany I was not as naïve as previously.'

Despite the restrictions on alcohol, there was booze aplenty smuggled into the Village. Bribed guards turned a blind eye to the athletes' consumption, as they did to the prostitutes who rendez-voused with athletes in the forests around the complex.

If a few of the Australian men smoked, drank or smuggled women into the camp, they transgressed quietly. By and large they behaved well. The same cannot be said for Aussie the kangaroo. More than once he bounded out of his enclosure, and the Austral-ians and the young German guides were sent out in search of the errant marsupial. One day, after being overfed meat, vegetables, fruit and cake by well-meaning athletes, he developed an alarm-ingly distended stomach. The mascot pulled through, and signs in three languages were posted on his cage, forbidding feeding by anyone other than approved personnel.

What were *not* banned were the Nazis' noisy nightly war games around the Village. Garrard heard 'German armies marching at night time, they marched and sang. You could hear them for miles and miles around.' And while no aircraft was permitted to fly directly over the Village, 'high above and not far from the Village we saw Luftwaffe planes having mock dog fights'.

Sculler Cec Pearce told Harry Gordon that while the rowers were in the Olympic Village, 'All night you'd hear guns, machine guns, there must have been a range somewhere round about. And the general topic next morning was "Did you hear those guns last night?" One fellow said, "Yeah, looks like Germany is getting ready for war." And of course it was.' Dunc Gray noticed that 'all the windows and doors were double-glazed'. Attaché von Benda claimed it was to keep the cold out, but the cyclist believed the double-glazing was a precaution in case 'they had a war on and they started to drop poison gas around. There were signs everywhere that war was coming. I was never happier than when I crossed the border out of Germany.'

'Hitler *was* getting ready for war,' said pole vaulter Fred Woodhouse. 'There was a great display of might, the armoured cars and tanks in the streets of Berlin, planes flying overhead. In the Village was a cellar that I believe now was an air raid shelter. In there they kept camouflage sheets which I reckon were to be hooked up to the roofs in the event of attack.' Woodhouse became suspicious when the Village doctors quizzed him on the height from which he landed when vaulting, the weight he was carrying, and the effect that hitting the ground had on his frame. He believed that 'the information they were hoping to get from me was to help them train paratroopers, teaching them to take the jarring of a fall'.

So disturbed was Woodhouse by Germany's military escalation that during his time in Berlin he wrote to *The Times* of London, expressing his regret that the English didn't seem to be taking seriously the threat posed by the Germans, who were making great industrial strides and mobilising for war. The Brits were being 'lackadaisical' and not 'fair to themselves' by letting all this happen on their doorstep, and if Britain 'didn't pull up its socks it may have some serious trouble with Germany in the near future'. The letters editor of *The Times*, where the editorial policy was to appease

Hitler, wrote back to Woodhouse regretting that space restrictions prevented his letter's publication. Said Woodhouse, 'They just didn't want to publish it.'

As well as such diversions as fireworks and a light show, classical musicians and entertainers performed for the male athletes each night at the Village's Hindenburg House with its stage, orchestra pit and concert seating for 1000. The venue also had a state-of-the-art projector and sound equipment so that films—after being vetted by the Reich Film Chamber—and newsreels could be screened.

There was a radio in each house, and a Village newspaper delivered each day. And, in another first for the Olympics, there was television. 'None of us had laid eyes on TV before,' said Dickinson, 'and it caused quite a fuss.' The German Post Office Department equipped a special mobile van and Hindenburg House each with a small television, and programs—usually a sporting documentary or a film lauding the Third Reich—were beamed in daily between 8 and 11 a.m. and 3 and 8 p.m. When the Games were underway, proceedings from the Reich Sports Field were transmitted. Reception was fuzzy, but such was the novelty of the new medium that nobody minded.

Before they left for Germany, athletes and officials of every competing nation had been asked to fill in a questionnaire sent by the Organising Committee inviting them to list the food they'd like served in the Village. Consequently, the dining rooms offered a plethora of cuisines, prepared by chefs from the German shipping line Norddeutscher Lloyd.

The Australians opted for 'English-style cooking, three meat meals a day with grilled beef, mutton and veal preferred; salads, milk and tea'. The Argentines wanted steak *à la plancha* or empanada *à la creole* once a day; chicken with saffron rice and risotto with fish; small portions of veal and pork; spices, including sweet paprika and garlic; oodles of oil; tomatoes; vegetables; and *mate* in the afternoon.

Germans stipulated beef, sausage, tomato juice, cream cheese with linseed oil, and their favoured beverages such as Ovaltine and Dextropur. The Indians ate 'curry, meats including mutton, veal, lamb and fowl but no beef, pork or beef suet', and Dutch athletes dined on 'warm meals only in the evening; ample quantities of vegetables, potatoes and fresh salads; for breakfast, Dutch cheese; for lunch, cold cuts of various kinds, sausages, eggs, Dutch cheese, bread'. The Yugoslavians were easily pleased, needing only 'dishes cooked in oil'. Alderson called the food his men were served 'excellent and, above all, the tea is good. They are much the best meals we've had since leaving home. The menu is especially suited to athletes and agrees closely with the wishes we expressed before leaving Australia . . . All the men have splendid appetites.'

The Hitler Youth and the Honorary Youth Service were in the Village to help the athletes post letters at the Village post office, use the Village bank, wash clothes in the Village laundry, make calls at the telephone exchange and find their way around the Village and Berlin. 'Their attitude generally towards Nazism was unquestioning, as strong as any religious faith,' recalled Metcalfe. 'I had afternoon tea with a member of the Berlin University Youth Group . . . I tried to draw him into a political discussion and he said in a way that indicated that he was not prepared to discuss the thing at all, "Mr Metcalfe, in Germany we have one leader, that leader is Hitler, and we love our leader."'

The athletes grew used to the Village officials' weapons and uniforms, their constant marching and *Sieg Heil* saluting. So close did the soldiers and young guides stick to the teams that competitors suspected they were being spied on, and they probably were. Some athletes, including Australians, complained when letters from home were opened by guards before delivery. They were told that such practice was routine to prevent foreign currency and messages critical of the regime entering Germany.

The Village guards and officials didn't seem to mind that when they greeted an Australian with the Nazi salute and a 'Heil Hitler!' they received in return an irreverent 'Heil Joe Lyons!', 'Heil Selassie!' or 'Heil Mary full of grace'. The Americans responded with 'Heil Roosevelt!' and the British with 'Heil King Edward!' One evening in the rowers' barracks a food fight, involving the Australians, broke out and a portrait of Hitler was pelted; there were no repercussions.

Pearce, however, found some of the Germans assigned to the athletes to be 'ruthless bastards . . . There was one incident . . . They had the German army driving the buses that took us around. One bloke would be driving and the other bloke would be his offsider. Now, apparently Berliners on bicycles were not allowed to ride three abreast, so the offsider had a [club and he'd] lean out of the bus and go *whack* and knock the [offending cyclists] arse over turkey.'

There was another unpleasant moment when Nazi fanaticism surfaced. A German War Ministry film was screened to the athletes equating athletics with war and illustrating how certain physical exercises were good training for throwing bombs and hand grenades. The audience booed and cried, 'Militarisation of sport!' The officers angrily ordered the hecklers from the auditorium. The athletes held their ground and demanded to see a different film. 'Cinema audiences are entitled to express their dissatisfaction,' protested one Swede. The officers insisted: the film night was over and there might be no more. The protesters reluctantly left, grumbling, 'All right, we're going now.'

It was not all one-sided. Some of the Australians, often after a few illegal drinks, considered it a lark to abuse the guards, to be openly rude about Germany, its customs and National Socialism, and even indulge in petty theft. Hitler Youth daggers and swastika flags found their way into more than one set of luggage. Not only did Gray stash in his bag the Australian flag he carried at the Opening Ceremony, he would also say, 'I've got a knife, fork and spoon that I pinched while having a meal. I put them in my pocket, and most of the others did too.' Wal Mackney wasn't at the Village long before leaving with his fellow rowers for Köpenick; yet he still found time to relieve a dozing Hitler Youth of his knife.

Some of the Australians' larrikin behaviour made Metcalfe and Dickinson squirm. 'It's a characteristic of Australians . . . there's perhaps a humorous side but it also can be embarrassing,' remarked Metcalfe. 'It certainly was embarrassing at the Village when the Germans waiting on the tables asked us the English words for various things, and some of us told them the most disgusting words, which the waiters [not realising they were obscenities] went on to use at other tables. The fellows at fault had to be pulled up over it.'

Dickinson was irritated by the crass parochialism of some of his teammates. 'So many in the Australian team were forever saying how terrible the Germans and Germany were and how wonderful were Australians and Australia. They criticised a place and a culture they knew nothing about. They bragged endlessly how Australia won World War I. Some didn't stop whinging. Dunc Gray had too much to say about certain things, too much to say about Hitler and the Nazis. He constantly denigrated them—it was "the bloody Germans" this and "the bloody Germans" that. There were guides everywhere, and no doubt spies as well, and he could have landed himself, and those of us he was speaking to, in serious trouble. I held my peace. The longer I was in Berlin the more I was aware of Germany's dark side, and realised that National Socialism could cause the world some serious strife. Yet I had no chip on my shoulder about everyday Germans, who could not have been kinder and nicer, nor the German athletes, who were good blokes, just like ourselves.'

Like Dickinson, all the Australians grew increasingly unsettled by Nazism. The Village newspaper was little more than a Nazi rag, and the Australians, more knowledgeable now about what was going on in Germany, scoffed at its blatant propaganda. Sometimes, against the rules, Australian, British and American newspapers found their way into the Village. These would have contained reports of National Socialists breaking up a meeting of non-Nazi citizens in the largely German-populated city of Danzig, Poland, beating them so viciously that 50 were hospitalised. Following the modus operandi that Hitler would use again to excuse future invasions of Czechoslovakia and Austria, the regime claimed that German forces now had no choice but to invade Poland to protect the German citizens of Danzig, who were being persecuted by 'a divided minority'.

That same week, as the Nazis were radiating Olympic bonhomie in Berlin, another article read: 'Spokesmen, representing nine nations at a European conference in London, gave details of brutality and torture of political prisoners of the Nazis.' The conference had drawn up a manifesto calling on civilised people throughout the world to unite and protest officially to Germany. Figures were produced showing that one million people had been arrested since the Nazis came to power, and 10,000 had been driven to suicide. Ellen Wilkinson of Britain's Labour Party told how there were 105 concentration camps, in which were 40,000 prisoners. At Dachau, punishment included whipping, beating the soles of the feet with iron rods, branding with lighted cigars, and beating with rubber hose pipes. At Sachsenhausen (just kilometres from the Olympic Village and the Reich Sports Field) a man was forced to stand with his arms extended until he fainted. At Heuberg a man was made to work until he collapsed. When icy water was poured on him, he died.

Again in July, at the worst possible time for Nazi propagandists, France's respected General René Tournes Duffour sent a shudder through his countrymen and the world when he said what many governments suspected but were too afraid to voice: that beyond all the Games hype, Germany's mission was ultimately to wage war.

The German army—the army that was not even supposed to exist—was now the strongest in the world. Aerodromes were sprouting up all over Germany to facilitate the bombing of Paris, London, Brussels and Geneva. The roads leading from Berlin to France, Austria, Belgium, Switzerland and Czechoslovakia had all been widened and improved to accommodate armoured vehicles and troops.

On 9 July, Goebbels suspended all Nazi political meetings in Germany for five weeks. He explained that party members needed 'time to recuperate for the task that lies before them'. He did not specify what that task was. The Berlin correspondent of the usually pro-Nazi *Times* of London wrote: 'It has long been believed that after the Olympic Games—not immediately, but about the middle of September or the beginning of October, when most of the foreigners have left—a period of intense Nazi political activity will set in. Dr Goebbels' order is the first official confirmation of this. All signs point to further drastic measures against Jews, non-Nazis and the churches, but the predominant idea of the new campaign is apparently to force the issue between the Nazi party and those who have remained outside it, either through opposition or indifference. Outsiders will be given the option of joining the party or being branded definitely non-Nazi, and suffering serious disadvantages under the citizenship law.' All of which came to pass.

As Metcalfe had discovered, talking politics with the locals was a no-go zone. Should an athlete question a guide or attaché in the Village about National Socialism, the smiles faded and the subject was swiftly changed. With good reason: one group of German women who dared to discuss life in the Third Reich with Olympians was reported by eavesdroppers and arrested by the Gestapo.

If the hosts refused to answer hard questions about National Socialism, some of the regime's victims had no such qualms. Underground anti-Nazi groups found ways to alert the visiting athletes to the injustices they were being subjected to. Letters and leaflets clandestinely handed or mailed to the athletes at their lodgings called the Games a sham, and revealed the Nazis' brutality and how Germany was rearming for war. Maps were circulated detailing the locations of political murders and concentration camps. The leaflets begged the athletes to bring world attention to the situation by refusing to compete. Dickinson said that the Australian team received such correspondence but quickly disposed of it for fear of getting into trouble. Jewish women employed at Friesian House confided to Doris Carter that they feared for their safety. Even Freifrau von Wangenheim admitted to Carter that she had no time for the Nazis but was too scared not to follow orders.

'It was very obvious that Hitler was preparing for war, more than every second person wore a uniform of some sort,' Carter would tell the authors of *A Proper Spectacle*. When she asked Berliners why the regime was mobilising, she was informed 'that they were very afraid of the Russian bear and had to be ready to prepare for any invasion from that direction. Hitler, of course, was very cunning. He was, as we learned later, really facing in the opposite direction and he planned accordingly.' Carter was puzzled by the many tunnels in Berlin, and later learned that they were 'air raid shelters for the Berliners if needed'.

Just days before the Olympics commenced, the regime discovered that Village commandant Captain Wolfgang Fürstner, who had transformed the drab army barracks into a paradise for the athletes, was a *Mischling*, half Jewish. He was immediately stripped not only of his command but also of his uniform and his German citizenship, and replaced by hardline Nazi Lieutenant Colonel Werner Albrecht von und zu Gilsa. To avoid a scandal, his accusers permitted Fürstner to remain in the Village in the token role of assistant commandant. He knew that as soon as the Games were over, so might be his life. (Two days after the Closing Ceremony, he attended a banquet honouring his successor, then shot himself. The regime broadcast that Fürstner had died in a car accident.)

One balmy twilight, as Alderson looked the other way, a few of the Australians joined the Japanese for a clandestine cigarette on the secluded back veranda of Worms. Perhaps an illicit beer was shared as well, for surely it would not have been a dry party with such a resourceful rascal as Fred Woodhouse in the team. In five years' time, these men, the Australians and the Japanese, would be mortal enemies. But for now they sat together, perhaps, because of the language barrier, not conversing, just sharing the moment, as machine gun fire and the vengeful songs of the Hitler Youth rang through the surrounding wood. This was the most pure Olympic moment, the moment most in keeping with Olympic ideals, that the 1936 Australians ever knew.

CHAPTER 11
INNOCENTS ABROAD

When they were not training or relaxing, the Australians took excursions into Berlin, to shops, galleries, museums, theatres, cafes and music halls, to go boating on the sweetly meandering Spree, or strolling or cycling in the squares and parks or the leafy countryside. Soon after arriving, Basil Dickinson had suffered a heel injury from running and jumping on the hard and unfamiliar cinder training track; he did as much sightseeing as the searing pain in his foot allowed.

The athletes, who benefited from an Olympians' currency rate that saw them pay less for goods, shopped for themselves and their loved ones in Berlin's cavernous department stores, many of which had been built and run by Jews until the Nazis evicted them.

Dickinson also recalled a night at the Berlin State Opera House to see Puccini's *Madame Butterfly*. Neither he nor any of the other Australians were aware then that Jewish musicians employed at the magnificent 200-year-old building had been dismissed or had fled, and so, blissful in their ignorance, they enjoyed the opera. 'Oh, it was marvellous,' Dickinson said. 'The music, the costumes. Some of us were dragged kicking and screaming . . . and most ended up enjoying it. The Opera House, of course, was bombed to smith-ereens in 1945. At the Wintergarten theatre, whose ceiling was covered in lights to resemble a starry sky, we saw Johann Strauss II's opera *Die Fledermaus*. The Wintergarten was bombed too.'

The Australians visited the zoo and cradled lion cubs, and strolled in the leafy expanses of the Tiergarten; police caught them walking on a manicured lawn. Nobody had understood the sign that said '*Verboten!*' They were warned by armed officers that if they walked on the grass again they'd be arrested.

The Australians soon learned the meaning of '*Verboten!*' Norton told authors Stephanie Daniels and Anita Tedder of the time when she and Argentinian swimmer Jeannette Campbell sneaked into the Reich Sports Field stadium. 'No one was allowed in [at that stage], only tourists and their guides, and Jeannette and I hit on the idea to mix with the tourists and when they drew opposite an entrance to the stadium we would duck in. All went to plan, we got in, but not surprisingly we were chased by a storm trooper shouting "*Verboten! Verboten!*"'

'There was a strong Nazi presence in the streets of Berlin,' said Dickinson. 'I didn't like the blokes in brown shirts with their badges and night sticks and revolvers. Unlike the fellows at the Village, these city storm troopers had a chip on their shoulder and found it difficult to act friendly. I personally didn't see any violence to Jewish people . . . I learned later that it was all done out of sight.' The American sportswriter Grantland Rice wrote that these guardians of National Socialism didn't stroll, they strutted, and they didn't speak, they growled.

Percy Oliver was more bemused than scared by the presence of so many armed men in uniform. 'It all went over my head,' he told an interviewer late in life. 'I was seventeen, all I knew was school, swimming and Perth. I was naïve about world politics and what was happening in the 1930s in Germany. I was just an athlete at the Olympics. I was too busy thinking about swimming well.'

In Berlin, Evelyn de Lacy was like a child in a lolly shop. Her diary speaks of many treats. On 30 June, she, Kitty Mackay, Doris Carter and Mary Fergusson took a bus to Potsdam, south-west of central Berlin, and at one time the home of kings and kaisers. On 9 July, de Lacy's diary detailed shopping with Fergusson at Woolworth's department store. Lunch was 'jolly good'. Afternoon tea was taken at Charlottenburg Palace. 'Oh boy! What a place! Dotted all over were chairs and tables and in the centre was a marble dance floor and the orchestra in between dance music played marvellous classical music. We had strawberries and cream and coffee, while the little birds flew all around us. We stayed in this paradise in the heart of the city until half past six . . .' Just seven years into the future, Charlottenburg Palace, too, would be battered by bombs.

With her teammates, de Lacy had tea in the Tiergarten and swam in the River Havel alongside 'small boats like canoes with engines making them miniature speed boats'. On 15 July they watched a vaudeville show at the Wintergarten. 'We were welcomed and had the spotlight put on the whole team. Each of us got a tiny mouth organ. The Chinese acrobats doubled themselves in four and a magician suspended a woman in the air and made an elephant disappear . . .' On a visit to the swish Eden Hotel on 17 July, de Lacy ate an omelette filled with mushrooms and drank fruit and apple wine. She was aghast at the daily room rate: 'Seven pounds a day! Just imagine, 49 pounds a week! But it would be like living in a palace . . . And what do you think—I saw George Raft the film actor and I'm not too sure but I think he was with [Norwegian actress] Greta Nissen.'

One morning, while they were scurrying about Berlin, a photographer approached de Lacy, Mackay and Norton, and took their photo. A few days later there was hubbub in their dormitory when the *Berliner Illustrierte* magazine arrived and there were the girls grinning out of a double-page spread.

Boxer Harry Cooper wrote home to his family boasting that he was hobnobbing with the high and mighty in Berlin after spotting George Raft and Johnny Weissmuller. He mused, 'After this vast organisation and seeing the wonderful buildings especially erected for the Games, I could not suppress a smile when I thought of the person who said to me, "Why don't they hold an Olympic Games in Australia?" Of all the crazy ideas.'

There was a treat, too, on 26 July for boxers Cooper, Harley and Cook and wrestlers Garrard, O'Hara and Scarf when they were driven to Tempelhof aerodrome to join the welcoming party for world heavyweight boxing champion Max Schmeling, who had flown home on the *Hindenburg* airship after KO'ing Joe Louis in their fight at New York's Yankee Stadium. Schmeling, a genial man, ignored the demands of officials and hysterical fans at the airport reception lounge to chat to them and instead spent time with the Australians talking about boxing, with the aid of an interpreter. Schmeling was no real supporter of National Socialism, but as one whose family and work were in Germany he had no choice other than to allow himself to be used as a flesh-pressing propaganda stooge. Hitler and Goebbels, unsettled by the fast times recorded by African American runners Jesse Owens and Ralph Metcalfe, trumpeted Schmeling's KO of Joe Louis as yet another victory for the master race over lesser breeds.

On 19 July, the Australians laid a wreath of white lilies and oak leaves at the war memorial in the imperial guardhouse on Unter den Linden to honour Germans and their own countrymen who had fallen in battle. The wreath was inscribed: 'As a gesture of peace and goodwill from the Australian Olympic team.' After a minute's silence, a large crowd which had gathered by the eternal flame applauded.

De Lacy wrote that when the women called in at Grünau to watch the rowers training on the Langer See, 'Hitler's men came down and the people sang two national anthems and raised their hands in salute and said, "Hail! Hail! Hail!"' (What they were really saying, of course, was '*Heil! Heil! Heil!*')

Along with athletes and officials, politicians, sports fans and celebrities came to Berlin from all over the world to revel in the great Olympic festival. American aviator and staunch isolationist Colonel Charles Lindbergh was in Berlin at Göring's invitation to view the (illegal) Luftwaffe. As he showed Lindbergh the airfields and aircraft factories, Göring puffed out his barrel chest. Snaring Lindbergh was a publicity coup for the Reich, for, nine years after making the first solo flight across the Atlantic, 'Lucky Lindy' (who had been anything but when his baby son was kidnapped and murdered in 1932) was still one of the world's most famous and admired people. Back in the United States after the Olympics, Lindbergh reported, 'From the inspection trips I made through those factories I knew war planes were being built to fill those [air] fields . . . For the first time war became real to me. The officers I met were not preparing for a game.' Impressed by Hitler's 'character and vision', he believed Germany had the largest air force in the world, and one capable of destroying that of any other country. During Lindbergh's visit, Göring lectured him that there were only three truly great people in history: Buddha, Christ and Adolf Hitler.

The wealthy US-born British politician and socialite Sir Henry 'Chips' Channon was the guest of newly appointed German ambassador to Britain Joachim von Ribbentrop and lapped up his hospitality. He would write in his published diary that even though he was amused by Hitler's resemblance to Charlie Chaplin, he 'was more excited to see [him] than I was when I met Mussolini in 1926 in Perugia, and was more stimulated, I'm sorry to say, than when I was blessed by the Pope in 1920'. Channon was 'conscious of the effort the Germans were making to show the world the grandeur, the permanency and respectability of the new regime'. British Fascist leader Sir Oswald Mosley was a ubiquitous guest at the official balls and banquets over the Olympic period, with his fiancée Diana Guinness (née Mitford) and her sister Unity Mitford, who was besotted by Hitler and in Berlin as the Führer's guest. During the Olympics, Mitford stayed with Goebbels and his wife Magda. Royals at the Games included the King of Bulgaria, the Crown Prince and Princess of Italy, the Crown Prince of Greece, the Duke of Hamilton, Prince Philipp of Hesse and his wife Princess Mafalda of Savoy, who within the decade would die in Buchenwald concentration camp. Mussolini's sons were in town, and so too the British Nazi apologist Lord Londonderry, who had called on Hitler in the past. Emil Jannings, star of *The Blue Angel*, was there, though another star of the movie missed the Olympic festivities: Kurt Gerron, the rotund Jewish actor, singer and director who memorably played the magician, had fled Nazi Germany. He was later arrested in the Netherlands and gassed in Auschwitz in 1944.

The only senior Australian politicians in Berlin for the Games were Dr Earle Page—federal minister for commerce, who would be caretaker prime minister for three weeks in 1939 after Joseph Lyons' death—and NSW premier Sir Bertram Stevens. Aside from Stevens, the two most prominent Australian visitors in town were AOF officials James Taylor and Jim Eve.

The rich and famous who flocked to Berlin were, remembered Bavarian-born Jewish journalist Bella Fromm, 'spoiled, pampered, flattered and beguiled'. VIP guests of the Reich, while in all probability under surveillance by their hosts, found themselves invited to a seemingly endless round of lavish parties. The regime basked in the glow of the famous blow-ins, because in their eyes the celebrities' attendance in Berlin validated National Socialism.

There had never been any love lost between powerful Nazis Goebbels, Göring and Ribbentrop. Each revelled in undermining the others and vied shamelessly for their Führer's favour; now, over the course of the Olympics, they competed for bragging rights as the host of the most outrageously opulent Olympic party.

Ribbentrop was the first to pop the corks when he opened his mansion in Dahlem to 600 glittering guests of the Reich on 11 August. A former champagne salesman, the vainglorious and abrasive Ribbentrop—who, it was said, had bought the 'von' in his name and married his wife for her money—ensured that Pommery flowed like water and strutted among the guests, including the IOC, most of the Nazi leadership and prominent French, Italians, Poles and Britons. While the senior members of the British government remained in London in July and August 1936, there were peers, minor MPs, diplomats and their partners aplenty savouring Ribbentrop's hospitality. Wrote Ribbentrop in his unpublished memoir: 'It all looked like fairyland . . . the beautiful lawn of which we had always been proud, the swimming pool covered in water lilies, the gorgeous rhododendrons and the festively laid tables.'

Ribbentrop did not have long to wallow in his triumph. He was one-upped just two days later by Göring, whose party was held in the grounds of a government building. Encased in a bright white uniform weighed down with gold braid and medals, Göring greeted 800 guests while perched regally on an outsized lounge alongside his actress wife Emmy. He had ordered built in the floodlit grounds a miniature eighteenth-century French village with inn, bakery and tavern, and a Bavarian carnival with merry-go-round, sideshows, shooting galleries and bars where barely clad women poured wine, beer and cocktails. In the twilight skies above, Göring's Luftwaffe entertained the guests with daredevil aerobatics. Singers and dancers from the Berlin Opera performed. Swans glided among waterlilies strewn across an Olympic-sized swimming pool illuminated by underwater lights. (It has been reported that Eleanor Holm, the disgraced American swimmer, swam nude in the pool that night. This may or may not have been the reason Göring presented her with a silver swastika brooch. She would recall to a *Sports Illustrated* journalist, 'I enjoyed the parties, the "*Heil* Hitlers", the uniforms, the flags. Göring was fun. He had a good personality. So did the one with the club foot [Goebbels].' That night, and at other times, her path crossed that of Avery Brundage, no longer in a position to stop her smoking and drinking. 'I was invited to everything in Berlin,' she said, 'and he would be there, too. He would be so miserable because I was at all these important functions. I would ignore him, like he wasn't even alive. I really think he hated the poor athletes. How dare I be there and take away his thunder? You see, they all wanted to talk to me.')

At one point, the obese Göring rode a mechanical horse on the merry-go-round and as his medals flashed in the party lights, he waved to his applauding guests. Chips Channon would tell his diary: 'It was fantastic . . . roundabouts, cafes with beer and champagne, peasants dancing . . . vast women carrying pretzels and beer, a ship, a beer house, crowds of gay laughing people, animals, a mix of Luna Park and Old Heidelberg and the Trianon . . . The music roared, the astonished guests wandered about . . . Goebbels, it appears, as well as Ribbentrop, was in despair with jealousy.'

If so, the minister for propaganda and enlightenment got even with his nemeses a few days later when it was his turn to play host. The venue for Goebbels' grand Italian-themed party for 2700 guests—including the US, British and German Olympic teams—was the picturesque Pfaueninsel (Peacock Island) in the Havel River near Potsdam. He had assigned noted Reich stage designer Benno von Arent to decorate the site as a sumptuous film set, replete with sweeping lawns, romantic forests and the plumed birds which gave the island its name. Three dance bands played.

Like Ribbentrop and Göring, Goebbels used money from government coffers to pay for his party. He had had constructed a pontoon bridge over which 'everybody who was anybody' crossed onto the island before being greeted by topless actresses brandishing flaming torches and serving canapés and champagne. Hanging in trees were huge butterflies constructed of glowing lanterns. The evening was capped by fireworks which bloomed high into the sky. The display reminded American ambassador to Berlin William E. Dodd, who had advocated that the Games be boycotted, of a pitched battle.

The widely syndicated and influential journalist William L. Shirer was invited. 'Never before, to my knowledge, had the Nazi bigwigs put on such extravagant parties,' he wrote in his book *20th Century Journey*. 'The propaganda minister's "Italian Night" . . . gathered more than a thousand guests (including even me) at dinner in a scene that resembled the Arabian Nights. While the best food and wine I had ever tasted in Nazi Germany were being served to the immense throng on a broad terrace overlooking the lake under a spreading canopy of 5000 Chinese lanterns, we listened to the Berlin Philharmonic Orchestra and stars from the State Opera and watched dancers from the Opera ballet.'

Late in the evening the party became an orgy as drunk guests chased the dancers and actresses through the undergrowth. Despite having an abnormally large head, puny body and club foot, Goebbels was a renowned Lothario, and lived up to his reputation by pursuing the actress Lida Baarova, who would soon become his mistress, despite the presence of Baarova's husband and Goebbels' wife Magda, who was pregnant with their fourth child.

Hitler, a teetotaller whose favourite repast was boiled vegetables, avoided these bacchanals. He abhorred drunken ribaldry and excess, and carefully nurtured his image as one too busy saving Germany to do anything so trivial as enjoy himself. The Führer did hold a sedate formal dinner for 150 senior Nazis, German captains of industry, and sympathetic international royalty and statesmen in the state dining room of the Reich Chancellery, and made fleeting appearances at a select few of the almost nightly banquets and receptions. He even steeled himself to drop in briefly on a dinner Göring was hosting for Baillet-Latour, Brundage and other members of the IOC in the Reichstag Presidential Palace.

The Australians, while not on Goebbels' guest list, were invited to Olympic celebrations before and during the Games. 'One of these, a British Empire reception at the mansion of the British ambassador to Berlin [Sir Eric Phipps], proved disastrous,' recalled Dickinson. 'We arrived by bus, all immaculate in uniform, with the British, South Africans, Indians and Canadians, and as we entered the reception hall we were introduced by the first and second footmen in their livery and then a third footman presented each of us to the ambassador. There were many members of the British aristocracy in their medals and finery. When everything settled down a bit we formed groups, and a few had too much to drink. The waiters were walking around holding trays of drinks on high. A couple of our fellows thought it was funny to follow behind the waiters and sneak a drink off their tray without them noticing. It was pretty infantile behaviour. Eddie Scarf was furious. He read the riot act to us, and in taking the glasses from the drunk blokes he knocked into one very well-dressed woman who turned on him and said, "Oh, you Australians are so crude." This was unfair because only a few were acting up, and Eddie of course was just trying to do the right thing. He wasn't going to put up with being spoken to like that so he looked the woman straight in the eye and retorted, "Madam, you know right where you can go!" Well, from that point, Eddie let the blokes run riot. The bloke among us who played up the most was Fred Woodhouse. Fred only had to smell a cork and he'd be plastered. We took him back to the bus to keep him from landing himself, and us, in any more trouble, and he kept breaking out and staggering back to the party to make more mischief.'

Two days before the Opening Ceremony, Goebbels hosted a dinner for the 1200 journalists, broadcasters and cameramen who would be covering the Olympics. Seated at the top table, just a few places from Goebbels, were Sir Bertram Stevens and James Taylor, who was representing the Commonwealth International Olympic Federation. Goebbels began by smoothly regurgitating the anodyne pronouncements with which he had been force-feeding the international community for the past two years about how Germany had nothing but goodwill towards mankind. He then gave a glimpse of the Nazi zealot that lurked behind his Cheshire cat grin. Without warning, he chastised those at the dinner who had criticised in their reports the National Socialist dictatorship and its policies of aggression and repression. The foreign press had no right to criticise a regime they did not understand, he said. 'You will realise that [the German government has] more important things to do than give absolute liberty. As we respect your opinions, it is only just that you should respect ours in the new Germany. That is a response which all journalists, whether from democratic or autocratic countries, should take,' he stormed. Then, after a pause during which he registered the effect of his words on his audience, he reverted to a quieter, conciliatory tone. 'We have been reproached for employing the Olympic Games as political propaganda. As Minister for Propaganda, I know of no such intention, but we want you to see for yourselves, and you will see smiling faces everywhere. We have been reproached for not allowing free public opinion. You will see what the new Germany wants. I hope the Olympic Games festival will be a peace contribution to the happiness of all nations.'

CHAPTER 12
OLYMPIC COUNTDOWN

'We were true amateurs in every way,' said Basil Dickinson. 'Our physical and technical shortcomings, and our attitude, were brutally exposed in Berlin in 1936.'

For the Australian Olympians of 1936, the honour of representing Australia in an Olympic Games and then competing fairly and to the best of their ability was more important than medals. So they did not train with the intensity of the Germans, Americans and Japanese, to whom winning was everything. It was in the Americans' DNA to excel at every endeavour, the Japanese were terrified of shaming their homeland, and the Germans were motivated by fear of the Nazi enforcers and extreme fealty to the Fatherland.

Harry Alderson, in his official report, would assure the AOF that his team 'carried out as much training as it could on the five-week voyage aboard the *Mongolia* and then quickly settled down to work in Berlin but . . . much of the time was taken up in regaining lost fitness and getting used to the changed conditions'. Indeed, most of the athletes were kilos heavier and considerably less fit than when they'd left Australia—and after they'd arrived their preparation was hamstrung by injuries and illness.

Only jumper Jack Metcalfe trained as hard or as often as the athletes of the Olympic powers, but instead of following Metcalfe's example, his teammates by and large were happy to sit back and marvel, considering him a freak. 'Jack Metcalfe was an astonishing person,' said Fred Woodhouse. 'He was extremely intelligent . . . He did everything we didn't believe in in those days. We were scared that if we trained too hard we'd burn ourselves out. We didn't push ourselves. I for one used to thrive on very little exercise. I tried for quality rather than stamina. As well as his high jumping itself, Jack did extreme sit-ups and leg exercises and had enormously muscled thighs and calves, which he felt gave him take-off power in the high jump and also speed when running in to the broad jump and hop, step and jump. He would train as hard as a ballet dancer, and that made sense because he was keen on art and music. Like a dancer, he could [pirouette]. He could do one-legged squats 20 times on each leg. He was only 5ft 10 [1.77m] but could jump 6ft 6 [1.98m] with his eastern cut-off.'

When criticised for training too intensely, Metcalfe countered that he could only achieve peak performance in a major event if he'd trained hard. 'You get out what you put in . . . I don't believe you can just turn on a great performance when you need it. It's not consistent with the rules of probability.'

Another thing Metcalfe was accused of was misplaced generosity; he assisted his main hop, step and jump Olympic rivals—the Japanese athletes Kenkichi Oshima, Naoto Tajima and Masao Harada. 'I trained on a smaller oval not far from the Village, the one where the women were staying and where the women trained,' Metcalfe said. 'Before she was injured, I jumped with Doris Carter. A few other athletes trained there, including the Japanese hop steppers. We certainly exchanged tips, but I don't think anything I said [helped them to win], they would have won anyway. They were better jumpers and were certainly better trained. They'd had three months competing in Helsinki and doing pre-Games training in Japan before coming to Berlin. This was true of the whole Japanese team, the swimmers too. But they were doing the event that I did and I enjoyed the experience of performance even if we were only in training. They seemed to be the same. One of them, Oshima, spoke good English. We did discuss things but it was in no sense me coaching them. It was simply a matter of talking about our sport. And goodness me, anyone in those days who was prepared to talk about athletics, they had to wear ear muffs if they wanted to get away from me.' When two German officials saw Metcalfe lending a hand to his Japanese friends, they reported him to manager Alderson, who told them that if what they were saying was correct, then Metcalfe's good-heartedness gave him as much pleasure as if Metcalfe had won a gold medal. Oshima and Metcalfe met again at the Melbourne Olympics in 1956, where they reminisced. The Japanese gave the Australian a photograph inscribed: 'In sweet memory of Berlin—from K. Oshima to Mr J. Metcalfe.'

The Australians did notch up a victory before the Games. Cyclist Chris Wheeler challenged a Peruvian to a 100km road race but the Peruvian became exhausted and waved the Australian on. Later that evening when the Peruvian had not returned to the Village, Wheeler and a rescue party set off to find him. They came upon him asleep on the roadside 20km from the Village.

Gerald Backhouse typified the laidback Australian mindset. Training was anathema to him. Recalled Woodhouse when interviewed by Harry Gordon: 'He'd say, "I don't feel in the mood [to train] today. I think I'll go and have a look around Berlin." He said, "You have got to be like a great artist, you must be in the mood or you won't succeed." He'd go out and have a little jog for a quarter of an hour, about half a mile, and, right, that would do him. The only times we saw Gerald running was when he ran back to the Village from a party in Berlin at two or three in the morning and he'd be wearing his black tie and tails. He went to Geelong Grammar like I did and was a real gentleman, a wonderful person, wonderful personality. One athlete at the village, I don't know what country he came from, approached Gerald and said, "What about having a trial race over the half-mile or mile" (I don't remember which), and Gerald said, "I don't feel like it today, I'm going into Berlin." The fellow kept on and on at Gerald, who finally said, "All right, I'm feeling like it today," and Gerry beat him over the distance in a better time than he'd ever run in Australia.'

Evelyn de Lacy's diary records the women's relaxed pre-Games attitude. 'Today we all slept in. Jumping out of bed at nine o'clock, I quickly awakened the others and we hurried through our coffee and rolls and went off down the pool with our little guides . . . The Japanese swimmers are marvellous. Can they swim! We are learning a few things off them all right! It's great to watch their easy movements in the water. On land they all do exercises for about half an hour before entering the water, then they float away with the greatest of ease. We lunched at a cafe at the Olympic stadium and paid 40 pfennigs for a great feed. Then we retired out on the lawns and slept it off.'

While other nationalities honed their times and style, to the Australians, weekends—and inclement weather, too—meant no training. 'Weekends off!!!!' exulted de Lacy. 'Today is Saturday so Kitty and I went to town shopping. We had such fun and stayed in town for lunch and more fun ordering our food. We arrived home at 3. Had a hot bath and a sleep. After dinner we had a visit from the American athletes and had a musical evening.' Just three days from the Opening Ceremony, it was 'very, very wet . . . we fooled around today'.

On 30 July, de Lacy 'slept in and rested'. On 31 July, the day before the Opening Ceremony, 'we went to the open air theatre [at the Reich Sports Field] and saw a play. Wonderfully acted and gorgeous dresses. Retired about 11.'

The five track and field athletes—Metcalfe, Dickinson, Wood-house, Backhouse and Watson—left the Village to fly to London to compete in the British Championships on 15 July. Alderson and Metcalfe believed they would benefit from international competition before the Olympics. The flight was bumpy and terrified the athletes, only one of whom—Metcalfe—had ever flown. Dickinson promised himself while bouncing about high in the clouds that if he were ever lucky enough to be on land again, his first flight would be his last.

More than 40,000 spectators packed White City sports field for the two-day meet. The Australians did well enough on what Dickinson called 'a horrible cinder track'. Metcalfe won the high jump and the hop, step and jump, while Dickinson placed second in the hop, step and jump and fourth in the broad jump. He worried that his concentration on the former had cost him a place in the latter. Watson ran second in the 440yd hurdles. Backhouse kept pace with the leaders in the mile, but cinder track–induced shin soreness saw him fall behind as the race wore on. Woodhouse, clearly hampered by a strained side muscle he'd suffered training on the Village field, nevertheless vaulted well and was pipped for first. When Metcalfe telephoned Alderson in the Village from London to report on their performances, Alderson called the rest of the team to the phone to give the track and field men a rousing cheer. The manager was sure that 'these results will put new mettle into them'.

After their rough flight over, the group refused to fly back and instead returned to Berlin by ferry and then train. All were seasick on the ferry crossing and felt every bit as ill as they had in the aircraft.

Seasickness was not all that ailed Dickinson. He was homesick and lonely in London. 'I took the chance to do some sight-seeing and visited the British Museum and it was very interesting, but loneliness began to creep up on me. I was the youngest and felt excluded by the others. I didn't confide in my mate Jack. He was four years older than me and highly educated, so apart from athletics and us both having been Sydney High students, we didn't have too much in common. Jack and I had different personalities. He was self-confident. He was studying to be a lawyer and his family was well off, his father being a successful businessman, whereas I came from the low end of the middle class. Jack was a likeable fellow, a private man in many ways, very much more developed mentally and physically than I was at that stage. He'd had many trips, been to the London Empire Games in 1934, to New Zealand. It took Jack extra years to finish university because he was always going skiing in Europe. He competed in the javelin and shot put as well as the jump events. He received the publicity. I always came second to him. And, in turn, the state barrier divided Jack and me from the Victorians Woodhouse, Backhouse and Watson.'

The Australian rowing eight had a London sojourn of their own when they accepted an invitation to compete in the prestigious Grand Challenge Cup at the Henley Royal Regatta. Unfortunately, after the squad arrived, the organisers invoked a rule that 'anyone who is, or has been, for trade or employment for wages a mechanic, artisan or labourer' was barred from rowing in the Challenge Cup because those who did manual work had a physical advantage over gentlemen who did not. To the organisers, policemen were deemed to be labourers. Wal Mackney was not amused. 'My father, who was very left wing, saw the ban as a Tory plot to disadvantage the workers,' says Mackney's son Kim today. Although the British rowers had no say in the edict, the Australians vowed to get even with them with oar—and if the chance arose, fist—at the Olympics the following month.

There were times in July when the Australian athletes' dorms resembled hospital wards. From the moment they arrived in Berlin, they needed time to regain fitness and shake off the lingering effects of their long and inactive voyage. As Alderson reported, 'The swimmers did their training at the Reich Sports Field in the main swimming pool and a practice pool situated close handy. Both pools were of excellent construction, with fresh water, the main pool being heated. Unfortunately the lack of fresh water pools in Australia placed our swimmers at a disadvantage . . . as a good deal of valuable time was lost getting used to the changed conditions. The different floating powers and buoyancy of salt and fresh water required a change in the technique of the swimmers.' The cyclists had to acclimatise to racing over the longer metric distance and the wooden cycle tracks and the wrestlers and boxers had to learn different international rule interpretations and point-scoring systems. For the track and field athletes, there was the issue of running and jumping on the unfamiliar cinder tracks. Metcalfe and Dickinson were performing well until the cinder track took its toll and both suffered foot, ankle, shin and knee strains. 'My first experience on a cinder track was in London [in the 1934 Empire Games] and I just couldn't manage it at all, it's a different experience,' said Metcalfe. 'On the take-off of my first high jump in London . . . I landed on my back. I tried to adjust my style to cinders but I was never able. In Australia, I used to do a show-off feat where I put the high jump bar at 6ft 2 [1.88m] and had the athletes stand under it and I'd jump over them. I had no difficulty, I had all the confidence in the world. I couldn't jump that high on cinders in Berlin.'

Dickinson displaced a bone in his heel running and jumping in his running shoes with two spikes on each heel that were made for grass and were largely useless on cinders. 'I didn't have enough money to go into Berlin and buy a proper pair of shoes,' he said. He was instructed not to jump on cinders before his actual event to avoid worsening his injury. This was sound advice but no way to prepare for the hop, step and jump of his life. A specialist athletics coach, such as were employed by the other nations' teams, would have been valuable.

With hurdler Alf Watson the only track and field athlete not hobbled by the tracks, Alderson became more determined than ever that Australia introduce cinder tracks so that the problems he and his team were facing were never repeated. When Sir Bertram Stevens visited the Village, Alderson pleaded with the premier to consider installing such tracks for athletes in New South Wales and suggest to other state premiers that they do the same. Stevens sympathised, but that was all he did.

Before he left Australia, Woodhouse had been working his way up to vaulting 13ft (3.96m) with a view to achieving 14ft (4.26m), which he hoped would be high enough to win an Olympic medal. Then, on his first day of practice in the Village, he strained the muscles in his right side; the injury grew worse despite diathermy treatment.

For as long as he lived, Woodhouse cursed the amateurism of the Australians' preparation. He resented that he'd not been given adequate advice on preparation when selected in the team, and that the five stir-crazy weeks on *Mongolia* weakened him to the extent that the first time he used his abdominal muscles to vault he damaged them. 'On the boat we did everything that was foreign to us. I was unable to pole vault, so instead I tried to keep fit by tossing medicine balls, sparring with the boxers, a little bit of high jumping with Metcalfe.' Training at the Village, he said, 'I took off and felt a ripping inside. The doctor applied strapping and told me, "You must rest it."' Woodhouse defied the doctor's orders and competed in London in mid-July. When back in the Village, the strain would not heal. The doctor had no choice but to rule him out for a month, which eliminated him from the Olympics.

There is a photograph of Woodhouse slumped disconsolately outside Worms, ruefully nursing his vaulting pole. The doctor had just dashed his Olympic dream. 'Aw, couldn't the period be reduced to a fortnight?' he had pleaded. Years later, his bad fortune still rankled. 'It left a scar because I felt I had a chance.' He may or may not have been serious when he claimed that had he been fit, he could have beaten American Earle Meadows' winning vault of 4.356m. 'Not being able to compete in Berlin was one of the saddest moments in my life.'

Though the cinder track caused Backhouse some shin soreness, he was still running well. Perhaps his dislike of regular training had worked in his favour. In an 800m race before the Games he covered the distance in 1 minute, 53.5 seconds, a personal best. His time was only 3.7 seconds short of the existing Olympic record.

Carter was another casualty of the cinder track; her take-off leg was affected by shin splints, and she was able to train only intermittently. Though she jumped well when she could practise—once clearing 1.57m, just 7.5cm shy of the Olympic record—she spent most of July nursing a hot pack to her leg. For some months after the Olympics she would walk with a limp.

The avalanche of injuries showed up the shortcomings of masseurs McKay and Morrison. 'They were hopeless,' was Dickinson's verdict, 'they just slapped our legs and had no clue about the treatment of various injuries and the needs of athletes of different sports.' Because there were no specialist masseurs for rowers, sculler Cec Pearce had to be rubbed down by heavy-handed German masseurs who specialised in massaging cyclists.

Injuries weren't the only setbacks the athletes had to contend with; illness also plagued the team. At Grünau, Bill Cross came down with strength-sapping tonsilitis and Pearce was felled by the flu. Although the angry boils on boxer Les Harley's arm had been lanced, the infection worsened and Village doctors admitted him to Berlin General Hospital where he was placed on an antibiotic drip in a ward for Olympic athletes. For a while it seemed likely that Harley's arm would have to be amputated. Even though the boils finally responded well to antibiotics, the blood poisoning he'd suffered had weakened him and stripped 7kg from his frame. In those days before diet supplements and specialist weight training programs, all the boxer could do was gorge himself on food to try to stack on weight in time.

Harry Cooper was making better progress. The broken hand he'd sustained shadow-boxing was by now, he reported, 'still swollen but well on the mend'. He was strengthening the damaged fist by squeezing a hard rubber ball. 'My mitt is bigger than before,' said the irrepressible fighter, 'and all the better to hit with.'

Eddie Scarf developed painful swelling on his shin and a high temperature; he was hospitalised and treated with antibiotics. When released, he trained with the boxers to prevent his injured leg being twisted by his fellow wrestlers.

The swimmers were also in the wars. On 9 July, Pat Norton—whom Harry Nightingale had been cossetting so as not to overtrain her—developed swollen glands behind her ear and was ordered not to train until the infection responded to treatment. This kept her dry for more than a week. Back in the swim, she backstroked 100m in a creditable 79 seconds. If she could improve just a little on that, Nightingale thought, she might stand a chance. Soon after Norton's ear trouble was cured, Ron Masters and Nightingale himself contracted ear infections. The chloride in the water was blamed.

Bill Kendall was stricken by a bad cold that persisted for weeks. Kitty Mackay, too, spent days in hospital on antibiotics for flu. It was late July before she was fit to swim, and when she did she found it more difficult than her teammates to adjust to racing in fresh water. She was capable of swimming faster than her best Berlin training time of 70 seconds for the 100m freestyle.

Yet another hurdle that the small Australian team faced was limited access to training facilities once the other athletes arrived. Sheer weight of numbers, and IOC influence, ensured that the Olympic big guns trained where and when they wanted. The Australian team were also outgunned when it came to the number of coaches accompanying the team. Springboard and high tower diver Masters discovered that the German diving boards had less spring than those he was used to. An American diving coach who was coaching the Germans helped Masters to learn to control the German boards. Had Masters had a coach, he surely would have accomplished this long before. The American divers faced the same issue with the unforgiving German boards, but had the prescience to bring their own, which they browbeat the organisers into allowing them to use in Olympic competition. Adding to Masters' problems, he had to recalibrate his style and timing to dive 10m instead of 10yd.

Percy Oliver fell out with coaches Nightingale and Harry Hay and was left to his own devices. Thankfully, the confident young man had always been his own sternest critic and had a realistic view of how he would need to perform to be competitive in his event, the 100m backstroke. He made the late decision in Berlin to alter his technique to emulate that of American Adolph Kiefer, the finest backstroker in the world. Oliver had no qualms about spying on Kiefer. 'My sister always taught me that if I saw good style to learn from it, try it, sort it out and if it feels good to develop it . . . I had no coach. There *was* a coach of the team, but we disagreed. He wanted to change my training regime and I wouldn't change, so he said, "Train on your own," and I did, for six weeks. I'd been reading of Kiefer for two years . . . and when the Americans arrived I hurried to the pool to watch them swim, particularly to see what this Kiefer did. His action was radically different to mine, and I figured as the world record holder he must be doing something right. [But] Kiefer's action required more power. I couldn't replicate his action exactly, as he was bigger and stronger than me. He was a very big man at 1.8m and 82kg, and I was a little boy of 66kg, so I had to work out a way to bring my arms through the water similar to him and so I developed a bent arm action at the elbow and brought it through in a free state, and this made a difference to my time over 100m of two seconds. So at the Sydney Empire Games in 1938 I swam the time that would have won me silver in Berlin. I only had two weeks after Kiefer arrived in Berlin to perfect the new action. It took a lot of practice and I just didn't have the time. I *nearly* got it right.'

The cyclists were also experiencing problems. Along with the new timber surface of the tracks, which contracted and expanded in the moody Berlin summer weather, they had a setback with which the rowers could sympathise: the crate containing their racing cycles had gone missing in the chaos of the Marseilles strike, and frantic efforts to locate it had failed. Dunc Gray, Chris Wheeler and Tassie Johnson were forced to train at the cycle track 12km east of the Village on borrowed bikes. Finally, word came that the bikes had been found and were on their way to Berlin by rail. They arrived on 14 July, three weeks after the cyclists.

As for the rowers, the eight were registering 40 strokes per minute, compared with the 42 they estimated they'd need to be competitive with the crack United States, Italian, British and German squads. Coach Mackenzie admitted that his rowers were still 'somewhat green' after the long voyage from Australia. He was keen to enlist the services of well-regarded former professional sculler Tom Sullivan, an Englishman who also coached the Berliner club, to help train the Australians. Sullivan began work, only to be told by a German rowing official that because he was being paid by a German club he was not permitted to assist foreign teams.

On the eve of the Games, Australia's knowledgeable sporting experts gave the team little chance of returning home with the great haul of medals predicted by the boosters back home.

The Referee's chief Olympic pundit, 'The Ranger', was in Berlin reporting for his newspaper. After observing the Australians at close hand, speaking to them and to Alderson, and then studying the form of rival athletes, he filed a considered Olympic preview. His predictions were essential reading for Australian sports fans, who in the fortnight to come would be poring over the morning paper or tuning in on their wireless sets for Olympic updates.

The Ranger could not decide who would win the 100m, which vied with the 1500m as the Olympics' track and field glamour event, but he was sure it would be an American. 'Both Owens and [Eulace] Peacock had bettered the present world's record of 10.3 seconds for 100m held by their countrymen [Eddie] Tolan and [Ralph] Metcalfe. They have shown brilliant form in the last 18 months. Owens has put up some marvellous performances over 100 yards. This year he set a new world record for the classic sprint distance with 9.3 seconds. Last year he turned in a 9.4 seconds effort and followed it up with another 9.4 clocking and then his world record. There is no doubting his sprinting class. But there are some strange things about Owens. He is not only a sprinter. He holds the world's records for the running broad jump and the

220 yards hurdles. In his sprinting style he disobeys the canons set down by English and Australian students of sprinting. He sprints with his body almost vertical to the ground. There is no comfortable incline of his body at an angle to the ground. And his arm action is high. His long, lean legs pound out far ahead of him. Metcalfe and Peacock are of more solid and compact build, but will measure every stride with Owens on the Berlin Stadium.' The journalist predicted that Owens and Ralph Metcalfe would also fight out the 200m. With so little separating the champions, the result of the race would probably be settled by how well they started.

Then, perhaps to give Owens' and Metcalfe's rivals a ray of hope, The Ranger indulged in a little wishful thinking. There was always 'a decided chance that by the time of the actual races, the American stars will have burned themselves out. They take part in intensive tests in preparation for the Olympic Games. It has often been noticed that during these tests the Americans have reached the peak of their form. They break many world's records. They *have* to get into their Olympic team. But a reaction sometimes set in and by the time of the Olympic Games they were unable to reproduce their test performances.'

As for the other track and field events, in the 400m the experts' consensus was that the winner would come from among Great Britain's Godfrey Rampling, Bill Roberts and Godfrey Brown, who, in contrast to the American runners, had built up slowly to a peak, training to produce their best when it mattered. African American Archie Williams was deemed the US's best chance of a medal, with his fellow American Jimmy LuValle and South African Denis Shore also chances.

Australia's little terrier, Backhouse, although an outsider in the 800m, had muted support among the sporting intelligentsia. He was respected for his fighting spirit and cool head, and was perfectly capable of beating his previous best time for the distance, which he would have to do to pose a threat to the favourites—the beautifully balanced Ben Eastman of the United States and the Italian greyhound Mario Lanzi. Backhouse had a track record of coming from behind to win.

The 1500m was wide open. The British and American runners, in particular the current world record holder Glenn Cunningham, were all consistent performers. Backhouse was given scant hope. New Zealander Jack Lovelock was many pundits' pick. Lovelock had confided to Metcalfe and Dickinson at the British Championships in London earlier in July that his medical studies had kept him from performing at his best, but now he was ready to give his all. The wiry Lovelock was a magnificent runner, marvellously durable and mentally tough, typically devising a strategy for each race and relentlessly sticking to it.

Watson, although unscathed by the injuries and illness dogging his teammates, was given little hope in either the 100m hurdles or the 400m hurdles, his times being well below those of the Americans, and in particular the favourite, Glenn Hardin, who had blitzed every event in which he had competed in the past year. The Americans and the English were expected to win gold and silver respectively in the 4x100m and the 4x400m relays.

Just as he was favoured to win the 100m and 200m, few experts could see Owens being bested in the broad jump. Peacock, the Japanese Harada and Chuhei Nambu, and Australia's Metcalfe and Dickinson (whose best jumps averaged around 30cm inside Owens' regular 7.6 to 7.9m leaps) would possibly do battle for silver and bronze.

The Australians Metcalfe and Dickinson had proven themselves to be among the world's best in the hop, step and jump over the past two years, so figured in most experts' calculations for the event, with Metcalfe rated the better chance. The main competition would come from Japan's Harada, Oshima and Tajima, the athletes with whom Metcalfe had exchanged friendly tips.

Although his personal best 1933 jump of 1.98m was marginally higher than the existing Olympic record, Metcalfe was an outsider in the high jump, and as the Games loomed he was tempted to scratch himself from the event, to concentrate on the broad jump and hop, step and jump.

Australia's main high jump hope was Carter, despite her leg injury. Her best recent jumps were world standard, with the champions Dorothy Odam of Great Britain and Ibolya Csak of Hungary notching only around 2.5cm higher in their lead-up competitions.

In the swimming, Norton was a possible medallist in the 100m backstroke. Though undone by her ear infection, she had swum well since arriving in Berlin. Although the Dutch world record holder, seventeen-year-old powerhouse Hendrika 'Rie' Mastenbroek, and her compatriot Nida Senff would provide formidable opposition, Eleanor Holm's banning was seen as a chance for the Australian to take bronze. Mackay would also be in the 100m backstroke, and her practice times were improving. Mackay was entered in the 100m freestyle, as was de Lacy, and both had recorded solid times. Those who knew the uncompli-cated, sunny-natured Australian pair believed they had the right temperament to rise to the occasion on the Olympic stage and swim faster than they ever had. Despite this, in the 100m free-style they would have their work cut out to beat the formidable Mastenbroek, Gisela Arendt of Germany and Argentinian Jean-nette Campbell. De Lacy was also entered in the 400m freestyle, in which Mastenbroek was again the experts' pick.

Masters had at last conquered the unfamiliar diving boards in Berlin and was as well prepared as he was ever going to be for his 3m springboard and 10m high tower events, but he, too, faced stiff competition from the Americans—Dick Degener, known as 'the Fred Astaire of diving', and Marshall Wayne.

Still struggling with a heavy cold, Kendall was not expected to do well in the 100m freestyle against the Japanese swimmers Masanori Yusa and Shigeo Arai, who had stunned onlookers at training with their intensity and speed.

Oliver had the brio to surprise the more fancied swimmers, but he was up against his hero Kiefer, the first ever to break 60 seconds for the 100m backstroke. It was thought that the Berlin experience would steel Oliver to go all out for Olympic glory in the Tokyo Games in 1940.

Although Gray had won 1932 Olympic gold, no Australian was regarded as a threat in cycling's 1000m time trials and scratch sprints to the formidable Dutchman Arie van Vliet or the rough-riding German Toni Merkens. Wheeler would have to go head to head with the French champion Robert Charpentier, who was an unbackable favourite for the race.

Australian boxing authority Jim Donald held out little hope for the fighters: 'Cook, Cooper and Harley do not, in my opinion, measure up to the Australian amateur boxing standard set by [previous Olympians] Reg "Snowy" Baker, Duncan Parberry, Frank Fitzjohn and Dave Smith. Certainly the present trio won their championship spurs in open competition and no doubt are the best men available. Which is the most I can say for them . . .'

Australia had no competitors in the women's diving. According to those in the know, the springboard diving and tower diving spoils would be divided among the Americans—Marjorie Gestring, Katherine Rawls, Velma Dunn and the Olympic veteran Dorothy Poynton-Hill, who was expected to add to her stash of medals in Berlin. Nor was Australia represented in the 100m sprint, where the American Helen Stephens was a popular choice for the gold medal, with Germany's Käthe Krauss and

Poland's Stanislawa Walasiewicz (Stella Walsh) fair chances of upsetting her.

On the evening of 30 July, Alderson and some of the athletes made a radio broadcast for the ABC that was heard around Australia. Alderson sent a mixed message. On one hand he was 'optimistic' about Australia's chances of winning medals and promised that the team would give a good account of itself. Then he reminded listeners that the athletes competing in Berlin numbered nearly 5000, including 359 (313 men and 46 women) from the United States, 450 Germans (403 men and 47 women), and 208 from Great Britain (comprising 171 men and 37 women); pitted against these legions was Australia's tiny team of just 33, so it should be appreciated by all at home that the quest to win medals was a daunting one. Too, Alderson continued, there had been 'mishaps and illness' since the squad arrived five weeks ago. Metcalfe took the microphone to tell the nation that the athletes were in great spirits and were vowing to do their very best. As the first Australian scheduled to compete (he had 'the honour of opening the innings for Australia . . .'), Harley assured the nation that his boils had now cleared up. Woodhouse mourned that his strained side had not.

On the eve of the Games, Norton and Mackay were interviewed by a journalist from *The Australian Women's Weekly*. Each was on tenterhooks because, as swimmers, they would have to wait more than a week to compete. 'What a trying time it is going to be between now and the day we meet the best from all over the world,' exclaimed Mackay, whose first race would be the 100m freestyle on 8 August. Norton's backstroke event would be held on 12 August. 'We are terribly excited already and it is going to be worse,' Mackay continued. 'Still, it is good to be that way. I suppose it shows we are getting up to concert pitch. Even the American girls, who have been in lots of big races, are excited. They mightn't say so, but their manner says they are. Though excited, we are not suffering from nerves. At least I don't think so. Excitement and nerves are two different things. Of course we may have nerves when *der Tag* [the day] comes, but even world champions suffer from nerves then.'

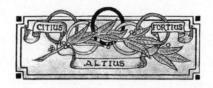

CHAPTER 13
THE OPENING CEREMONY

On Saturday, 1 August, the day of the 1936 Summer Olympics Opening Ceremony at the Reich Sports Field, rain tumbled from glowering skies and the wind blew on Berlin.

The Australian male athletes whiled away the morning at the Olympic Village before an army bus convoy arrived at 1 p.m. to take all the competitors to the May Field adjoining the stadium to be organised into ranks before marching into the arena. The athletes were nervous and champing for the day's gala to begin and end so they could finally compete.

Harry Alderson called together senior men Dunc Gray, Jack Metcalfe and Eddie Scarf to discuss how the team would comport itself when, as the fifth of the 49 nations, it marched past the Führer. It had been strongly suggested to Alderson by attaché Captain von Benda that it would be an appreciated show of respect to Hitler and Germany if as well as dipping the flag to the leader of the host country as was Olympic custom, the Australians honoured Hitler with a straight-arm Nazi salute. Alderson, who was becoming increasingly troubled by the encroachment of politics into sport at these Games, refused. He knew that giving the salute could be misinterpreted as an endorsement of Nazism. Every member of the squad agreed with his stand. 'We just didn't think it was the right thing to do,' said Percy Oliver. Basil Dickinson recalled 'so much hoo-hah over the salute the athletes were supposed to give. We were aware of the brownshirts watching us intently to see what we would do. I'm glad to say we refused to buckle under, and our refusal was unanimous.' Said Metcalfe, 'We *would* remove our hats and hold them across our chest and give eyes right in [Hitler's] direction. We'd dip the flag. As far as I know only the Americans didn't dip, and they never do. [American custom is for its flag to be lowered to none but the president.] But Australians giving a National Socialist salute just wouldn't have been appropriate.'

Feisty flag-bearer Gray opposed even dipping the flag to Hitler, but Alderson insisted. Alderson canvassed the other countries' managers. The British and Americans would not be performing the straight-arm salute, nor would the Kiwis or the French. If Australia's refusal caused offence to the hosts, they were in good company.

There was also the matter of the Australians being clueless about marching in lockstep. Occasionally on slow days at the Village, Alderson had corralled the men into an open area and attempted to have them march in an orderly fashion, to no avail. One problem was that flag-bearer Gray was a small man who took small steps, which caused the taller competitors bringing up the rear to concertina and skippety-skip to avoid a pile-up. To avoid an embarrassment at the Opening Ceremony, Alderson brought in a drill instructor. 'He tried to knock us into shape,' said Fred Woodhouse, 'and then went, "Hopeless! You'll have to take your chance on the day."'

At around the same time as Alderson was rousting his men from their bunks, Berlin was beginning a day of festivity in and around the capital as well as at the Reich Sports Field that had been plotted by Hitler, Goebbels, Frick and the Olympic officials for more than a year.

The celebrations started in the heart of the city at daybreak, when around 100,000 Berlin schoolchildren marched in perfect step in calibrated ranks—unlike the Australians, they'd been drilled so well that marching presented no challenge for them—to local playing fields for athletics, tennis and soccer matches and folk dancing. Before the children began to play they were required to hear a speech from a teacher or councillor about the importance National Socialism placed on health and fitness.

On the streets surrounding the Lustgarten—the square and gardens near the Berlin City Palace which for centuries had been the scene of ceremonies, demonstrations and pitched battles, and where the Great War had been declared—an enormous crowd gathered to witness the rites to come.

From 8 a.m., infantry bands performed martial music on Unter den Linden by the Hotel Adlon, where Count Henri de Baillet-Latour, Avery Brundage and the other foreign Olympic officials had spent the night. Right on 9.30 a squad of cars descended on the Adlon and sped the dignitaries to church: the Catholics to St Hedwig's Cathedral and the rest to the Evangelical Berlin Cathedral.

After worship, the VIPs laid a wreath at the war memorial while the resident war memorial infantry battalion goosestepped. Then the party proceeded to the Old Museum in the Lustgarten, where Göring, in a sky-blue Luftwaffe uniform, Goebbels, in a white suit, and other senior Nazis escorted the officials to a ceremony in the oval room in the museum's roof. When the group returned to the square, which had been empty fifteen minutes before, it was filled with 28,000 members of the Hitler Youth in 40 ranks standing erect and still.

Nearing midday, the 3330th and penultimate Torch Relay runner loped up Wilhelmstrasse to the Lustgarten where, surrounded by the guests, he lit a cauldron on the Old Museum steps. That cauldron would burn until 4 p.m., when it would ignite the torch of the final relay runner, Fritz Schilgen, who would dash along the Via Triumphalis to the Reich Sports Field and the Opening Ceremony. In the slipstream of the Aryan Pied Piper would be 25,000 young athletes in white tunics.

Lustgarten festivities over, Hitler treated the politicians and Olympic officials to a banquet at an outsized horseshoe-shaped table in one of the dining halls at the Chancellery, where Baillet-Latour effusively thanked him for the 'stupendous preparations' for what was sure to be an impressive Olympics that would make a massive contribution to human culture.

Hitler could be unctuous when it suited him: 'I am deeply grateful to the International Olympic Committee for having allotted the Festival of the XIth Olympiad of modern times to the capital city of the German Reich, thereby affording Germany the opportunity of furthering the eternal Olympic ideals. Germany gladly assumed the task of preparing for the present competitions in a manner which aspires to be in keeping with the ideals and traditions of the Olympic Games, and hopes that she has thereby contributed to the strengthening of the principles of international understanding upon which this Festival is based,' responded the dictator who could hardly wait to go to war.

After being transported to the May Field at 1.30 in 170 buses, the Olympians milled around together before being mustered into national ranks according to the order in which they would enter the stadium for the march-past. The rain had eased and now fell only intermittently. When it did, Evelyn de Lacy recalled, it was in 'great big heavy drops'. Commander of the march-past Major Feuchtinger gathered together the flag-bearers and briefed them on their role.

At 3.18 p.m., the official Olympic party left central Berlin for the Reich Sports Field—Nazi bigwigs Göring, Frick, Blomberg,

Hess, Ribbentrop, Himmler and Heydrich departed first in gleaming black Mercedes-Benz cars. Next were cars bearing the IOC and the German Olympic Organising Committee. Finally, dramatically stage-managed to the moment, came the Führer. In military uniform—peaked cap, tunic with swastika armband, white shirt and tie, heavy leather belt and knee-length jackboots—Hitler stood upright in the front footwell of his open black Mercedes limousine, right arm outstretched. British *Daily Mail* journalist George Ward Price watched Hitler's car pass and would describe in his memoir *I Know These Dictators* 'the streets of the city, lined with dense crowds from which went up an unceasing roar of "*Heil! Heil! Heil!*" It beat upon our ears like the surge of the sea. Every window was hung with flags and crowded with onlookers. Hitler remained on his feet all the time, raising his arm in salute . . . I studied the serried ranks on either side. All ages and types of people wore the same expression of ecstatic delight.'

Thomas Wolfe also witnessed the motorcade, and later wrote that when Hitler swept past 'something like a wind across a field of grass was shaken through that crowd', and the cheering that greeted him was 'the voice, the hope, the prayer of the land'. The salute of the small, dark man with the comical moustache was a 'gesture of blessing such as the Buddha or Messiahs use'.

The streets through which the cavalcade moved were lined fifteen to twenty deep with hundreds of thousands of spectators—many of whom had claimed their spot the day before—and tens of thousands of Hitler Youth, military guards and storm troopers. It must have seemed to visitors as if Germany was mobilising for war rather than celebrating a sporting event.

The author of the Organising Committee report had no qualms about attributing supernatural powers to his Führer. 'A few drops of rain did not dampen the enthusiasm and the weather cleared up at the same moment as the German Chancellor entered the Reich Sports Field.'

Inside the stadium, 110,000 spectators who had been filing in since 1 p.m. were entertained by the Olympic Symphony Orchestra, comprised of musicians from the Berlin Philharmonic and the National Orchestra, as well as half a dozen military bands and a choir of 1000 white-gowned singers. The airship *Hindenburg* meandered 100m above the vast bowl, gleaming silver whenever the sun deigned to emerge from behind the clouds. The fuselage and tail fins of the 245m-long *Hindenburg* were decorated with swastikas, the Olympic rings and the inscription 'XI Olympiade Berlin 1936'. An Olympic flag fluttered from the gondola on the airship's undercarriage. Dickinson was mesmerised as the *Hindenburg* drifted overhead. 'Majestic and dreamlike is how I would describe the airship. It was the most wonderful sight I had seen in my life.' Its spectacular cameo at the Berlin Olympics was to be perhaps the *Hindenburg*'s finest moment, for less than a year later, on 6 May 1937, it was destroyed by fire when attaching to its mooring mast at Lakehurst, New Jersey.

For twenty minutes before the Führer arrived at the Reich Sports Field, loudspeakers in the May Field and the stadium blared, 'He is coming! He is coming!' As Hitler disembarked from his car outside the arena, the Olympic fanfare was played by a military band. At 3.50, Hitler, Baillet-Latour, Tschammer und Osten, Lewald, Diem, Frick and Blomberg met in front of the bell tower and were joined by a military battalion of honour. After reviewing the battalion, Hitler and the others inspected the assembled athletes, and some of the Germans and Japanese were so overcome that they broke ranks and mobbed him. Hitler appeared flustered by the clamour.

By the time he reached the Australians he had regained his usual steely composure. Oliver described how 'Hitler walked past most of the teams but stopped and gave us a close once-over. He walked up and down our ranks specifically. We were the only team he stopped to inspect. I have no idea why. Perhaps it was because of our record during the war. He passed two metres from me. This was Adolf Hitler, the feared leader of the German nation, but I felt nothing . . . I just gazed at him and thought, "He's not much".'

The Führer shook wrestler Dick Garrard's beefy hand. 'It was only a fluke,' Garrard assured Harry Gordon. 'When we lined up . . . it was the tall men at the back and the shorter men in the front, and because I wasn't so tall I was in the front and Hitler . . . stopped in front of me, shook hands and said something in German, just a casual remark I couldn't understand, and continued on. It was as quick as that.' (This was not Garrard's only close encounter with Hitler. 'Another time he was leaving the swimming stadium and I happened to be leaving at the same time and I picked up my camera and went *bang*. I didn't know whether I got a photograph of him or not but it turned out rather an excellent picture. It looks like he's saluting me, but he's not!')

Pat Norton, too, was unimpressed by the German chancellor. She later recounted, 'We four girls in our team stood without rest for two hours before entering the stadium . . . the air of excitement and noise among the teams drove our tiredness away . . . the teams suddenly became quiet at the sight of Hitler and his entourage striding down between the teams . . . It was my first direct look at the man who was the talk of the world, and a more uninspiring-looking person would be hard to find.'

Gray later said that as Hitler strode past him, he considered skewering him with the end of his flag: 'I could have saved the world a ton of trouble.' He only decided against it when he realised that the pole wasn't sharp enough to inflict much damage—and, perhaps, that he would be riddled with bullets by Hitler's seven uniformed guards and two dozen plain-clothed bodyguards.

Years later, Gray confessed that he kept the Australian flag he carried that day, along with its swastika decoration on the pole. 'I didn't pinch it, I just souvenired it. Brought it home with me. Harry [Alderson] should have given it to the Olympic Federation. They'll have to buy it now if they want it.' (Until wear and tear disintegrated the flag, Gray used the pole as a clothesline prop in his backyard.)

Shortly before four, the arena announcer dramatically informed those present and the millions listening to radio broadcasts all over the globe, 'The masses wait feverishly for the moment when the Führer will appear.' And then his voice rose several octaves and he shrieked, '*Achtung!* The Führer now enters the stadium!' The multitudes stood in their seats and gave a mass Nazi salute, and from their throats there came a thunderous roar of '*Sieg Heil! Sieg Heil! Sieg Heil!*' that rolled in waves around the stadium. Said de Lacy: 'The people went mad. It was hysteria.'

Following their leader was an entourage of around 100—Nazi chieftains, officers of the Wehrmacht, the SS and SA, and Hitler's personal protectors. Many visitors found the uniforms and guns grossly out of place. A couple of paces behind Hitler were Baillet-Latour and Lewald, each tall and bald and wearing a silk top hat, a black frock coat, striped formal trousers and gold ceremonial medals and chains. (Göring mused that the duo resembled flea circus directors.)

On the pitch, Hitler was greeted by five-year-old Gudrun Diem, daughter of Carl Diem, dressed in blue, her buttercup-yellow hair gathered in a band of flowers, who curtsied and presented him with a bouquet of roses, a Nazi salute and the greeting '*Heil, mein* Führer'. Hitler, eyes glistening with emotion, said a few words to her and awkwardly tousled her hair. The scene evoked more screams of '*Heil* Hitler' from spectators.

To the strains of a theme by *Olympia* film score composer

Herbert Windt, Hitler climbed the steps and took his seat between Baillet-Latour, Lewald and, puzzlingly, the Crown Prince of Italy, on a speaker's balcony bristling with microphones mounted on lecterns decorated with a German eagle. As he did so, the orchestra played 'Deutschland Über Alles' and the entirely inappropriate 'Horst-Wessel-Lied':

> Flag high, ranks closed
> The SA marches with silent solid steps
> Comrades shot by the red front and reaction
> March in spirit with us in our ranks
> The street free for the brown battalions
> The street free for the storm troopers
> Millions, full of hope, look up at the swastika
> The day breaks for freedom and for bread
> For the last time the call will now be blown
> For the struggle now we all stand ready
> Soon will fly Hitler-flags over every street
> Slavery will last only a short time longer.

As most in the crowd—*not* NSW premier Sir Bertram Stevens— sang along lustily, the flags of the nations were hoisted to the top of the poles ringing the arena. (Happily, Sir Bertram was not one of those spectators ejected from the arena by sharp-eyed SS and SA men for failing to sing the Nazi song.)

Then, for the first time that day, the Olympic bell was rung, softly and slowly at first, then building in volume and tempo, heralding the Games of the XIth Olympiad. Around the mammoth arena, close to 100,000 arms were extended in the Nazi salute towards Hitler. Almost eighty years later, the photograph of that disquieting scene typifies the Berlin Olympics as surely as Jesse Owens flashing across the finish line.

Filming it all was Leni Riefenstahl and her 45 cinematographers. The beautiful and ambitious one-time actress, photographer and dancer had endeared herself to the regime as a director with her documentary on the Nazis' 1934 Nuremberg Rally, *Triumph of the Will*, and it was at Hitler's invitation that she filmed the Berlin Olympics. Later, Riefenstahl falsely claimed that she had been commissioned by the IOC. Before the Reich's fall, Riefenstahl's admiration for Hitler was boundless: 'To me, Hitler is the greatest man who ever lived . . . totally without fault.' The Führer called *her* 'the perfect woman'.

Olympia remains a terrifying and exhilarating achievement. Terrifying for its scenes of Hitler-worship and Nazi pageantry, exhilarating for its chronicling of the sporting events, especially those featuring Jesse Owens in full, glorious flight. Riefenstahl's stated aim was to cover the Olympics 'from every conceivable angle . . . [make] the impossible possible . . . to shoot the Olympics more closely, more dramatically, than sports had ever been captured on celluloid'. She utilised groundbreaking techniques such as slow-motion and tracking shots, the latter achieved by attaching cameras to a rail alongside the track and the pool to keep pace with the runners and swimmers. She invented startling camera angles and new ways of lighting. She attached cameras to horses' saddles and strapped them around marathon runners' necks to shoot their feet pounding the road. Her extreme close-ups of competitors left no bead of sweat or expression of euphoria or despair unrecorded. She dug trenches to achieve low-angle camera views and erected towers for high perspective. To impart the sheer spectacle of the Olympics, she placed her cameras in balloons, dirigibles and light planes. Riefenstahl had a camera trained constantly on the Führer to film his reactions, and her crowd shots—the massed '*Sieg Heils*' and Nazi salutes—leave no doubt about the thrall in which Hitler held the nation. Riefenstahl shot more than one million feet of film, which took eighteen months to edit. *Olympia* was released in April 1938 to acclaim and condemnation.

The report of the Organising Committee credited Riefenstahl's task as 'the strangest, most incalculable ever entrusted to a director and [her] cameramen at any time in the history of film. There was no precedent to go upon . . . It was impossible to arrange for photographs to be taken at a time when the weather and light promised a certain amount of reliability . . . What took place before the lens during the few minutes of the contests was past beyond recall because no subsequent posed photograph, even if it had been possible, would have been able to reproduce the excitement, the fever, the expression of the competitor, his attitude in the last tense efforts, the excitement of the public . . . Innumerable incidents of all sorts had to be reckoned with. Nobody expected that the German women's relay team would lose the gold medal by dropping the [baton] at the last change-over. It speaks volumes for the meticulously exact distribution of the photographers that this completely unpredictable incident was recorded, and on a slow motion film, although the hundred thousand spectators experienced a tremendous surprise during the few seconds of it happening . . . The intention was that the beauty of sport should be recorded side by side with the sporting contest itself. The aim was to . . . render eternal in the film the special charms of the various kinds of sport, their special beauties, their grace and their power . . . as well as the Olympic idea . . . of peacefully competing nations.'

Watching Riefenstahl's riveting footage, there is no sense that she filmed it while feuding bitterly with Goebbels. The propaganda minister, jealous that Hitler admired Riefenstahl more than himself, and miffed that she had more than once rejected his advances—she revealed how Goebbels would come to her office, grope her breasts and 'sob with desire . . . his face contorted with lust'—continually put obstacles in her way. One of their biggest bust-ups came just before the Opening Ceremony when she attached sound cameras to the official rostrum to film Lewald and Hitler as they declared the Games open. She diarised: 'Goebbels entered the rostrum. When he saw me and the cameras, his eyes flashed with rage, and he screamed at me, "Have you gone mad? You can't stay here! You're destroying the whole ceremonial tableau. Get yourself and your cameras out of here immediately!" I was shaking with fear, fury and indignation, and the tears were streaming as I stammered, "Herr Minister, I asked the Führer for permission way ahead of time—and I received it. There is no other place from which we can film the opening address. This is a historic ceremony, it cannot be left out of an Olympic film" . . . Goebbels seemed to be incandescent with rage.' Right then Göring entered the rostrum. Riefenstahl's diary continued: 'I was especially unhappy that Goebbels was in charge of arranging the guests on the rostrum—and our cameras were standing on the very spot that he had reserved for Göring, one of the best seats in the first row, and they were blocking the view. To justify himself to Göring and demonstrate his innocence, Goebbels screamed at me even more loudly, but Göring raised his hand—and Goebbels fell silent. Then [Göring] turned to me and said in a conciliatory voice, "C'mon my girl, stop crying, there's room here even for my belly." Luckily Hitler hadn't yet arrived. But many of the guests had witnessed this embarrassing scene.'

Duly summoned by the great bell, the 4783 Olympic athletes marched onto the arena, their bright uniforms vivid in the leaden gloom. The Greeks wore blue blazers and white flannel slacks; the Americans white shoes, white trousers, dark blue blazers and white straw boaters; the Egyptians red fezzes; the Chinese and Bermudians solar topees; the Italians black shirts; the Afghans turbans. Betraying the priorities of the Nazi organisers, German athletes

Australian flag bearer Dunc Gray leads the Australian team onto the arena for the Opening Ceremony march-past. The 33 Australians were among 3962 athletes from 49 countries. Immediately behind Gray march team manager Harry Alderson and chaperone Mary Fergusson.

After inspecting the athletes, Hitler opened proceedings. Olympic protocol ensured that the Fuhrer was limited to a few words: 'I proclaim open the Olympic Games of Berlin, celebrating the XIth Olympiad of the modern era.'

Jack Metcalfe warms up before the hop, step and jump, under the watchful gaze of German track and field officials.

Hitler's favourite film-maker, pioneering director Leni Riefenstahl, cajoles the appropriate reaction from an American athlete. Her cameramen make sure it's captured for *Olympia*, her chronicle of the Berlin Games. (Corbis)

US sprinter Jesse Owens demolished the Nazis' claims to Aryan athletic superiority by winning gold in every event he entered: the 100m, the 200m, the broad jump and the 4x100m relay. (Getty)

A sea of Nazi salutes. The fanatical adulation of Adolf Hitler by his countrymen at the Olympics shocked and dismayed many of the visiting athletes and spectators. (Getty)

An aerial view of the Olympic arena and swimming and diving complex with the Games in full swing. Despite suffering some damage in the war years and after, Hitler's Field of Dreams remains largely intact today.

The NSW Police rowing eight: Merv Wood, later police commissioner of NSW, stands third from right. The colourful Wal Mackney, whose ears and nose bear testament to his other athletic pursuits, rugby and street fighting, is seated on the left.

While his police rowing colleagues offered traffic advice to Paris's gendarmes, Merv Wood preferred to sightsee from the Eiffel Tower. (Courtesy of John Wood)

Cyclist Dunc Gray, who had won gold at the 1932 Los Angeles Olympics, was no fan of National Socialism and didn't care who knew it.

Basil Dickinson gave it his all in the hop, step and jump in Berlin. (Courtesy of Pauline Watson)

Hitler's sports czar, the Nazi zealot Hans von Tschammer und Osten (right, charming Argentinian swimmer Jeannette Campbell and Australian boxer Len Cook) was instructed to ensure that the visiting athletes' every whim was met.

Australia's swimming and diving team at the Olympic pool (from second left): Bill Kendall, Kitty Mackay, Pat Norton (flanked by German attendants), Evelyn de Lacy, Percy Oliver and Ron Masters. Harry Hay (left) and Harry Nightingale (right) were the team's unofficial coaches.

Bondi comes to Berlin. Elfin swimmer Pat Norton with her long-time friend and coach, the dashing lifesaver and surfer Harry 'Salty' Nightingale. (Fairfax)

While scouting locations at the Olympic pool, Leni Riefenstahl was much-impressed by the strapping Bill Kendall and photographed him in action. Kendall cherished the snap shot until his dying day. (Courtesy of Brooke Ryan)

Pat Norton endured tragedy later in life, but the former Olympian always found the time (here in 1949, at Dee Why rockpool) to teach youngsters to swim, just as Harry Nightingale had once taught her. (Fairfax)

Basil Dickinson, in his eighties, was persuaded to don his 1936 Olympic uniform. His old-style cap, blazer and tie seem timeless when compared with the designer garb of the sportspeople of the day. (Courtesy of Pauline Watson)

who were members of the armed forces wore uniform rather than traditional whites and marched ahead of the civilians. The entire team were adorned with swastika necklets.

As per Olympic custom, Greece—the land where the Games began—entered first, then, alphabetically, Egypt (the German spelling of which is 'Ägypten'), Afghanistan, Argentina, Australia, Belgium, Bermuda . . . down to the United States, then the host nation took its traditional position as the last to enter the stadium. Practising their marching in the May Field before the ceremony, the German athletes had impressed as being by far the best marchers. 'We had the last laugh,' said Dickinson. 'When the German team entered the stadium, the crowd was yelling so loud for them that the marchers couldn't hear the beat of the band and so they were all out of step, and being out of step in front of Hitler was not wise.'

As all teams did their best to avoid offending against protocol or falling out of step, there was a serious edge to proceedings. 'I don't think it's ever been like that since [Berlin],' Woodhouse would say in the wake of the joyous 2000 Sydney Olympics. 'There has been a friendly mood, the athletes and officials waving and smiling to friends and the crowd, a lovely feeling about Opening and Closing Ceremonies. But not in Berlin in 1936. [It was] just nations outdoing each other, showing how high precisely they could march and how much they worshipped Hitler.'

The teams marched once around the stadium—all but the Americans dipping their flag, and giving their chosen salutes as they passed the Führer—then reassembled in their ranks in the centre of the stadium facing the speaking dais.

The spectators' reception to each team was telling. Whether a squad greeted the Führer with the Nazi salute or not was regarded as an indication of its country's support for the Reich. Teams which gave the straight-arm salute—Afghanistan, Bermuda, Bolivia,

Estonia, Iceland, Italy, Turkey and Bulgaria (whose team members also goosestepped)—were applauded, while those who did not were met with whistles and howls of disdain. The recalcitrant Americans were dealt the latter. Over the years, some of the US athletes have claimed that as they marched they irreverently sang 'Hail, Hail, the Gang's All Here' and joked with each other about Hitler's resemblance to Charlie Chaplin and Göring's to the rotund comedian Oliver Hardy. One American who was not laughing was Eleanor Holm. The expelled swimmer wept as she watched her former teammates parade without her.

The crowd knew not what to make of the Swiss team, whose flag-bearer tossed his flag into the air and caught it repeatedly, like a drum major.

The New Zealand squad mistook a diminutive uniformed gent with a toothbrush moustache for Hitler. Dickinson recalled: 'New Zealand stuffed up. There were only seven of them, Jack Lovelock was flag-bearer. Fifty yards from Adolf Hitler, who was standing on a platform about a third of the way up the stadium, they raised their hats and did eyes right and Jack dipped his flag. Problem was, the bloke they saluted wasn't Hitler. By the time they reached the *real* Hitler their hats were back on and the flag was upraised. It looked like a snub. When the poor old Kiwis got back to their dorm, the lights in their kitchen wouldn't go on.' The New Zealanders' gaffe was missed by the spectators, though clearly not by Nazi officials. Hitler, if he was aware, did not react.

Woodhouse recalled that the cheers for the Australians were barely audible. There was 'almost, well, complete silence, except for a few people we knew, friends who recognised and acknowledged us. We received no encouragement [from the crowd] . . . It didn't worry us.' Some spectators later said they'd been disappointed when Aussie the kangaroo wasn't included in the Australian marching contingent.

A German scribe reported that the applause for the French team was so prolonged and heartfelt that he 'had the feeling that a great moment had arrived in the history of the world'. And another remarked that 'Never was the war threat on the Rhine less than during these moments. Never were the French more popular in Germany than on this occasion. It was a demonstration, but one of comradeship and the will for peace.' Hitler, it has been reported, could not help briefly recoiling when the German audience applauded his hated France.

Metcalfe was keen to see how the French would respond to Hitler as they marched past him, 'because of the political situation at the time as far as France and Germany were concerned. There was an extraordinary atmosphere. As the French team approached the dais there was absolute silence, not a sound, as everyone was watching to see what they would do. When they gave what most thought was a Nazi salute the cheer that went up was deafening. It could have been heard miles away . . .'

The German crowd's approbation of the French was misplaced. The French team had more reason than most countries to refuse to honour Hitler and instead opted for the traditional Olympic salute. The two salutes closely resemble each other: for the Olympic salute, the right arm, palm down, is extended stiffly to the side; the Nazi salute is a straight right arm, palm down, extended to the front. The German spectators mistakenly believed that the French were paying homage to the Führer and his regime. Other nations who gave the Olympic salute were later accused of being Nazi sympathisers. Bizarrely, some Austrian team members gave the Olympic salute while others, including every woman, offered the Nazi version.

The ceremony continued. At 5 p.m. a recorded message from Baron de Coubertin, in the second-last year of his life and too unwell to be in Berlin, was broadcast from the arena's loudspeakers in French, the official Olympic language. An English translation was projected onto the announcement screens: 'The important thing in the Olympic Games is not winning but taking part; the essential thing in life is not conquering but fighting well.'

On the speaking platform, as Hitler grimaced and fidgeted beside him, Lewald stood to deliver the Olympic address. After battling so hard to win the Olympics for Germany, then suffering the ignominy of being dumped as Organising Committee president when his Jewish connection was discovered, now was Lewald's moment to make his mark on the ceremony, and he made it with an interminable address. For twenty minutes he blithered platitudes. He referred to Hitler, whom he had come to fear and despise, 'respectfully and gratefully as the protector of these Olympic Games to be held in this stadium, built according to your will and purpose'. Lewald declaimed: 'To be an amateur means to follow sport free from selfishness and the commercial spirit, with only one aim: perfection; and only for the sake of developing those mental and bodily qualities which state and nation have a right to expect from their citizens. The amateur principle is a lofty and a sacred one.' Lewald knew from painful personal experience that there was little that was lofty or sacred about the way Germany was conducting these Games. Hitler managed to maintain a straight face when Lewald declared that 'such a festival as this may be devoted to sport only so long as sport is not pursued with selfish aims but as a moral duty'. Then he called on the Führer to proclaim open the Olympic Games.

Hitler obliged with a response that struck many—including Dickinson down in the arena—as churlish, but which was all IOC law permitted the leader of a host nation to say: 'I proclaim open the Olympic Games of Berlin, celebrating the XIth Olympiad of the modern era.'

At that, as the lesser dignitaries gathered to the right and left of the speaker's balcony, Major Feuchtinger ordered that the Olympic flag be hoisted to the top of the mast at the stadium's western end. Riflemen fired salvos and 20,000 carrier pigeons flew free from cages. The swirling, swooping cloud of birds was recalled by American runner Louis Zamperini (whose Olympic and wartime exploits are recounted in the book and film *Unbroken*): 'We were on the infield on the grass all lined up military-style when they released 25,000 [*sic*] pigeons. The sky was filled with pigeons. They circled overhead. Then they shot a cannon which scared the poop out of the pigeons. We had straw hats on and you could hear the pitter-patter on our hats. We felt sorry for the women because they got it in their hair.'

A trumpet fanfare introduced the Olympic hymn, performed by the orchestra and 3000-strong choir and conducted by its composer Richard Strauss (ironically neither a lover of sport nor a fan of National Socialism). Goebbels had commissioned the famous composer. As one who had seen the toughest storm trooper dissolve in tears at the playing of 'Deutschland Über Alles' and 'Horst-Wessel-Lied', Goebbels knew the value of music in touching the hearts and minds of the public and, hopefully, overseas guests. At its end, the crowd, as it had been instructed to do, hollered again and again, 'Festival of peace! Olympia!'

And then came the Opening Ceremony's pièce de résistance, as the final participant in the Torch Relay—middle-distance runner Fritz Schilgen—appeared at the east gate in the stadium grandstand, bearing aloft the flaming Olympic Torch that he had borne from the Lustgarten. Schilgen remained briefly at the top of the steps, his classic Aryan profile silhouetted against the sky, then pranced into the arena past the teams in formation on the field. With rapid, fluid strides he ran up the Marathon Steps to the altar. There he raised the torch high and at 5.20 p.m. plunged it into the bowl of the urn. Reported the Organising Committee: 'It was a moment in which every heart beat faster, an occasion which in its solemnity impressed all alike.' As Schilgen's torch kissed the altar, an enormous yellow flame leapt into the sky. Another roar came from the crowd.

Next into the spotlight stepped Spyridon Louis, the 63-year-old Greek winner of the marathon at the 1896 Olympics, to hand Hitler an olive twig from the sacred grove on Mount Olympus. 'I present to you this olive branch as a symbol of love and peace,' he said through an interpreter. 'We hope that the nations will ever meet solely in such peaceful competition.' The Führer, clearly more moved by Spyridon's gesture than he'd been by Lewald's oration, self-consciously flicked at his forelock and wrung the old Olympian's hand. Perhaps this moment sprang to Hitler's mind as he ordered the invasion of Greece in April 1941.

At another command from Major Feuchtinger, the flag-bearers of each nation formed a semicircle at the base of the speaker's platform. Each dipped his flag when Rudolf Ismayr—who had won a weightlifting gold medal for Germany at the Los Angeles Olympics—grasping, possibly by mistake, the swastika flag instead of the Olympic standard, took the Olympic Oath: 'We swear that we will take part in the Olympic Games in loyal competition, respecting the regulations which govern them, and desirous of participating in them in the true spirit of sportsmanship for the honour of our country and for the glory of sport.' As he recited, every competitor joined in.

At the oath's completion the choir and the spectators sang the 'Hallelujah Chorus' from Handel's *Messiah*. As the last strains were heard, the flag-bearers rejoined their teams and, again in order, filed from the stadium into the May Field, where they dispersed and took buses back to their lodgings.

De Lacy wrote that night that 'the whole affair was very impressive and the only thing that was the matter was we couldn't understand what they were talking about'.

At 6 p.m., the Führer departed to massed 'Sieg Heils' and Nazi salutes from the spectators. He was driven in his limousine back past the crowd and the storm troopers still lining the Via Triumphalis to the Reich Chancellery for dinner with cronies. By then Goebbels had informed him that the Opening Ceremony was being hailed around the world as a stunning triumph. To the end of his life, Hitler remembered this as one of his best days.

The Opening Ceremony did not end with Hitler's departure. At 8 p.m., as twilight gathered, 20,000 children surged through the Marathon Gate and down onto the field to dance, sing and play games and enact a five-act Olympic Pageant, *Olympic Youth*, penned by the versatile Carl Diem, which, inevitably, ended in a duel to the death. When the curtain rang down, searchlights around the stadium created 'a magnificent dome of light'.

Time magazine was awed by the Berlin Opening Ceremony and remarked that it made the Los Angeles ceremony in 1932 seem as interesting as a couple of fleas running around the brim of a hat. To *The New York Times*, it was the most beautiful pageant ever staged in any country.

Summing up the Opening Ceremony many decades later, Dickinson was impressed but less ecstatic. 'It was nothing like the mass entertainment it has become today, with pop stars, dancers and crackers going off everywhere. In Berlin it was a militaristic, formal event. SS and SA officers were everywhere, and, to me, as impressive as the spectacle was, it was more about glorifying Hitler and his Reich than celebrating sport. Hitler, Goebbels, Göring and Ribbentrop were cheered to high heaven.'

Now, at least until the Closing Ceremony in sixteen days, it was time for the warlords to withdraw to the wings and for the athletes to command centre stage. Let the Games begin.

CHAPTER 14
DAYS OF GRACE AND FURY

DAY 1: SUNDAY 2 AUGUST

Not Hitler, not Goebbels nor the Aryan athletes . . . United States quadruple-gold-medal-winning sprinter and broad jumper Jesse Owens was the star of the 1936 Olympics. With his sublime performances, Owens shunted Nazi politics to the sidelines. There were many other stellar performances as well, today regarded as Olympic milestones. Meanwhile the Australians did their best, accepting defeat, injury and bad officiating stoically and, with just a few exceptions, in good heart.

It is Olympic tradition for the first week of the Games to be largely devoted to track and field, while competition in the pool takes its turn in week two. The athletics began at 10.30 a.m. on a drizzly day, with the first heats of the 100m sprint: twelve races comprising five or six runners, the fastest 24 of whom would progress to the second round of heats that afternoon. Hitler took his seat in his enclosure at 10.20. As the heats began, he looked to be in high spirits, laughing and chatting with his guests and flunkies, like a lion anticipating a kill, licking his lips in expectation of the avalanche of Aryan triumphs that would surely come.

Owens' recent 100m times had been excellent and his popularity with Berliners was obvious to all, so the regime's spin doctors had sought to discredit him by demonising him. Suddenly German commentators were calling him '*der Neger*' ('the nigger'). Yes, went the propaganda line, he *was* fast and strong, but this was because, being black, he was more animal than human (to emphasise the point, caricatures were published of Owens as an ape) and so held an unfair advantage. Even so, the reports claimed, Germany's best sprinter Erich Borchmeyer was faster and stronger, and being smarter than Owens would plot a strategic race and humiliate the American. Ironically, Owens and Borchmeyer—a decent man who would not have enjoyed being used as propaganda fodder and whose most prized possessions included an autographed photograph of Owens—were friendly and respectful of each other. The pair bantered good-naturedly as they took off their tracksuits and limbered up beside the cinder running track, awaiting their turn to run.

Owens had a superb running style: upright, relaxed, elegant, his face composed, appearing to glide without effort; one observer said that he seemed to be 'running on feathers' and another lauded the 'machine-like exactness of his leg movements'. In his heat he cruised past his straining, flailing rivals, beating the second placegetter by 7m and equalling the world and Olympic record of 10.3 seconds. Evelyn de Lacy saw all of Owens' races, and Owens running 'with such beauty and grace, he was so beautiful to watch' was her abiding memory of the 1936 Olympics.

Hitler's good mood evaporated. He sat sullen and glum, stunned by the ease of Owens' win in the heat. A group of storm troopers in the grandstand hissed and heckled the American, only for their catcalls to be drowned out by a deafening cry of '*Yess-say*

O-vens! Yess-say O-vens!' from 100,000 spectators. The regime's campaign to discredit Owens had failed. Owens himself looked surprised by the adulation and responded with a self-effacing smile and an awkward wave. American 800m runner John Woodruff remarked after the Games that ordinary Germans had treated visitors, including African Americans such as himself and Owens, 'royally . . . They were very friendly, very accommodating, very gracious, very cordial.'

Owens won his second 100m heat in a remarkable 10.2 seconds. This new world and Olympic record was not recognised because a strong following wind assisted his time. Still, he was 0.3 of a second faster than the nearest competitors—Ralph Metcalfe, Borchmeyer and Lennart Strandberg of Sweden.

In that second preliminary heat, Owens nearly sustained an injury that would have ended his Olympics. It was Leni Riefenstahl's fault. To film Owens' performance, Riefenstahl wrote in her diaries, 'One of our [camera] pits was located some 70 yards behind the finishing line of the 100m sprint, and a cameraman and a photographer were standing in the pit . . . Owens swept along the track with incredible grace and ease . . . At the run-out, Owens couldn't slow down, and he almost plunged into our pit. It was only because of his swift reaction that he managed to leap aside in time to prevent a mishap. After that, we not only had to fill in this pit, but all the others.'

Those with tickets for the following day's 100m semifinals and final must have sensed that they were in for something special from the man they called the 'Buckeye Bullet'.

National Socialist precision fell down at Deutschland Hall. The Australian wrestlers Garrard, Scarf and O'Hara left the Village at 7 a.m. for the 10km bus trip to Deutschland Hall to weigh in on time at 8 and be ready to compete at 11, only to be told that the order of bouts had changed and they'd be called to the ring 'sometime' later in the day. The trio spent hours on tenterhooks in a steamy dressing room, not knowing whom they'd be wrestling or when. 'More temperamental wrestlers than the Australians might have magnified their treatment into a source of violence,' reported *The Sydney Morning Herald*. 'The Australians, realising that their experience was not isolated, eventually treated it as a bitter joke, as they ate sausages brought to their dressing room. Their fellows in misfortune included the Japanese, one of whose wrestlers, wakened from a sleep, was brought to speedy defeat.'

While all agreed that the Opening Ceremony was memorable, the wrestling bungles and inadequate drainage on the cinder running tracks that left pools of water after rain were signs, observed one visitor, 'that the organisers had concentrated on stage management rather than on sport'.

At 2 p.m., Dick Garrard, competing as a lightweight, learned that he was on. He lost his first match to Italy's Paride Romagnoli on a points decision after appearing confused by many of the referee's rule interpretations, and in his second, on the following day, he was eliminated from the competition when thrown by Hungary's Karoly Karpati in 2 minutes, 45 seconds. Years later, Garrard mused to Harry Gordon, 'I was stiffed . . . [but] the rules are the rules. We can't go blaming the rules all the time. The fellow I met won the gold medal anyway, the Hungarian, and he put me out pretty early in the piece.'

Welterweight Jack O'Hara did well after being given the runaround by officials. For his first bout, he was summoned to the ring midmorning, and when he arrived psyched up and ready he was told to go away and not return until 2 p.m. He lost his first match narrowly to the formidable German Sepp Paar. At one point, the grapplers tumbled off the mat and into a pack of journalists. In his second match two days later, on 4 August, O'Hara convincingly defeated the Czech Alois Samec. O'Hara's third match, that same afternoon, was his Berlin swan song. The Swede Thure Andersson won in 1 minute, 53 seconds. At least O'Hara could hold his head high knowing he'd been defeated by world-class wrestlers. Andersson would win the silver medal, and Paar ranked sixth.

Bitter protests were aired about the incompetence and bias of the wrestling judges. London's *The Daily Telegraph* wrote: 'Already we have had incidents. There is serious trouble among the wrestlers. England, Canada and Australia have joined in a protest against three of the wrestling judges. There is dissatisfaction also with the method of judging. To overcome the language difficulty, wrestlers are not distinguished by name but by anklets of coloured ribbon. More than once, it is said, the anklets have been issued to wrong competitors, and obvious losers have been judged winners.' In his protest, Harry Alderson insisted that Garrard had decisively beaten the Italian Romagnoli but that the judges—an Austrian, a Czech and a Hungarian who had seemed more interested in the bout on an adjoining mat—had mixed up the winner's and loser's anklets and had wrongly crowned the Italian the winner by 13½ points to 1½. 'No wrestler alive could beat Dick by that margin,' scoffed Alderson. In Garrard's match against Karpati, the fall was wrongly given against the Australian. 'I was at ringside . . . and am of the opinion that although Garrard's back touched the mat in rolling over, his shoulders were never down.' As for O'Hara, he had the better of Paar, 'but he failed to register points, as his methods did not count with the judges'. Alderson made clear that O'Hara had been beaten by Andersson fair and square. The Australian manager said that his men's unfamiliarity with the international rules under which the matches were contested cost them points. All three Australian wrestlers were puzzled when the judges awarded more points for footwork than mat skills, when in Australia the opposite was the case. It beggars belief that nobody had told the Australians that international rules would apply in Berlin and explained those rules to them.

Held concurrently with the 100m sprint heats on the first morning was the men's high jump elimination trial. To proceed to the semifinal, jumpers needed to clear 1.85m. Eighteen failed to do so; among those who succeeded was Jack Metcalfe, in the first appearance by an Australian at the Games. The semi was held at 3 p.m., and this time Metcalfe, who did not make the required 1.94m, was ousted. He would be placed equal twelfth. Metcalfe refused to blame the knee injuries he'd incurred jumping on cinders for his elimination. He had often jumped higher than 1.94m; however, even fit and well he would not have troubled the eventual winner, the 1.95m tall American Cornelius Johnson, whose winning jump was 2.03m, nor Johnson's fellow African Americans Dave Albritton and Delos Thurber who placed second and third, both of whom registered 2m.

Metcalfe encountered Johnson in the Village restaurant on the evening of Johnson's broad jump triumph. 'There was Cornelius sitting alone at a table. I went over and sat down and had a yarn with him . . . You'd have thought he'd have lots of friends to be with. There was a fair amount of racism in the United States team.' The Australian asked an American coach why African Americans such as Johnson and Owens were so successful, and after explaining 'anatomical differences' between the races, the coach conceded that there might be another reason. 'The American negro has difficulty achieving in so many ways in America that when he gets onto something where he can get somewhere, he grabs it with both hands.' Johnson would die of pneumonia in 1946, aged just 32.

Gerald Backhouse—the eccentric, dilettantish Australian 800m and 1500m runner who trained how, when and where he pleased, and seemed more comfortable in a dinner suit than running gear—surprised everyone that first track and field day. There were some who felt his easygoing training routine—even by the lax Australian standards—and his late night returns to the Village after partying in Berlin gave him no hope of a good show. Backhouse proved them wrong.

At 4 p.m., he won his heat in the first round of the 800m. Not only that, but he beat the man considered the best in the world, nineteen-year-old Woodruff. Backhouse's time of 1 minute, 57.7 seconds was the slowest of the six heat winners, yet it was fast enough to win him a place in the second round of heats. It had been a typical Backhouse psych-out: early on he lagged in fourth or fifth place, surged up onto the heels of the frontrunners, fell back again. Then, his rivals having written him off as a spent force, he accelerated past them to win. Woodruff also made the cut.

In his second heat on the following day, despite a sodden track, Backhouse improved on his previous day's time. He ran second in a fine 1 minute, 53.2 seconds. Woodruff, who contested another heat, also lifted his game, winning easily in 1 minute, 52.7 seconds. Both men qualified for the final on 4 August.

When they lined up for the 800m final, the ground had dried. Woodruff started strongly, while Backhouse was trapped in a cluster at the rear. By 400m, the Australian had moved up to third place and seemed to be running strongly and on course for an upset. 'Although I wasn't good friends with Backhouse,' recalled Dickinson, 'I was on my feet and yelling for him. I knew he was known for his ruthless strategy and ability to play mind games with rivals, then speeding past them, as he had done in his heat. I wondered could he do that in the final against the best in the world.' He couldn't. As Backhouse faded, Woodruff was tussling with Italian Mario Lanzi and Canadian Phil Edwards. Each took a turn in the lead, but at the finish it was Woodruff first in

1 minute, 52.9 seconds. Backhouse came eighth out of nine, and as soon as he crossed the finish line he threw his arms around each of the other runners. Like Metcalfe, he said nothing to reporters about the shin splints he'd suffered on the cinder practice track. 'The heat I won was the easiest run I've ever had in a half-mile, but in the final it was different. I couldn't get near the pole line at any time.' The American runners had done marvellously but, Backhouse continued, 'they aren't supermen. Physically they are no better than we are, but they are products of nationalised sport, and that makes the difference.'

What with the successes of Owens and Ralph Metcalfe, Johnson, Albritton and Thurber, the Nazi belief in Aryan superiority was on shaky ground. The relief of Hitler and his fellow racial supremacists was extreme when Germany's Tilly Fleischer, a winsome blonde whose daughter years later claimed that she was the result of a love affair between her mother and the Führer, won the gold medal for the women's javelin throw with a new Olympic record of 45.18m, and Berlin policeman and SS officer Hans Woellke placed first in the shot-put final, also setting an Olympic record. In fact, so relieved was Hitler that he summoned the pair to his box for effusive congratulations. The crowd applauded the German gold medallists as fervently. They were in awe of Owens, but Fleischer and Woellke were countrymen.

A gold medal was not beefy blond policeman Woellke's only reward. Thumbing his nose at Olympic amateurism, Göring promoted Woellke to lieutenant, and later to captain in the SS. When the Australian rowing eight, composed completely of policemen, learned this, they wondered if Commissioner MacKay would promote them if *they* won gold. (Woellke would be slain by partisans in Khatyin, Soviet Belarus, in 1943. His death led directly to the reprisal slaughter by the Nazis of 149 Khatyin villagers.)

Jack Metcalfe was in the stands when Hitler hailed Fleischer and Woellke, and also when they mounted the dais to receive their gold medals. 'When a victory ceremony was held and the gold medal winner was a German, they played the national anthem ["Deutschland Über Alles"] and also the "Horst-Wessel-Lied", both in their entirety, and it took quite a long time to play through the two and the German spectators all stood, giving the Nazi salute. I was standing next to a German and towards the end of the second anthem I put my hand under his elbow and looked to him to indicate I was prepared to help him hold his arm up because he couldn't be expected to do it very much longer. He took it alright. He smiled down at me. I was just having a little crack at him.' Only a few bars of other nations' anthems were played.

Hitler on that first day also entertained in his box the blond and blue-eyed Finnish 10,000m gold, silver and bronze medal winners Ilmari Salminen, Arvo Askela and Volmari Iso-Hollo, ostentatiously grasping their hands and patting their backs. Yet the patron of the Games did not invite up black American high jump gold medallist Johnson. Indeed, Hitler left the arena minutes before Johnson mounted the winner's dais.

Although Johnson was not offended, stating 'there's nothing in the program stating that we winners are to be received by him. I'm not kicking', there were accusations by the international media that Hitler had insulted the African American. In response, the next day the Chancellery explained that the Führer had had an important appointment that evening and could not afford to be delayed in the traffic snarl of spectators leaving the Reich Sports Field. Overnight, Baillet-Latour despatched Karl Ritter von Halt to remind Hitler that he could not pick and choose those gold medallists he deemed worthy of public congratulation. Only IOC-designated people were permitted to personally congratulate gold medal winners in an Olympic venue. An exception might be made for the Führer as head of state of the host nation, but for permission to be given he would have to shake the hand of every gold medal winner, Aryan and non-Aryan alike. Hitler bridled. In that case, he would not shake the hand of any athlete. By taking this stand, he had cunningly found a way to avoid international wrath for refusing to congratulate athletes of 'inferior' races.

At the close of the first day of track and field, while notions of Aryan superiority had been challenged by the African Americans, still the Reich had won gold medals. Goebbels revelled in the 'awakening of national pride' and called the first day 'a beautiful day, a great day, a victory for the German cause'. By the same time on the next day, Goebbels' smile had vanished. Owens had wiped it from his face.

DAY 2: MONDAY 3 AUGUST

The greatest moment of the Berlin Olympic Games, and possibly in Olympic history, came at 5 p.m. on the second day of track and field. The semifinals of the 100m men's sprint had been run at 3.30, and as the final neared, the six qualifiers trowelled out purchase footholds on the starting line (there were no starting blocks then), and stretched and cantered nervously. The finalists were Borch-meyer, Strandberg, Martinus Osendarp of Holland, and the three Americans Metcalfe, Frank Wykoff and Owens. The 23-year-old Ohio State University student Owens was a hot favourite for the gold medal, and for excellent reason. In his semifinal he had not exerted himself, running only as fast as necessary—a time of 10.4 seconds—to place first. Owens looked composed and calm, breathing evenly as he prepared to do battle for the gold medal. In the grandstand, Hitler twitched and shifted in his seat, cold blue eyes darting, nervously flicking at his fringe. Beside him, Göring and Goebbels in their finery, looking like peacocks alongside their khaki-clad leader, also betrayed edginess. Their champion Borchmeyer had qualified for the final, but at the slow time of 10.7.

With spectators perched on any available vantage point, the official starter cried, *'Auf die Plätze!'* ('On your mark!'). The atmosphere crackled. The crowd roared, *'Yess-say O-vens!'* Owens clasped his hands above his head and gave a goofy grin. Hitler continued to writhe, knowing that Aryan superiority was about to be put to the test before the world.

The six fastest men on earth crouched at the starting line. Owens, in the inside lane, swallowed, then breathed deeply. His eyes were focused hard on the finish line at the end of the track, which was again sodden after more rain. He would later say that he could not hear the stadium din, only silence. The starter yelled, *'Fertig!'* ('Set!') and the runners rose on their fingertips and held statue-still. Then *crack*! The starter fired his pistol.

The crowd sprang to their feet. For the first 30m, Owens trailed Wykoff and Strandberg. At 50m, he drew level, and at 60m he was 2m in the lead, with Wykoff, Strandberg, Osendarp, Borchmeyer and Metcalfe labouring in his slipstream. Owens ran brilliantly, head back, shoulders high, back straight, arms low, legs churning like pistons, every limb and muscle in magical harmony. Suddenly Metcalfe burst free of the other runners and for a second or two threatened Owens, but Owens held him off and won in 10.3 seconds, equalling the world and Olympic record. If the track had not been heavy he would have run at least 10.2. Metcalfe's time was 10.4, and 'Flying Dutchman' Osendarp (10.5) came third. After he broke the tape, it took Owens all of 65m to bring himself to a halt. The crowd yelled themselves hoarse for a minute or more. Hitler and his party rose and left the arena.

Down at the finish line, Owens clasped hands with the other competitors and was congratulated by US sprinter Helen Stephens, whose semifinal was the next race to be run. Owens mounted the victory podium between Metcalfe and Osendarp and, as 'The Star-Spangled Banner' was played, was presented with his gold medal and a wreath of oak leaves. When a reporter asked him his secret, he said, 'Imagine you are running on a red-hot stove, that's the secret of speed. Keep the foot relaxed, and the toes slightly spread, then snap hard with those calf muscles immediately the foot touches the ground. Don't think it didn't take years of practice for me to catch that knack. I have been doing nothing else since I was thirteen.' Then he dropped a line to the press that was the root of the trouble that dogged him after the Olympics: 'I intend to retire from athletics within a year. I am married and want to earn some money.'

If Owens' 100m win was the greatest episode in Olympic history, what happened almost immediately afterwards may be the most controversial. As Owens flashed to victory, eyes swung to Hitler in his box as people tried to gauge the Führer's response. Over the years there have been conflicting versions of Hitler's reaction, and because there is no film footage of it—for once Riefenstahl's camera missed the moment—the truth can never be known.

Some say that as the arena erupted in cheers, Hitler sat stock-still, his hands in his lap, his pasty face showing no emotion, then he rose from his seat and left. Some have written that the Führer grimaced and pounded his thigh with his fist, that he kneaded his hands in rage. Others say that a sour-faced Führer pointedly turned his back on Owens when he won. The accepted wisdom is that Hitler did *not* contain his hatred of Owens, and that before he stormed off to his limousine he actively snubbed him.

Hitler Youth leader Baldur von Schirach, who was sitting with Hitler during that 100m final, said that Hitler was never going to perform what to him would have been the most distasteful of tasks: publicly congratulating Owens. Von Schirach claimed that he and Tschammer und Osten had tried to persuade the Führer to salute Owens. Hitler had slapped them down. 'The Americans should be ashamed of themselves, letting negroes win their medals for them,' he fumed, according to von Schirach. 'I shall *not* shake hands with this negro.'

In his memoir *Inside the Third Reich*, Hitler's confidant and architect Albert Speer asserted that the Führer was 'highly annoyed' by Owens' Olympic success. 'People whose antecedents came from the jungle were primitive,' Hitler had said with a shrug. 'Their physiques are stronger than those of civilised whites. They represent unfair competition and must be excluded from future Games.' Hitler indicated to Speer that black or Jewish victories would not be a problem Germany would have to endure for long, because in a short time, the Fatherland would be the permanent host of the Olympics and in a position to impose whatever racial restrictions on competitors it saw fit.

Yet Owens himself—a genial man who courted no Olympic controversy and who since coming to Berlin had been treated with more respect by everyday Germans than by many whites back home—insisted that, far from snubbing him, Hitler had saluted him with a friendly wave from his box. Woodruff backed up Owens, telling *Hitler's Olympics* author Christopher Hilton in 1987 that the champion and the chancellor had exchanged greetings from afar. Later, when reporters suggested to Owens that Hitler had treated him shamefully by not acknowledging his triumphs, Owens replied, 'Hitler didn't snub me—it was our president [Franklin Roosevelt] who snubbed me. The president didn't even send me a telegram . . . Although I wasn't invited to shake hands with Hitler, I wasn't invited to the White House to shake hands with the president either.'

All his life, Dunc Gray repeated the story that as an elderly man he would tell Olympic historian Harry Gordon. According to Gray, he was with a group of Australian teammates in an enclosure 'adjoining Hitler's' where the athletes could watch the events. Gray had a guest, 'a nice little German girl', who was 'thrilled' to be sitting 30m from the Führer. Gray told how at the end of the 100m final, Hitler had gone down to the winners' dais when they received their medals. He had shaken the hand of the bronze medal winner, the Dutchman Osendarp, then 'just walked past the negroes and went and sat down and when he did my German lass said, "Did you see what Hitler did? . . . Not very nice."' Gray's version of events is puzzling, for at no stage did Hitler descend to the track after the run. Others in the Australian team would report that they had a close view of Hitler and that if he was aghast at Owens' victory he did not show it. Merv Wood recalled 'being with all my teammates in the competitors' section of the stadium when Jesse Owens won the 100 yards [*sic*], and the competitors' section was just 15 or 20 yards away from Hitler's box, which was open and gave us a good view of him, and none of us noticed anything untoward'.

Then as now, scandal sells newspapers, so the American press went ballistic. 'HITLER'S SNUB TO JESSE!' and 'NAZIS HUMILIATE OWENS!' were two headlines the following day. *The Pittsburgh Courier-Journal* gave the Führer both barrels: 'an individual envious of talent, suspicious of high character, devoid of chivalry, bereft of culture, a cowardly effeminate who proved incapable of being a gentleman even at the Olympic Games where prejudice and politics are traditionally taboo'. Later, when he found out what the journalists had written on his behalf, Owens was embarrassed: 'I think the writers showed bad taste in criticising the man of the hour in Germany.'

Dickinson got to know Owens a little. 'Both Jesse and Ralph Metcalfe were nice men. I met Jesse this way. Sometime before the Berlin Olympics I corresponded with an American athletics coach named Charles Riley in Cleveland, Ohio, where Jesse lived. Charles had coached the young Jesse at Fairmont College and recognised his ability and worked with him in the early stages of Jesse's development as a sprinter until he was given an athletics scholarship at Ohio University . . . Anyway, when all the selection scandal was going on in Australia in early 1936, I wrote to Riley and said I was hoping to go to Berlin and told him about the frightfully unfair way our team was being picked. He wrote back and was sympathetic, and added that Jesse . . . would be competing in Berlin and that I should make myself known to him because he was a good bloke. In the Olympic Village, I approached Jesse and he *was* a lovely fellow. We talked athletics, mainly broad jumping. For a while it looked like we'd be jumping against each other at the Games until I withdrew to concentrate on hop, step and jump when I hurt my foot.

'We bumped into each other a fair bit at the Village, and again in London after the Olympics. By then Jesse had been sacked from the American team because he'd refused Avery Brundage's demand that he compete in a US tour of Sweden. Jesse was lonely, just like me, wanting to get home to be with his wife Ruth and daughter and to get a job so he could provide for them. This was a slap in the face to Brundage because Jesse was his star athlete and was making him look good. So Brundage sacked him. Back in the States they treated Jesse as a traitor for turning his back on amateur athletics. He did receive a ticker-tape parade in Manhattan, but it was a tawdry affair. He had been offered all kinds of good jobs when he was on top of the world, but of course these offers were withdrawn when he was no longer an Olympian. He ended up racing against greyhounds and horses in carnivals, and doing odd jobs to make a dollar. In 1955, President Eisenhower came to Jesse's rescue when he put him in charge of youth development in Chicago, and in 1956 the president sent Jesse to the Melbourne Olympics as his personal representative. I was a judge in Melbourne and I couldn't get near him.'

On the same day as the 100m final, Alf Watson managed third place in his heat of the 400m hurdles in the respectable time of 54.5 seconds. Unfortunately for him, only first and second places qualified for the semis. Watson would recall that Hitler took his place in his enclosure just as the hurdles heats got underway and watched them intently. It may have been a consolation for the 29-year-old veteran that his heat time was faster than those of some who qualified for the semis, and that the two men who beat him, Miguel White of the Philippines and Johnny Loaring of Canada, respectively won bronze and silver in the final. The event was won by the American Glenn Hardin in 52.4 seconds, two seconds slower than his own world record of 50.6, which would stand for nineteen years. Three days later, Watson competed in the 110m hurdles but was unplaced in his heat.

'I had to change my style because of the metric distances and to learn to start from the foot opposite to that which I've been used to,' Watson explained to reporters after he bowed out. 'Not that that made any great difference. I'd like to suggest that in future we bring a couple of running coaches and employ trainers from overseas.' Another key to doing better, said Watson, was to have more international competition. 'What chance have we against the athletes of other countries who are competing internationally right up to the time they go to the Games?'

Meanwhile at Deutschland Hall, light heavyweight wrestler Eddie Scarf faced off against the tough Belgian Julian Beke in his first heat. Scarf's poisoned shin had healed and the LA Olympics bronze medallist was rated one of Australia's strongest medal chances in Berlin. Knowing how Garrard and O'Hara had been thrown by the international rules and the judges' decisions, Scarf went in fast and aggressively, reckoning that if his match was close he'd probably be denied the decision. The Belgian was on the back foot from the start and never recovered. Scarf threw and body-pressed Beke for the victory in 11 minutes, 36 seconds.

The next day, in his second-round bout Scarf found himself up against not only Hubert Prokop of Czechoslovakia but also biased judges. Although he battered and bloodied the Czech, two of the three judges awarded the bout to Prokop. Alderson's hackles rose: 'This was a very doubtful decision, and caused much comment from many of the nations. In the first place, Prokop was given time to have his nose dressed on two occasions, and on our timing the bout lasted 20 minutes, 40 seconds, whereas the rules provide for fifteen minutes of wrestling, and a maximum of time off of five minutes, so that 40 seconds had been allowed to Prokop longer than the time allowed by the rules. At the conclusion of the bout, Prokop had to be helped from the ring, while Scarf appeared as though he had been untroubled by the bout. I decided, after consulting other representatives, to protest . . . but some officials were of the opinion that the five minute maximum could be claimed each time a competitor claimed it for a bleeding nose, and to my surprise I found that my protest would be heard by the "Jury of Honour" which included some of the judges who officiated in the match under discussion. Under these conditions it would [have been] futile to protest.' Scarf himself was philosophical. 'I've seen enough matches here,' he grinned, 'to know that any result is possible.'

The redoubtable Scarf, however, had accumulated enough points to progress to the third round later that evening. Although the bout with the German Erich Siebert, who would win bronze in the final, was evenly fought, two of the three judges plumped for Siebert. Lamented Alderson, 'Under the rules a draw is not possible, otherwise I am certain one would have been given in this case.'

DAY 3: TUESDAY 4 AUGUST

Two American athletes made 4 August a day to remember. One was Owens, who won the broad jump gold medal. The other was Helen Stephens, of whom one scribe wrote: 'She is not a lip-sticked Atalanta [the beautiful virgin huntress of Greek legend], as are the majority of the American and Canadian athletes who turned out with their hair exquisitely curled and cheeks artistically tinted.' Her victory in the 100m women's final was compelling in its own way.

Stephens was known as 'the Fulton Flash', after her hometown in Missouri. Life was difficult on her parents' farm in the Depression—food and money were scarce, and at nine she was raped by a relative. Running gave her the strength to cope. She honed her speed and stamina by running to school each day hanging onto the stirrup of her cousin's horse. When she first competed in the 1935 Amateur Athletic Union championships the seventeen-year-old astonished the world of American athletics by winning the shot put, setting a new world record in the broad jump and the 200m, and equalling the 50m world record. From that day until she gave athletics away after the 1936 Olympics, Stephens never lost a race.

In the 50m she had vanquished no less than the winner of the 100m at the 1932 Los Angeles Olympics, Stella Walsh. The lantern-jawed, muscular Walsh was born Stanislawa Walasiewicz in Poland in 1911 and had made her home in America, changing her name in the process. So upset was she at being beaten by a no-name schoolkid that she lambasted Stephens as 'a greenie from the sticks'. From that point it was daggers drawn between the pair, and when they faced off in the final of the 100m at the Berlin Olympics each was determined to grind the other into the red cinders. Walsh, for the Games, reverted to her Polish name and represented her country of birth. Germany's great blonde hope in the 100m final was yet another large-boned and powerful athlete, the 1.9m-tall Käthe Krauss.

Having recorded a new world record of 11.4 seconds in her heat—though, as with Owens, it was ruled invalid because of a strong following wind—the American was favoured to win. After a series of false starts by the nervous runners, she did exactly that. She led from the start and finished 2m ahead of Walasiewicz, with Krauss a distant third. By now the wind had dropped and Stephens' winning time of 11.5 stood. It broke her own world record of 11.6 seconds and equalled Walasiewicz's 1932 Olympic record.

When the three placegetters took their places on the victory platform—where Krauss threw a vigorous Nazi salute—it resembled a scene from *Land of the Giants*. Because of their size and strong facial features, there were whispers that the three athletes were male. Fingers were pointed at Stephens, not least by Walasiewicz, for her angular, flat-chested physique, square face and deep, gravelly voice. If her accusers had done their homework, they'd have learned that when she was a child on the farm she had tripped and fallen on an arrowhead while chasing her dog. It had punctured her throat, damaging her larynx and impairing her voice. Still, the rumours persisted. After her win, when a Polish journalist accused her of being a man, Stephens was tested by the IOC and her sex was confirmed. Krauss's sex was never tested.

Ironically, Stephens' accuser Stanislawa Walasiewicz/Stella Walsh *was* a man, or at least was found to have both male and female sex organs. The truth emerged in tragic circumstances. In later years, Walsh remained in demand for speaking engagements and guest appearance spots at US baseball and basketball games.

She beat men at arm wrestling, slamming their arms to the tabletop with a guttural grunt. One night in 1980, when she was 69, she stumbled into a robbery-in-progress and was shot and killed. At her autopsy it was discovered that she had male chromosomes and both male and female genitalia. (Another athlete at the Games, German high jumper Dora Ratjen, was also a male—real name Heinrich—competing as a woman. Ratjen's heavy beard was his downfall. Horrified fellow athletes alerted Olympic officials, who ordered the athlete—who had placed fourth in the final—to strip and his secret was revealed. After the war, Ratjen claimed that the Hitler Youth had bullied him into masquerading as a woman to win another medal for Germany.)

According to Stephens in an interview she gave late in her life, Hitler was not fazed by her appearance. Impressed by her win, he invited her to a room behind his viewing box where, if Stephens was telling the truth, a bizarre incident occurred. 'I believed he was gonna shoot me because I saw some of those black-shirts comin' in and they're testin' their Lugers, pulling 'em in and out of their holsters, and they arranged themselves around me. Hitler came in accompanied by an interpreter and gave me a salute, a sloppy salute. I didn't return it. I gave him a good ol' Missouri handshake and I put extra pressure on it and that gave him the wrong message because immediately he began to hug me and pinch me and squeeze me to see if I was real and he said, "How 'bout spending the weekend with me in Berchtesgaden?" That was his mountain retreat.' Stephens claimed she declined on the grounds that the 4x100m relay was to be held on the Saturday. She placated Hitler by asking for his autograph. As he was scribbling in her notebook, she claimed, a photographer tried to take a picture of her with the Führer. Hitler lost his temper when the flash went off, slapped the snapper and kicked his camera across the room. Then he smiled at Stephens as if nothing had happened. 'He pinched me and hugged me again and left.' (Interestingly, Stephens would also claim that Göring made a pass at her at his party on 13 August when he summoned her to his bedroom and she found him waiting for her in a black bathrobe.)

Jack Metcalfe and Dickinson were interested spectators at the broad jump final at 5.45 p.m. Both had planned to participate in the event but scratched themselves to save their sore legs and feet for their other events—in Metcalfe's case the high jump and the hop, step and jump, and for Dickinslon the hop, step and jump. 'We were both nursing injuries after training on cinders,' said Dickinson. 'It was a tale of woe. Jack had hurt both knees and I had bruising and a chipped bone in my take-off heel. My heel was really sore. Throughout July, I'd rest it for a few days and think it had recovered, then the first time I jumped or ran again on cinders it flared again. The hop, step and jump was two days after the broad jump and we thought we'd avoid aggravating our injuries.' Neither man would have survived the broad jump preliminaries, for the six finalists jumped further than either Australian ever had.

Analysing the much-anticipated duel between the two best broad jumpers who had ever lived, Owens and Germany's Luz Long, a German journalist indulged in the casual racism of those times. 'In the person of the Nordic type, [we find] a well-thought-out style, a systematic working towards the outside edge of the take-off point, in order to achieve an ever-better performance, a pulling together of the entire body. In the negro [we find] an unsystematic upwards rush of the body, almost like the elegant and easy jump of an animal in the wild.'

In that final, Owens and Long went jump for jump, upping the ante each time. Both smashed the Olympic record. Owens jumped a personal best 7.87m, and Long equalled it. The American hit back with 7.94m. Long was flustered, overstepped the starting board and was disqualified. Owens dealt the coup de grâce with an amazing leap of 8.06m, the first time the 8m barrier had been broken. This Olympic and world record would stand for 24 years.

After Owens won the broad jump (and his second gold medal) from Long, the African American and the German embraced and walked arm in arm along the track, then lay alongside each other on the grass awaiting the victory ceremony. The men's mutual admiration after their epic encounter was a magnificent and spontaneous display of Olympic spirit. Hitler was appalled.

Dickinson said that Long was responsible for one of the greatest acts of sportsmanship he had ever witnessed. 'Jesse was fouled twice in the qualification round when his feet had overstepped the jumping board at his first two tries. He was allowed one more jump, and if his spikes again came over the board, he would be disqualified. Long took him aside and said, "Jesse, if I were you I'd jump earlier and not worry about hitting the board." Jesse did as suggested and made it through and won his second gold medal. A few years later when Long was fighting in Russia he wrote to Jesse and asked him a favour. If Long didn't survive the war, would Jesse contact Long's son and tell him what kind of man his father had been.' Owens agreed, and after Long was killed on 14 July 1943, fighting with the Wehrmacht as the Allies invaded Sicily, he kept his promise. Until Owens' own death in 1980 he corresponded with Long junior.

At least German discus thrower Gisela Mauermayer gave Hitler something to cheer about when she won gold that day. Her mighty throw of 47.63m was a new world record, and a hefty 2m further than that achieved by the runner-up. Mauermayer, with her blonde good looks and statuesque frame, was an enthusiastic Nazi and remained unashamedly sympathetic to National Socialism all her life. She once told an interviewer that she had been proud to represent the Third Reich and, anyway, Hitler was less warlike than Winston Churchill.

DAY 4: WEDNESDAY 5 AUGUST

'Hitler weather' finally arrived at the Reich Sports Field. After four days of showers, the sun shone.

In a balmy twilight with gathering cloud, Dickinson watched Owens compete in the final of the 200m, and was as awed by this run as he had been by his performance in the 100m. In a centre lane, Owens blistered the track in a new Olympic record time of 20.7 seconds, ahead of African American Mack Robinson and Osendarp. 'Jesse's style was as close to perfection as it was possible to be,' said Dickinson.

This time there was no dispute. When Owens won his third gold medal, Hitler's expression was sour and he angrily pounded his knees with his open palms. Hitler's disposition was not helped by the fact that no German had qualified for the 200m final. Novelist Thomas Wolfe, close to Hitler in the box of US ambassador William E. Dodd and his daughter Martha, with whom Wolfe was having a fling, witnessed Hitler's rage. When American Wolfe let out a whoop of delight at his countryman's victory, Hitler had twisted in his seat to locate the culprit and glared at him.

The Führer's box was empty by the time Owens mounted the victory platform directly opposite. As the champion bowed his head, Baillet-Latour draped a gold medal around his neck and then with the assistance of a maid of honour placed an oak wreath on his head, handed him an oak tree in a pot and presented him with a commemorative book. The crowd again chanted, '*Yess-say O-vens! Yess-say O-vens!*'

'What really impressed me that day was Jesse's modesty,' recalled Dickinson. 'He had every excuse to throw his arms in the air and prance about, but he didn't. He was humble, and even as the crowd sang out his name he wore a genuine expression of surprise, as if to say that it was all down to luck that such good fortune had come his way.' As had happened when he received his other gold medals and heard 'The Star-Spangled Banner', tears tumbled down Owens' cheeks.

Like Hitler, *Der Angriff* did not try to conceal its displeasure at a black man trashing its much-trumpeted theory of Aryan superiority: 'But for America's black auxiliary tribes, the United States would have made a poor show at the Olympic Games.' Against all the evidence, the Nazi organ claimed that the United States had been eclipsed in the first days at Berlin. Had it not been for the unfair participation of 'negroes', Aryanism would have reigned supreme—'the German, Long, would have won the broad jump, Lanzi [Italy] the 800m, and Osendarp [Holland] the 100m'.

DAY 5: THURSDAY 6 AUGUST

Basil Dickinson had hardly slept. Nervousness, doubts over whether he even deserved to be in Berlin, and his excruciatingly sore heel all conspired to keep him awake. 'My mind was in turmoil. Occasionally I'd doze off, have a short dream and then wake up and be quite happy until I realised that later in the day I'd be competing . . . against the best in the world from Germany, the United States, Japan and Great Britain. I didn't panic, just lost confidence. All that I'd trained for over recent years, the loss of my job, the donations from supporters who couldn't afford it to fund my trip, and now it was time to make it all worthwhile. I had self-doubt. Despite being ranked among the world's best hop, step and jumpers, I'd managed to convince myself that I was in Berlin on false pretences and about to be exposed. Jack [Metcalfe] knew how I was feeling and came to me at midnight in my room with aspirin to calm my nerves.'

At 4 p.m., Dickinson gingerly limbered up for his hop, step and jump elimination trial to be held in 30 minutes. He was physically and emotionally drained and, if anything, even more pessimistic about his chances than in the dead of night.

In the trial, competitors had to hop, step and jump 14m or be eliminated. 'I fouled on my first two attempts by messing up my run-up and stepping over the edge of the jumping board. You have to take off from behind it. I was too agitated to know what I was doing wrong.' Just as Long had coached Owens in the broad jump, Metcalfe suggested to his troubled teammate that, 'If I were you, I wouldn't worry about taking off close to the board, even take off a foot before it so you don't even have to consider it. At least you won't be fouled a third time, and if you jump as well as you can, you'll get through.' Recalled Dickinson, 'It was so typical of Jack to help a rival.' Following his friend's advice, Dickinson managed 14m and, with Metcalfe, who had had no trouble exceeding the distance, qualified for the semi.

Only one Australian made it through to the final, and it was Metcalfe. Dickinson's best effort, 14.6m, saw him finish sixteenth of the 23 semifinalists. The extent to which his demons hampered him is evidenced by his Berlin leap, which was 1m short of the personal best of 15.6m that he'd set in Sydney eight months earlier. 'In the semi I fouled again and was eliminated. I simply lost my confidence in the run-up. I was flustered and couldn't concentrate on what I needed to do. I look back and think how stupid I was. But I was a naïve kid, just 21, and I was overwhelmed competing in front of a capacity stadium and there were all the flags and swastikas, and my heel was painful.'

Metcalfe mingled with his fellow finalists as the hands of the stadium clock neared 6 p.m. As well as the German Heinz Wollner and the American Rolland Romero, three Japanese had qualified: Metcalfe's practice friends Tajima, Harada and Oshima.

Riefenstahl's footage of the hop, step and jump final makes clear the different styles of the competitors. Heavily muscled Metcalfe is all power, starts his run-up slowly, almost lumbering, then gains momentum like a jumbo jet on a runway, before launching into his hop, step and final leap. The slighter Japanese sprint down the track as if rocket-propelled. As one commentator broadcast, 'Sheer physical speed and endurance enabled Tajima to [easily beat] Metcalfe's world record. The Japanese land flat-footed and seem impervious to the strain, perhaps because weeks before training begins they beat their heels against boards until the heels become so hard that the athlete can land on concrete without suffering.'

Tajima won the gold medal. His 16m smashed Metcalfe's existing world record of 15.78 and the Olympic record of 15.72. Harada placed second with 15.66, and Metcalfe won the bronze with 15.5.

The Australian was philosophical. 'My first effort in the hop, step and jump was as good as I could have wished for,' he said. 'After that, well, I just couldn't better that distance. Basil Dickinson and I soon found after arriving in Berlin that we would have to alter our style on cinders. We'd been used to landing on our heels, but had we gone on in that fashion we would have shattered our legs. The Japanese landed on the flat of their feet, and Jesse Owens [when he broad jumped] on his toes. They were used to the cinders, and knew what to do . . . Perhaps we'd have done better if we'd had a decent turf to train on, but that's a thing you seldom find in Germany.'

When Metcalfe mounted the victory platform, Dickinson was there to cheer him. 'I didn't expect to do well, so at that moment I wasn't too disappointed. I was so pleased for Jack. He didn't boast about winning his medal. He was a very natural person and a good man whom I wanted to do well. When I returned to the Village it finally hit me that after all the sacrifices and travelling so far my Olympics were over, and that there'd be no medal for me. I recovered, of course, knowing that in even competing I'd experienced something special that most people never did.'

On this day came another classic contest: the 1500m. Jack Lovelock, the New Zealand contender, was claimed by Australians, as they tend to do when Kiwis succeed.

The final got underway at 4.45. It was scheduled for 4.30 but Hitler, who was keen to watch it, arrived late at the arena, and the runners were made to cool their heels trackside for fifteen minutes until he took his seat.

There had been Australian hopes that Backhouse would qualify for the 1500m final. He had been advised not to compete because of shin splints. He finished seventh out of eleven in his heat and was eliminated. Afterwards the Victorian was inconsolable, believing he had let Australia down, and it was left to manager Alderson to tell reporters, 'We realised before the start of the race that Backhouse had not the remotest chance of winning, but he was so desperately anxious to compete that we allowed him to start.'

Lovelock was small and slight—just 60kg—with a wide, smiling mouth under a mop of unruly crinkly blond hair. Yet he was an achiever, a man blessed with brains and stamina and a steely determination to exceed his potential in whatever challenge he undertook. He had won the mile at the 1934 Empire Games, was on his way to a medical degree at Oxford University, and was an accomplished rugby player and boxer, a fine swimmer and an erudite and quick-witted debater.

Looking like a child among men, in his black shorts and vest with silver fern on the breast, Lovelock ran a magnificent race, dissecting the field as if conducting a medical experiment. Early on, he was content to alternate between seventh and eighth while German Werner Boettcher, Englishman Jerry Cornes and Italian Luigi Beccali vied for the lead. Then Glenn Cunningham hit the front. In the second lap Lovelock eased up to sixth. With 800m to go, he materialised in third place where he ran smoothly for another 400m. Sweden's Eric Ny now made his run. As the bell rang to herald the final lap, the early frontrunners faded. Ny was first, and looked to have the gold medal in his keeping. Lovelock was having none of that. He accelerated. Lovelock was known for his electrifying finishes, and now, when it really mattered, he *sprinted* past Ny. Cunningham and Beccali, arms pumping, tried with all their might to catch Lovelock. Cunningham, a huge and powerful man, seemed to be gaining. Then Lovelock sped up *again*. Because the crowd was making so much noise it was impossible to hear footfalls; 20m from the finish Lovelock quickly turned his head to the right to check that his rivals weren't mounting a last-ditch challenge. He needn't have bothered, the gold medal was his. He broke the tape 3m ahead of Cunningham. Lovelock set a new world and Olympic record of 3 minutes, 47.8 seconds. The crowd buzzed excitedly for fifteen minutes afterwards.

The 1500m final is there for all to see on film, with commentary by Harold Abrahams, the British runner who won 100m gold in the 1928 Olympics and was immortalised in the film *Chariots of Fire*. So excited was Abrahams by Lovelock's run that in the final stages his trademark stiff-upper-lip impartiality went out the window. 'Lovelock leads . . . Lovelock! . . . Lovelock! . . . Cunningham second, Beccali third . . . Come on, Jack! One hundred yards to go . . . Come on, Jack! By God he's done it! Jack, come on! Lovelock wins! Five yards, six yards, he wins . . . he's won! Hooray!' Abrahams, who was an old Oxford University friend of Lovelock's, was censured by the BBC for bias. He was unapologetic.

Lovelock's run was as ruthless as it was beautiful. For all of Owens' amazing feats, the 1500m men's race was the most nail-biting event at the Games. Afterwards Lovelock wrote, 'It was the most perfectly executed race of my career . . . a true climax to eight years' steady work, an artistic creation.'

Riefenstahl's footage of Lovelock's triumph does justice to his legendary run. It is both inspiring and—viewed with the knowledge of what befell the runner just thirteen years later when, at age 39, he fell under a train in New York and was killed—heartbreaking. 'He married an American girl and had two daughters and was . . . working in a hospital in New York,' said Dickinson, who treasured his times with Lovelock in England and Germany in 1936. 'Jack was ill. He'd had a fall from a horse and was badly injured. He suffered from dizziness. He was waiting on the platform of a station and collapsed in front of the train. There are stories he suicided. I choose to believe he fell.'

DAY 6: FRIDAY 7 AUGUST

As the reigning 1000m standing-start time-trial Olympic champion, cyclist Dunc Gray had every right to expect that he would be given the chance to defend his title in Berlin. Australian cycling brass had other ideas. In what may have been another case of interstate bias, they named Victorian Tassie Johnson to ride in the event in Berlin, shuffling Gray to the 1000m scratch sprint.

Gray, the outspoken rebel of the Australian team, gave the sprint his all. While in his first heat he was beaten by half a length, in the repechage (in which those who are defeated by a small margin in the heat are granted a second life) he rode strongly and came home a length and a half ahead in an excellent 13 seconds. This qualified him for the second round, and again Gray won, in an even faster 12.2 seconds. Now down to the final eight competitors in the sudden-death third round, it was the Australian's bad luck to be pitted against Holland's Arie van Vliet, arguably the best

1000m sprint rider in the world. Gray and van Vliet played cat and mouse for much of the distance before the Dutchman zoomed away and won by two lengths. 'Van Vliet,' said Gray years later, 'was the fastest amateur I've seen. There was nothing like him at Amsterdam or Los Angeles, [and] he was the toughest man I've met, anywhere.'

Van Vliet opposed the German Toni Merkens in the final and in the first of the best out of three races had Merkens beaten until the German ran the Dutchman into the barrier fence. In the second race, Merkens won fairly and claimed gold. Gray was at trackside barracking for van Vliet. 'Merkens beat van Vliet but he had to put him in the fence to do it. He was found guilty of bad sportsmanship and fined 100 marks but still won the race.'

Ironically, Johnson performed poorly in Gray's pet event the following day. His 1 minute, 15.8 seconds was not in the winner van Vliet's class—the Dutchman won the gold medal in 1 minute, 12 seconds. 'My trouble was that I reached my top form about a fortnight too soon,' explained Johnson. 'I broke the record in training.' Yet in the heat 'I was flat or pretty close to it'. As for Gray's defeat in the sprint, 'It was lack of competition and experience that beat Dunc . . . Those continentals know too much!'

The Australian cyclists took their failures to heart. *The Sydney Morning Herald* could not help but notice 'the deepening pall hanging over the Australian camp'. On 10 August, Johnson and Chris Wheeler would finish unplaced and far behind the leaders in the 100km road race. In the event, which sped the cyclists through Berlin's glorious lake district and past the Olympic Village, the clutch on Wheeler's three-speed gear mechanism failed after 50km as he bumped and bounced over cobblestones. By the time he repaired it, the race was lost. Later he hinted at sabotage. 'I was going well and felt I had a chance until I had trouble with my variable gear,' which, he added acidly, 'was fitted in Berlin'. Also, 'those continentals keep jamming all the time! However, it's all in the game.'

Riefenstahl's cameramen were at the velodrome and on the road to capture the cycling. She was not. Her priority was to be at the Reich Sports Field to film the men's decathlon, a gruelling two-day series of events: 100m, broad jump, shot put, high jump, 400m, 110m hurdles, discus, pole vault, javelin and 1500m. What made the decathlon all the more enticing for Riefenstahl was that it featured a young US athlete who had caught her unashamedly amorous eye, the muscular and handsome Glenn Morris. Morris and fellow Americans Jack Parker and Bob Clark ran, jumped and threw to the point of collapse. One American reporter observed Morris in the final and decisive event, the 1500m: 'His features were strained and drawn. Every step was painful, but still he came on, running only with his heart, his feet were leaden.' Even Hitler kneaded his hands in excitement when Morris staggered spent and delirious across the finish line, winning the gold medal. Morris's 7900 points was a new world and Olympic record, ahead of Clark with 7601 and Parker on 7275.

Riefenstahl captured the competitors' exhaustion and exhilaration. A photograph shows her lying on the grass with Morris during a break in the decathlon. They are looking into each other's eyes and laughing, apparently besotted with each other. The camera didn't lie. In her memoirs, Riefenstahl described the moment: 'With a towel over his head, Glenn Morris lay relaxing on the grass, gathering strength for the next event . . . we looked at one another, we both seemed transfixed. It was an incredible moment and I had never experienced anything like it. I tried to choke back the feelings surging up inside me and to forget what had happened.' The director wrote, apocryphally because not a soul seems to have seen the incident, and had they done so would hardly have forgotten it, that Morris 'grabbed me in his arms, tore off my blouse and kissed my breasts, right in the middle of the stadium, in front of 100,000 spectators. A lunatic, I thought. I wrenched myself out of his grasp and dashed away. But I could not forget the wild look in his eyes . . .' What is *not* apocryphal is that Riefenstahl and Morris had an affair in Berlin.

DAY 7: SATURDAY 8 AUGUST

The day before the swimming events began, Australia's de facto swimming coach and Pat Norton's chaperone Harry Nightingale wrote to a Sydney friend. He had been shocked by the power, speed and training intensity of the American, Dutch and Japanese swimmers. 'What impressed me most [about them] was this—there is no fixed stroke. I have seen many of these champions putting elbows in first, fingers wide open, head submerged, and dozens of things which, according to our critics in Australia, are quite wrong. So . . . my ideas have changed a good deal.' Considering the fast times of foreign swimmers, 'It is obvious that we put too much style into our work and not enough brute strength . . . Our swimmers look like models with their even strokes, but it means nothing here. The amount of work done by the other champions would kill our swimmers.'

Nightingale was awed by Holland's Mastenbroek, who would be swimming in the 100m and 400m freestyle, the 100m backstroke and the 4x100m relay. 'She is a girl of tremendous strength' who utilised an 'entirely new' power stroke which 'we have never seen employed in Sydney, or, I should say, Australia. I intend to try it out when I return. Mastenbroek has a pip of a turn and gains a good start on her opponents.'

The Australians were doing as well as they could under the circumstances, but Nightingale knew they'd have their work cut out. 'Pat Norton looks forward to the battle with great heart . . . I expect her to be near the winner. Kitty [Mackay] has had a keen struggle to make the grade, but we—and I say *we* because I can honestly say I've given more time to her than any of the other girls—have made a big improvement. She could not get below 1 minute, 13 seconds in the fresh water for the 100m with that salt water stroke she employs. But after three weeks hard training and alterations, she is returning 1 minute, 10 seconds.

'No doubt you'll recall that I have always maintained that de Lacy is a world-beater. Well, she could not handle the fresh water at all, so she decided that something had to be done. After a quiet talk, she decided to put herself entirely in my hands. The improvement in four weeks has been amazing and now, a day before the 100m heat, she is returning 1 minute, 9 seconds. Her improvement has been just as wonderful over the quarter mile [400m] . . . To say I am pleased is putting it mildly. I don't want any thanks, I have received my reward by the improvement she has made. Perhaps I am storing up a heap of trouble when Evelyn and Pat meet in the national titles!'

On the evening of 8 August, de Lacy diarised: 'Today was the day [of my 100m freestyle heat]. It was cloudy but got brighter . . . Had breaker [breakfast] in bed. Up about 10 to stretch my legs, wandered around, played Ludo but the morning seemed endless. At 12 had a beef steak and then rested. At quarter past 2 went over to the Olympic stadium, now feeling a bit go-ey. At quarter to 3 had costume checked, at 3 the first [heat]—Mastenbroek of Poland [*sic*] first, Arendt of Germany second, Rawls of America third. Then mine. Den Ouden of Holland first, *de Lacy of Australia second*!!!'

The only swimmer in her heat not to wear a cap, de Lacy was cheery and composed before her event. Her pet race would be the

400m on 13 August, so lining up for the 100m she wasn't nervous, not even when she drew the lane beside the champion Willy den Ouden. At the starter's pistol, the Australian's dive was smooth; she surfaced beside den Ouden and sprinted for the 50m turn. At the turn, the Dutchwoman was a metre ahead. De Lacy, swimming faster than she had ever done, gained slightly, but den Ouden was too good and de Lacy finished 0.4 of a second behind in 1 minute, 8.5 seconds, the fastest time ever recorded by an Australian woman for 100m. The Western Australian would be back for the semifinal the following day.

Kitty Mackay did not fare as well in her 100m heat. In the minutes before her race she was paralysed by nerves. Some 18,000 spectators had packed the swimming stadium to capacity, and the Americans, Germans and Japanese had noisy and colourful cheer squads. 'Kitty found the occasion too much,' said Nightingale, and *The Sydney Morning Herald* observed that she was 'afflicted by stage fright'. As race time neared, the tall, usually confident swimmer trembled. Her mind was in such turmoil that she could not later recall the minutes before the starter's gun when she made her way to the pool and took her place alongside the other competitors. She placed fifth out of seven in her heat, swimming a poor time of 1 minute, 13.8 seconds. Central to Mackay's unravelling, said Alderson, was that 'Kitty found the fresh water more difficult than the other swimmers, and she had to change her style quite a lot to meet the altered conditions. After leaving Australia in the winter, a swimmer would require the whole of the six weeks at the venue of the Games to get perfectly fit, and when a change of style has to be made it does not give sufficient time when one has to meet swimmers who are able through special facilities to train all the year round.' Also, Alderson blamed a lengthy unexplained delay before her heat for making Mackay even more anxious. 'I swam one of those nervous swims for which I am known . . .' she later said in her honest and straightforward way. 'I faded away from nervous exhaustion.'

Sydney's 100m freestyler Bill Kendall swam a good heat, even with a heavy cold. With a time of 1 minute, 0.1 seconds, he placed third. The winner, to nobody's surprise, was Japan's best freestyler, Masanori Yusa. The Australian wasn't fazed, and assured teammates that he could improve on his time in the semifinal, to be swum at 3 p.m. True to his word, Kendall swam an Australian record and personal best, in 59.9 seconds. Unfortunately, Yusa and Shigeo Arai, who were in his heat, swam 57.51 seconds and 57.9 seconds. Kendall did not qualify for the final, which was won by Ferenc Csik in 57.6 seconds ahead of the two Japanese, but his was a gallant effort. 'Billy Kendall swam really well,' reported Nightingale. 'For a week before the race he was down with a heavy cold. He only failed by inches to get into the final. The fact that he did the best time ever by an Australian is the best indication of how well he swam.' Alderson, too, considered Kendall's effort a highlight of the Australian campaign. 'The outstanding performance [in the pool] was that of Kendall . . . When I state that Kendall is the only British subject who has ever broken the minute for the 100m, it shows the sheer merit of his performance, especially when we consider the populations of the British Empire and her dominions.'

Kendall learned from his Berlin experience and adopted elements of the Japanese swimmers' technique. 'I'll dip my shoulder more in future and with my stroke I'll not pull hard until my arm is actually well down in the water.'

Following her heat, de Lacy consoled Mackay, then after watching some more events and training in the warm-up pool for the following day's semi, she returned to Friesian House. 'Home for dinner,' de Lacy told her diary. 'Kitty played to us in the music room, then retired early.' It was a strength, and perhaps a weakness, of those young Australians that Mackay—level-headed, happy-go-lucky, knowing that competitive swimming, after all, was just one facet of life—could recover from her disappointing showing quickly enough to put it behind her and entertain the others.

While the Australian swimmers harmonised around the piano, relations in Olympic soccer headquarters that evening were anything but harmonious. Hours before, there had been an ugly second round match between Austria and Peru that ended in bitter recriminations and the early departure from Berlin of the aggrieved Peruvians. The game was ill-tempered from the kick-off. Austria led two goals to nil at half-time, then Peru scored two quick goals to equalise and the match went into extra time, the first fifteen-minute period of which remained scoreless. Early in the second stanza of extra time, a Peruvian player aimed a mighty kick at an Austrian, who collapsed as if shot, and was carted from the pitch and replaced. Recovered, he returned to the field and all hell broke loose. The outraged Peruvians ringed referee Peco Bauwens, screaming that since the Austrian had been subbed he should not be able to take any further part in the match. Bauwens, and the Austrian players, disagreed. A lengthy argument ensued, the footballers shouting and gesticulating. After some minutes of this, more than 1000 Peruvian fans leapt the barrier and, yelling and waving their arms, ran onto the field and attacked the Austrian team. When Bauwens saw one Peru player reach into his shorts pocket he assumed he was drawing a pistol and tackled him to the ground. In the chaos, with the Austrians more concerned with warding off the kicks and punches of Peruvian players and fans than playing football, Peru scored two more goals. When Bauwens blew the final whistle, the score was four to two to Peru. The match was broadcast in Peru, and the victory caused delirious celebrations. A message was sent to the team by President Óscar Benavides: 'With all the Peruvian people I share intense patriotic emotion for you in your triumph . . . your gallant achievements will lead to greater national prestige.'

Meanwhile, the Austrians had lodged an on-field complaint which was upheld by IOC and soccer officials, and the result was overturned. The match would be replayed on Monday, but to avoid further mayhem spectators would be banned from the stadium.

At this, Peruvian fans rioted in both Berlin and Lima. Olympic flags were burned. Anyone in lederhosen and a Tyrolean hat was at risk of being beaten up. President Benavides called his team home. On Monday, the Austrian footballers arrived at the stadium as they'd been instructed and lined up on the pitch, awaiting their opponents. They waited . . . and waited. The Peruvian team was already in Paris on its way home. The match was awarded to Austria. The Peruvian manager grumbled, 'We won the match against Austria . . . against dirty play and against dirty refereeing.'

Afraid that the furore would reflect badly on Germany, Goebbels released a press statement exonerating Germany from any involvement: the players were Austrian and Peruvian, the referee was a Dane and the match officials Belgian, Swede, French and Czech. Göring hilariously suggested that communists were to blame. Austria would down Poland in a semi but in the final they fell to Italy two goals to one, a result that would have been welcomed in Lima.

The soccer controversy aside, midway through the Olympics, the coverage of the Berlin Olympics in every country ranged from positive to glowing. The spectacular Opening Ceremony, the feats of the athletes, the images of Hitler as sports fan—the Reich had never enjoyed such positive press.

With the British government and media largely appeasing Hitler, and America determinedly isolationist, Australian Prime Minister Joseph Lyons felt it would be right and timely to speak out against the Third Reich in its moment of Olympic glory.

The prime minister, who had turned down an invitation from the German government to attend the Olympics, addressed businessmen in Melbourne on 8 August and warned that those countries 'in which authority has been substituted for individual liberty' could spark a second world war. Lyons had the Nazi regime in his sights when he said, 'Democracy, as it is constituted today, does not make war, because 99 per cent of the private citizens of the world hate the very thought of war, and in democracies private citizens can say what they think and enforce their views on the governments that rule them. If you have a state that is based on authority, where people think what they are told or what they are permitted to think, where the press is all one way and where the theory is universal that the rights of the individuals have no existence in the presence of the all-powerful state, then you reach something that has every possibility of causing trouble for the world.'

DAY 8: SUNDAY 9 AUGUST

De Lacy was back at the pool at 3 p.m. on Sunday for her 100m semifinal. Again she would be racing against den Ouden and Jeannette Campbell. The flame-haired, freckle-faced Australian was keen to do well for Australia because Mackay had faltered the day before, but could only place fifth, swimming 0.2 of a second slower than in her heat. 'Never mind,' she wrote, 'I still have the 400m.' The final of the women's 100m, won by Mastenbroek in an Olympic and world record time of 1 minute, 0.6 seconds, was a thriller. At the 50m turn, Arendt was ahead, with Campbell and den Ouden in close pursuit. Mastenbroek was languishing in fourth. Thirty metres from the finish, Campbell caught up to Arendt, then den Ouden caught Campbell and the trio swam stroke for stroke. A photo finish seemed certain. Then, as the spectators went wild, with only 15m to swim Mastenbroek churned past all three to win. The Australian women cheered lustily for their friend Campbell, who claimed the silver.

After her race, de Lacy joined teammates in the arena grand-stand to watch Doris Carter in the women's high jump. *Olympia* captures Carter's fluid style. Riefenstahl had shot footage of Carter practising. 'Why are you filming me?' the Australian had asked, and Riefenstahl replied, 'Because we've been watching them all, and we think you'll win.'

Shin splints were crippling her take-off leg, but Carter was resilient and pain was not going to stop her lining up with the sixteen other competitors at the jumping pit. She survived the first elimination round, clearing the minimum mark of 1.3m, and the second mark—1.4m—and the third, 1.5m. When the attendants lifted the bar to 1.55m, she soared over that as well, but 1.58m was too high and she crashed to earth. As de Lacy chirped, 'Doris came in the first six in the world, and that's pretty good!' So it was. Uninjured, Carter would have done better; back home, healthy and jumping on grass, she frequently had. The winner of the high jump was Ibolya Csak of Hungary, who jumped 1.6m, a height Carter had bettered in Australia.

That eighth day of competition—sunny, mild, with scant wind—provided some of the XIth Olympiad's stormiest moments. The Reich Sports Field's state-of-the-art media centre was a hive of feverish activity that day.

The previous morning, shortly before the men's 4x100m relay heats, US runners Sam Stoller and Marty Glickman were dropped from the team without warning. Their speed and mastery of the demands of the relay, such as effecting smooth baton changes, had helped their country to be the favourite; they had been training with fellow relay team members Foy Draper and Frank Wykoff for more than a year. They were replaced by Owens and Ralph Metcalfe, neither of whom had trained for the event. Stoller and Glickman were Jewish. Six decades later, a still-seething Glickman fumed to an interviewer at the Atlanta Olympic Games: 'We were called into a meeting [with] Dean Cromwell, the assistant track coach, and Lawson Robertson, the head track coach. Robertson announced that he had heard very strong rumours that the Germans were saving their best sprinters, hiding them, to upset the American team in the 4x100m relay. Consequently, Sam Stoller and I were to be replaced by Jesse Owens and Ralph Metcalfe. We were shocked. Sam was completely stunned. He didn't say a word in the meeting. I was a brash eighteen-year-old kid and I said, "Coach, you can't hide world-class sprinters." At which point, Jesse spoke up and said, "Coach, I've won my three gold medals. I'm tired. I've had it. Let Marty and Sam run, they deserve it." And Cromwell pointed his finger at him and said, "You'll do as you're told." And in those days, black athletes *did* as they were told, and Jesse was quiet after that.'

On the day of the final, 9 August, with America considered certain to win, the controversy exploded. The dumping of Stoller and Glickman saw Avery Brundage accused of sacking the Jewish runners to curry favour with his Nazi hosts. Brundage angrily denied this, insisting that he wanted the fastest four Americans in the team. The decision stood, he said. Although the United States won the gold medal in a world and Olympic record-breaking time of 39.8 seconds, 10m ahead of second-placed Italy, most observers thought Stoller and Glickman had been treated cruelly.

In 1996, Glickman was still blaming Brundage for snatching from him his one chance of Olympic glory, all because (Glickman believed) he sought to save Hitler the discomfort of having two Jews triumph in front of 100,000 Germans. 'In the entire history of the modern Olympic Games, no fit American track and field performer has ever not competed in the Olympic Games except for Sam Stoller and me—the only two Jews on the 1936 team . . . Watching the final the following day, I see Metcalfe passing runners down the back stretch, he ran the second leg, and [I thought], "That should be me out there. That should be me. That's me out there." I, as an eighteen-year-old just out of my freshman year, vowed that come 1940 I'd win it all. I'd win the 100, the 200, I'd run in the relay. I was going to be 22 in 1940. I was a good athlete, I knew that, and four years hence I was going to be out there again. Of course, 1940 never came. There was a war on; 1944 never came.'

Just fifteen minutes after the men's relay came another dramatic event. Tall Helen Stephens anchored the crack US women's 4x100m relay team in the 3.30 p.m. final. Stephens and her team-mates Harriet Bland, Annette Rogers and Betty Robinson had received a shock in the heats the day before when their time of 47.1 seconds was bettered by the German team of Emmy Albus, the equally tall Käthe Krauss, Marie Dollinger and Ilsa Dorffeldt, who set a new world record of 46.4 seconds. Great Britain, Canada, Italy and Holland also qualified for the final. After the German women's success in their heat, Hitler bragged that Germany would surely win the gold medal, and as the runners took their marks around the track for the final he appeared serenely confident. While the German throwers had done him proud, the runners had not, and now amends would be made.

Right until the final baton change, the Führer's confidence seemed justified. Thanks to the fleet-footed Albus and Krauss, Germany was a yawning 6m ahead of second-placed United States and looked certain winners. Stephens was faster than Dorffeldt, the German anchor, but not fast enough to make up 6m. Then, for Germany, disaster: at the changeover, Dorffeldt dropped the baton. Dollinger had approached too fast and Dorffeldt set off too slowly. The women were side by side at the change. There was a fumble. The baton fell. Riefenstahl's camera caught the anguish on the women's faces. As the crowd groaned and the other runners flashed past her, Dorffeldt's mouth gaped in a silent scream; she raised her arms to the heavens, then clutched her face. Stephens took advantage of her good fortune to win, ahead of the runners of Great Britain and Canada, in a new Olympic record of 46.9 seconds, which was half a second slower than the German women's world record time in their heat. Hitler, who had been on his feet rejoicing, looked incredulous when the baton fell, then furious. He slumped back into his seat, closed his eyes and pounded his right thigh with his fist. Goebbels, beside him, said something to him, and Hitler turned and expressed his disbelief to someone behind him. Nevertheless, the Führer invited the four German women, who had huddled weeping on the track, to the room adjoining his private enclosure. He adopted an avuncular tone, telling them not to dwell on the mishap and assuring them that they were the faster team. Later he ordered an enormous bouquet of flowers to be delivered to the disconsolate athletes. Göring eased their sorrow by inviting them to his Olympic party.

No sooner had the dust settled and the tears dried than the men's 4x400m relay final was on; like the events that preceded it, this was a race for the ages. In the heats, five teams had stood out—the United States, Germany, Sweden, Canada and Great Britain—and any of them could win gold. The starter pistol popped at 3.45 p.m. Lagging 10m behind after the first baton change, Britain's Godfrey Rampling summoned a burst of speed that shot him past the others into the lead. Rampling, who lived to be 100 and was the father of the actress Charlotte Rampling, was in the zone: 'I never felt so good as that day. I seemed to float around the track, passing people without effort.' Harold Abrahams called Rampling's run 'the most gloriously heaven-sent quarter mile I have ever seen'. In the third leg it was a two-horse race between Great Britain's tiny Bill Roberts and the hulking American Edward O'Brien. O'Brien passed Roberts, then Roberts passed *him*. The crowd were on their feet and roaring. O'Brien was 5m behind Roberts at the final baton change.

The British anchor runner was Godfrey Brown, America's was Alfred Fitch. Fitch came hard at Brown but could not peg him back. With 100m to run, Brown increased his speed and Great Britain won by 15m in 3 minutes, 9 seconds. The United States was second with 3 minutes, 11 seconds, and Germany was third in 3 minutes, 11.8 seconds. The overjoyed Englishmen somehow maintained stiff upper lips on the victory platform, even as the crowd hailed their efforts. Roberts and his fellow gold medallists didn't see the point of triumphalism: 'It was our view that winning wasn't everything. It was the way you won that mattered.' The Australians would have agreed.

All that remained in track and field now was the marathon, which had begun at 3 p.m. The race was a gruelling contest, with competitors collapsing and vomiting. LA gold medallist Juan Carlos Zabala of Argentina was everyone's pick. He hit the lead early as the 56 runners left the Reich Sports Field and ploughed through the Grunewald Forest. After 5km, Son Kitei, a small, thin man who ran without socks, set out after him, but the British marathoner Ernest Harper motioned for him to be patient and save his energy. At 30km, Zabala collapsed, and Son and Harper, whose shoes had filled with blood, replaced him in the lead. Soon, Son, hurting and disorientated on that warm dry afternoon, found himself in front. 'The human body can [only] do so much,' he later said. 'Then your heart and spirit must take over.' That they did, and Son entered the stadium to the cheers of 110,000 and staggered exhausted across the finish line in 2 hours, 29 minutes, 19.2 seconds, 2 minutes ahead of Harper.

Son stood on the victory platform, his head adorned with the oak leaf wreath, the gold medal around his neck, as the Japanese flag was raised and Japan's anthem was played. Yet Son, who had not even been considered a possible winner in the lead-up, showed no trace of joy; rather his lower lip jutted defiantly and he seemed about to cry. He clutched his oak tree pot in front of him to obliterate the Japanese emblem on his shirt, and bowed his head in what he later called 'silent shame and outrage'. For Son Kitei was Korean, not Japanese, and his real name was Sohn Kee-chung. In 1936, Korea had for 26 years been occupied by the Japanese Empire, which suppressed Korea's citizens, culture and language. Sohn's epic marathon win was glorifying the nation that had conquered his country and oppressed him and his loved ones. When asked to sign autographs he defiantly and at personal risk signed his Korean name and drew a little map of Korea alongside. That night, Sohn refused to attend the party Japanese officials held in his honour. Winning the gold medal for Japan was, he would say, 'an unbearable disgrace for me'.

Back in Korea, one brave anti-Japan newspaper ran a photo of Sohn winning the race but blurred his shirt's Japanese emblem. As punishment, the Japanese occupiers arrested and tortured eight of its journalists and closed the paper for nine months.

Sohn went on to live an illustrious life as an elite athletics coach and administrator, and was instrumental in Seoul being awarded the 1988 Olympics. He was the only possible choice as final torch bearer at Seoul, and when he ran into the stadium in front of 80,000 spectators, displayed on the screen was his real name, not its Japanese corruption, and with it the fact that he had won the marathon at the 1936 Olympics not for Japan but for Korea.

DAY 9: MONDAY 10 AUGUST

Harry Cooper was the first Australian boxer to compete at Deutschland Hall, the boxing venue. Like their wrestling counterparts, Cooper, welterweight Len Cook and light heavyweight Les Harley only learned after arriving in Berlin that they'd be fighting under unfamiliar international rules. It was no secret German plot; the news simply had not been passed on by Australian officials to the boxers. In Berlin, they would not be allowed to bounce off the ropes for leverage as was permitted in Australia; there could be no draws, each bout had to have a winner; and instead of the referee officiating from a platform at the side of the ring, he would be in the ring with the fighters, tapping and pulling at them, instructing and warning them as they battled.

Before Cooper's first elimination bout, he assured Alderson that he was fighting fit. His chill had cleared up, and the broken bone in his right hand had knitted. Nevertheless, when the bell rang, Cooper lacked his usual energy and protected his right hand, concentrating on attacking his Polish opponent with his left. This was never going to be enough. Cooper survived the first round. In the second, Edmund Sobkowiak came out fast and after 90 seconds knocked Cooper down with a vicious right cross to the jaw. The feisty, foolhardy Cooper leapt straight back to his feet, and instead of moving about the ring and avoiding the Pole's rushes until his head cleared, he waded in, punching wildly and hoping for a fluke knockout. The Pole unleashed another right cross to the Australian's jaw. The thudding blow was heard around the hall. Cooper was unconscious before his head hit the canvas. He was carried to his corner with blood spilling from his mouth. When able to speak, he told reporters, 'I knew nothing about the punch that beat me. The Pole was too good in every respect. I met a better man. I don't think I'll ever drop my guard again.'

Cooper, like Mackay, didn't dwell on defeat, and was back ringside to barrack for Cook when he fought later that afternoon. Cook, having witnessed Sobkowiak's demolition of Cooper and learning that he'd also been drawn to fight a Pole, was described as being 'highly strung [with] an understandable suspicion of Polish boxers'. Cook overcame his nerves and won on points to advance to the second round the next evening.

In his bout against the eventual gold medallist Stanislaus Suvio of Finland, Cook gave almost as good as he got in a ferocious stoush. The Australian persisted in throwing left hooks to Suvio's body, and the Finn had no trouble blocking or absorbing the blows. In the third and final round, Suvio pummelled Cook mercilessly with right jabs to the body and straight lefts to the jaw. Only his heart kept Cook on his feet. Alderson was bitterly disappointed by the points loss. 'It was a very close contest,' he opined, perhaps a little patriotically, 'and had it been possible under the rules a draw would have been a just decision, according to good judges. Suvio went on to win the final, and in his subsequent fights had rather easy victories. Had Cook not met Suvio early in the bouts, he would have undoubtedly been his opponent in the final, and to my way of thinking it would have been anyone's fight.'

Until just before his bout on 10 August, there was doubt over whether Harley was fit to compete. Apart from being excruciatingly painful when punched, the infected boils on his arm had sapped his strength and stamina. He was rated no hope. Harley proved the doubters wrong with two plucky performances. First, he had a decisive points win over Switzerland's Walter van Bueren. In his second match, against František Havelka of Czechoslovakia, Harley lost on points. The fighting was furious, and the judges thought the Czech's barrages of straight lefts and right hooks were more than a match for the depleted Harley's rights to the jaw.

At the same time, Australia's stocky, barrel-chested Ron Masters was diving in the 3m springboard competition, which began at 8 a.m. and continued through the day. Each diver was required to perform a set of 'compulsory' dives that day and 'voluntary' dives the following day. Masters' dives included a forward running somersault, a backward somersault, a running backward dive, a backward spring with half somersault, and a full screw with half somersault running forward. When the two days' points were tallied, Masters' combined score of 115.72 was 47.85 behind that of gold medallist Dick Degener of the United States, placing him fourteenth out of 24. *The Sydney Morning Herald*, perhaps betraying interstate bias of its own, was unforgiving of the Victorian. Under the heading 'Masters' Poor Dives', it groused, 'Masters, whose inconsistency during training was disturbing, struck a bad patch. His first two dives were particularly poor, and it was early apparent that he had no chance of gaining a place.'

Things did not improve for Masters in the 10m platform event, which was held on 14 and 15 August. He accumulated 86.95 points, and, though placed eighth after the compulsory dives, ended up fifteenth of 26 competitors, lagging 26.63 points behind the winner, dashing American Marshall Wayne.

There is a marvellous photograph of Leni Riefenstahl in her trademark beret standing on a 5m diving platform directly beneath the 10m platform, directing her cameraman as he films Wayne, who has just hurled himself into space executing what was described in the photo caption as a 'perfect dive'. Until the breathtaking television coverage of modern times, the beauty and danger of Olympic diving has never been captured as well as Riefenstahl did at those Olympics. Shooting up from her vantage point, artfully framing the divers against billowing clouds, her slow-motion footage of Wayne and Marshall, and the equally photogenic American women divers, is poetic and thrilling.

The women's springboard was won by thirteen-year-old Marjorie Gestring, still the youngest-ever Olympic gold medallist, and the high tower by the beautiful, ukulele-playing Dorothy Poynton-Hill, who had also claimed the gold in that event at the 1932 Los Angeles Games. The US divers won ten of the twelve available diving medals, including all four gold medals.

DAY 10: TUESDAY 11 AUGUST

After training for his 2000m single sculls event on the Langer See, Cec Pearce was approached by English rowing coach Tom Sullivan. 'This bloke said to me, "Pearce, if the water is as choppy as it is today in the Olympic races, you'll win."'

Unfortunately for Pearce, the day dawned still, clear and warm, and as the rowing events got underway, the Langer See was mirror-smooth. And it wasn't just the elements that conspired against Pearce; he was also suffering from a cold, which he blamed on the German cyclist masseurs who were brought in to massage the Australian rowers. 'They left my muscles sorer than when I went onto the rubbing table,' he said. 'Then they complained that the liniment my cousin [former Olympic rower Bobby Pearce] gave me was affecting their hands. Baloney! They started rubbing me with talcum powder, and it clogged up my pores and I caught a cold.'

Pearce was drawn in the second heat. He began promisingly but ran out of energy and finished listlessly in fourth place, second last. His time of 7 minutes, 27 seconds saw him squeak into the repechage next day, but in the fourth heat of the repechage he came second to the Canadian Charles Campbell. The final, on 14 August, was won by the man who had easily won Pearce's first heat, Germany's Gustav Schäfer, a blond Aryan poster boy.

Australian eights rower Merv Wood was so inspired by Schäfer's performance that he decided then and there that his future was as a sculler.

The seventeen-year-old 100m backstroker Pat Norton had swum well in Berlin, as fast as ever she had in Australia. As her event neared, her stars were in alignment. Of all the Australian swimmers, she had coped best with the transition from salt to fresh water and with the 50m pool, which was 4.4m longer than the 50yd pools she was used to back home. And unlike freestyle, breaststroke or butterfly swimmers, who swim face down and can see the underwater markers telegraphing the end of the pool, the backstroker, if there are no markings poolside, must guess when to prepare to turn, and Norton was gauging it right. Another benefit was her irrepressible nature, which ensured that she wasn't intimidated by Olympic pressure. She had even recovered from the swollen glands that had hampered her training. Then, the day before her heat, Norton was stricken by what the nurse at Friesian House told Nightingale was 'a virus' but was in fact her period. 'The lady doctor attached to the house where the women are residing advised that Pat be withdrawn from her heat [because of her virus],' wrote Nightingale to his friend in Sydney, but 'the old Norton would not hear of it and off she went'. Despite her discomfort, Norton swam 'with true grit and pluck'. She placed fourth. Her time of 1 minute, 22.3 seconds was the fastest of all the fourth placegetters across the heats, and she qualified for the semifinal. Mackay had swum in the first heat, and finished fifth in 1 minute, 24.6 seconds.

Nightingale, when he saw Norton's distress at the finish of her heat, considered scratching her from the semi the following day. She told him, 'Don't you dare!' In it, she came sixth out of six, but in a creditable 1 minute, 21.1 seconds, just 2.8 seconds shy of the Los Angeles Olympic record. 'Pat was very unlucky,' wrote

Nightingale. But Norton herself was too honest to gild the lily. 'My effort . . . was abysmal. It was a great disappointment to me,' she said years later. 'Losing a week's training with a swollen gland, then to be confronted with my period on the day of the race did nothing for my morale. Menstruation was not a subject for general discussion among us girls . . . let alone with a male swimming coach! I was lethargic and slightly depressed and my limbs felt as if they had been turned to lead. I managed to make the semifinal, and if I had repeated my Australian record I would have come third. Well, these things happen, and you only have one chance, and that's that.'

The winner of Norton's semifinal was Nida Senff of the Netherlands, who would pip compatriot Mastenbroek for the gold medal in the final. After the race there was conjecture as to whether the disgraced American party girl Eleanor Holm would have successfully defended her 1932 Olympic title, as her LA time was 0.6 of a second faster than Senff's.

After the final, with Mackay and Norton eliminated, Nightingale wrote that, 'Our girls can never hope to defeat the Dutch girls, because the latter swim like some of our big surf swimmers. Don't get the idea that they are in any way stylists in their stroking because they are not. It is pure strength, plus 100 per cent relaxation in all recovery movements. Boy, I have my ideas now and the spray is sure going to fly around the Bondi pool. Our swimmers must learn to get tough and train harder.'

That evening, Hitler temporarily abandoned his peaceful pantomime when he held court at the Reich Sports Field as a crowd of 100,000 spectators watched a spectacular, and ominous, salute to German military might. Searchlights caressed the swastikas on the stadium towers and raked the low-hanging clouds; massed flaming torches waved by 50,000 goosestepping storm troopers lit up the arena, as Hitler gloated over his army, navy and air force. Flanked by Göring, Goebbels, Frick, Ribbentrop and Blomberg, and his Olympic minions Tschammer und Osten, Ritter von Halt, Diem and Lewald (the latter pair in their formal attire looking discomfited, as though they'd rather be anywhere else), Hitler delivered a speech of threats and boasts about Germany's ability to wage war. Brass bands banged out the usual anthems and the Olympic orchestra performed works by Wagner. Trumpets blared fanfares from the arena's ramparts and drums thundered. The Olympic flame, which had come to symbolise the efforts and fair play of the athletes, in the *sturm und drang* of the Führer's celebration of war took on the sinister aspect of a pagan sacrificial altar. Hitler proclaimed that Germany's days as a whipping boy were over; under National Socialism it was again a strong and feared nation led by a great man.

All but Nazi true believers considered the Führer's warrior pageant boorish and grossly out of place at an Olympic Games. Richard Crossman, a British Labour politician of the future, was moved to write in his diary: 'Germany today is openly and defiantly a nation at arms. Hitler . . . has won the masses.'

DAY 11: WEDNESDAY 12 AUGUST

'When I came second in my heat in the good time, for me, of 1 minute, 10.2 seconds, I thought, "Well, this is a bit of all right,"' said Percy Oliver of his swim in the 100m backstroke heat. 'I truly didn't expect to win a medal in Berlin. I was only seventeen, and while I had trained hard, and even changed my style after seeing Adolph Kiefer in action, I was simply happy to be representing my country.'

The Western Australian's third place in the following day's semifinal in 1 minute, 9.4 seconds—the fastest he had ever swum and the fastest *any* Australian had ever swum 100m backstroke—won him a spot in the final on 14 August, and a showdown with his idol Kiefer.

Oliver was enjoying the moment too much to be nervous. He knew that Kiefer, who had swum a remarkable 1 minute, 6.9 seconds and 1 minute, 6.8 seconds to win his heat and semi respectively, would have to drown to be denied the gold medal. He was heartened, too, when on the eve of the final he received a typically taciturn telegram from his parents back in Perth: 'Good boy. Love Mum and Dad.'

In the final, Oliver placed seventh out of seven in 1 minute, 10.7 seconds, more than a second slower than his semi time. Kiefer broke the Olympic record in 1 minute, 5.9 seconds, and was photographed at the wall after he'd won nonchalantly looking back at the other swimmers who lagged metres behind. Yet Oliver, if he had been able to replicate his semifinal swim, would have come home fourth, a tenth of a second from winning a bronze medal. Working against him was his unfamiliarity with the Olympic 100m distance, when all his life he'd been swimming the shorter 100yd. In those days, unlike today when they twist onto their front to make the turn, backstrokers turned on their back: swimming blind, so to speak, it was crucial that they correctly judged where the wall was. 'I messed up my turn,' Oliver said. 'I had never had trouble gauging where the wall was when I turned at 50 yards, but this time when I went to turn, the wall wasn't there. There were no marks to tell me where the end of the pool was, and there was still around 2m to go. I miscalculated and started my turn too early. It cost me dearly. To that point I was swimming my best time.' A third problem facing Oliver was nerves. 'I had no coach for the five weeks before competition, so I just worked out what was best for me, but it all fell apart in the final. For the first time I was hit by an attack of nerves. I had no one to talk to me and I got a bad case of the flutters. There was no psychological support in Berlin. By the time I got into the water to start the event I felt as though I had just finished.'

In his last years Oliver joked that he fared as well as any of the other Australians in Berlin, 'no bloody good . . . Yet I was satisfied I'd made the final.' As with some of his other teammates who found themselves out of their depth in 1936, glory lay ahead for Percy Oliver.

At Grünau, the Australian rowers had had an unsettled preparation. There was the matter of their missing boats, and their misbehaviour—such as when they got plastered on beer and threw food at the photograph of the Führer on the wall of the mess at their barracks—robbed them of the serious edge they would need to be competitive at Olympic level. There are no reports of the Australian policemen exacting revenge on the British rowers after Henley had snubbed them as 'labourers' the previous month, but according to author Daniel James Brown in *The Boys in the Boat*, they did manage to land themselves in a stoush. According to Brown, the German and Yugoslavian rowing teams had been doing their best to rob the other squads of sleep by singing loudly outside their quarters in the dead of night. One day in the mess, the Yugoslavians broke into 'Yankee Doodle'. The Americans took offence at this desecration of a national song and charged into the Yugoslavians, throwing punches. The Australians took the side of the Americans and whaled into the Europeans. It is not hard to imagine Wal Mackney—who, according to his son Kim, enjoyed a fight as much as anything else in the world—enthusiastically joining the brawl.

Hitler, in his uniform and peaked military cap but with the addition of a flowing cape to cocoon him from the cold wind that whipped off the water, stood alongside propaganda minister Goebbels and Reich minister Frick at some part of each day of the rowing. He was there at 4.30 p.m. on 12 August, gazing down from his viewing platform when Bill Dixon and Herb Turner rowed for Australia in the first of two heats of the 2000m double sculls. Rowing in a boat significantly heavier than their rivals', they were in second place for the first 1000m before Poland overtook them, and came equal fourth with the United States in the heat, covering the distance in 6 minutes, 55.6 seconds. This time qualified the Australians for one of the two repechage heats, which they won in 7 minutes, 58.8 seconds.

Dixon and Turner lined up against the powerhouses of world sculling in the final on 14 August. From all reports, they were cocky before the race, feeling that a medal was possible. In the end, superior power and technique were decisive, and the British pair of bespectacled five-time Olympian Jack Beresford and Dick Southwood had that. The pair powered home in 7 minutes, 20.8 seconds, ahead of Germany and Poland. Dixon and Turner finished last in 7 minutes, 45.1 seconds. Not helping their cause was the throat infection suffered by eights member Bill Cross, whose hospitalisation had forced both scullers to abandon their own practice in order to substitute for Cross in the eight during training sessions.

The first round of the 2000m eights commenced at 5.15 p.m. on 12 August. Hitler was on his perch to see Australia—represented by the rambunctious NSW policemen Len Einsaar, Joe Gould, Merv Wood, Wal Jordan, Cross (now recovered from his throat ailment), Clyde Elias, Mackney, Don Fergusson and coxswain Norman Ella—compete in the second heat. After leading the field at 300m, the Australians fell back, and at the finish line were fourth of five boats, coming home in 6 minutes, 21.9 seconds—far slower than the teams that were expected to battle for the gold medal. Nevertheless, they had done enough to qualify for the next day's repechage. In the repechage, their second placing in 6 minutes, 55.1 seconds was not good enough to make the final, which was won by the Americans in 6 minutes, 25.4 seconds from Italy and Germany.

While acknowledging that they had not been good enough, Australia's eight said that their poor preparation had not helped their cause. They were justified in complaining that their boats had arrived late. What strained credulity was their claim that once the craft materialised, they had trained so brilliantly that they grew complacent, deluding themselves that European and American rowers were inherently inferior to Australian and that the gold medal was theirs for the taking. Then, they explained, they had seen the skill and power of the other teams and their confidence had faltered, and when on race days the smooth water did not play to their strength, they despaired and lost hope. *The Sydney Morning Herald*'s Olympic correspondent wrote that 'no hard luck story can explain the eight's defeat . . . and the experience points to the same conclusion regarding the whole of the Australian Olympic team, namely, that Australian standards have been at a standstill for the past four years, while those of other nations have improved'. Another rowing pundit wrote that in each of their races, the eight was 'unable to raise a finishing burst. Their rating and recovery was not fast enough . . . The Australians' work together was disappointing and lacked a polish comparable with the other crews. They had been regarded as faster than the Canadians on their performances at practice, but the Canadians beat them.' Back in the barracks, coach George Mackenzie mourned, 'Australia cannot realise the strength of the opposition here. The Australians rowed below form but nevertheless were unequal to the task. Their work was too sluggish.' In his report, Alderson pulled no punches. The eight 'was not up to the standard of the best crews of the other nations, and it would appear that Australia, to have any chance against the other countries, so well coached and trained as they were, must [in future] select the best eight-oar crew available'.

Hitler appeared to enjoy the rowing immensely, beaming and clapping the German victories in the single sculls, the fours with cox, the fours without cox, the pairs with cox and without, and even enjoying the closely fought final of the eights. He chortled when during a storm on the afternoon of 13 August, strong wind and heavy rain downed a tethered balloon in which press photographers were shooting the races. The snappers plunged into the water and had to be hauled to safety by rescuers in a motorboat. The Führer rocked to and fro with delight. Many present had never seen Hitler laugh before.

And he would laugh again at the men's 1500m freestyle final on 15 August at the swimming stadium when a Californian woman named Carla de Vries, described as 'plump and wearing a red hat', burst through Hitler's black-shirted bodyguards to hug and kiss him. The guards reached for their pistols and truncheons, but when they saw that Hitler, after a couple of seconds of being nonplussed, seemed to enjoy the woman's affectionate assault—grinning bashfully and giving her an autograph—they relaxed. As she returned to her seat Hitler applauded her, as did the spectators. A kiss from the Führer may have assuaged any disappointment the Californian felt at the result of the 1500m freestyle final, when Japan's Noboru Terada beat American Jack Medica (who'd won gold in the 400m) by 20m and set a new Olympic record. (Hitler may not have been quite as sanguine as he appeared to be about being smooched by Carla de Vries; he sacked the guards to whom she gave the slip.)

DAY 12: THURSDAY 13 AUGUST

In the women's 400m freestyle, Evelyn de Lacy was drawn in the third heat. Swimming strongly, the young Western Australian recorded 1 minute, 17 seconds for the first 100m, and kept pace with the leaders until the 200m mark, when she wilted. With 50m still to race she was fourth, and at the finish fifth and last. Her time of 5 minutes, 51.1 seconds was not in the league of the heat's winner, Grete Fredricksen of Denmark, who recorded 5 minutes, 39.5 seconds.

Mastenbroek would win the 400m final in a then-astounding 5 minutes, 26.4 seconds. As the finalists gathered in the dressing room before the race, Denmark's Ragnhild Hveger handed around chocolates, and pointedly offered none to Mastenbroek. The Dutch champion was hurt, then angry, and thought she would make her spiteful rival pay. Hveger led the final until the last 25m, when Mastenbroek, who'd been toying with her, easily reined her in and won by a metre.

Mastenbroek's Berlin medal haul was three gold (100m freestyle, 400m freestyle and 4x100m freestyle) and a silver (100m backstroke). The seventeen-year-old set new Olympic records in the 100m and 400m freestyle. If Jesse Owens was the king of the Berlin Games, Rie Mastenbroek, 'with shoulders like a mantelpiece', was the queen, and her achievement was all the more noteworthy because she was suffering from chronic low blood pressure.

De Lacy, who typified the carefree Australian attitude, was philosophical at how her Olympic campaign had panned out. She said she was proud to have even been in the same event as the great Mastenbroek. That night she recorded her memories of her 400m freestyle heat in her diary: 'Was very disappointed, as six girls with slower times than mine entered the semi finals, one girl being 23 seconds slower. I was really ninth fastest in the world, but because mine was a very fast heat [I] was put out of the semi final. I went to town with Pat Norton and we had a gorgeous time spending all our money.'

On 15 August, the day before the Closing Ceremony, de Lacy, Carter, Norton, Mackay and the Argentinian Campbell set off to the pool at the Reich Sports Field and talked the attendant into letting them have a last swim. 'We held up five fingers to let him know that we would only stay five minutes but 35 minutes passed before he called us out. We had a great time. Our antics from the 1m and 5m diving boards were priceless. Doris took pictures with Kitty's movie camera of Kitty swimming and the four of us on the springboards . . . After dinner, I packed (what a job!). My things just would not fit into my cases. Had such a headache, so a hot shower and off to bed.'

CHAPTER 15
THE DYING FLAME

The Closing Ceremony was the Nazi Olympics' last hurrah, the final chance for Hitler to impress the world.

The Olympic flame was supposed to be snuffed out at the precise moment when the sun sank below the horizon, at 7.37 p.m. on Sunday, 16 August, but the late finish of the timed jumping equestrian event and its medal presentation saw the Closing Ceremony postponed until well after nightfall. By then, there were more than 110,000 in the stadium. Hitler, Goebbels, Göring, Frick and Ribbentrop, international and German Olympic officials, assorted dignitaries, athletes (those who had not already left for home or holidays or to compete in the British Empire versus United States athletics meet in London) and the public keenly awaited what organisers termed the 'final act' of the XIth Olympiad.

Around 8.30 p.m., the lights in the arena went out and for 60 seconds there was darkness. Then a trumpet fanfare from the Marathon Tower heralded a performance by the Olympic Symphony Orchestra of Mollendorf's 'Parade March'. As the music swelled, the floodlights in the arena and around the perimeter of the stadium blazed, reaching to the heavens, and the flag-bearers of the participating nations led their teams from the Marathon Gate to the centre of the field where, in their ranks, they wheeled and faced the balcony of honour where stood Hitler and his guests. IOC president Baillet-Latour stepped forward. He declared the Berlin Olympic Games closed and called on the youth of every country to assemble in Tokyo in 1940 for the Games of the XIIth Olympiad.

The Closing Ceremony was reaching its crescendo. The orchestra played Beethoven's song of sacrifice, 'The Flaming Fire'. Then 51 women, the same ones who had been employed to place oak wreaths on medallists' heads, solemnly attached red-gold ribbons of remembrance and oak wreaths to the nations' flags. The director of processions Major Feuchtinger—who would command a German panzer division in the Normandy invasion in 1944, be tried by the Reich for treason, and then, on being spared execution, become a spy for Russia—commanded, 'Haul down the flags!' There resounded a barrage of rifle and cannon fire from the artillery division in the May Field. The Olympic flag dropped from its mast as if shot.

Awed spectators fell silent as the Olympic flame slowly subsided, gave a final flicker, and expired. For the final time, the Olympic bell sounded, softly, then building to a clamorous metallic din. After some minutes, the great bell fell silent. A bugle fanfare followed, and a scarlet rocket was shot into the sky; the multitude linked arms and sang a German folksong, 'Play's at an End': '*Sunsets that bid us their greeting/Rise up again for a meeting/Till then, farewell!/ Till then farewell!*' As the song was sung, the national flags on the arena were lowered in unison. The arena lights went out one by one. There was a minute's silence in the pitch black.

When interviewed for the *People's Century* television program, Robert Mitchell, of England's water polo team, remembered: 'The lights came down and the Olympic flame went out and then there was utter silence and utter darkness and it was really most impressive and then they started *"Sieg Heil!"* . . . 100,000 people going, *"Sieg Heil! Sieg Heil!"* and giving the Nazi salute. And I literally put my hands in my pocket to stop myself being hypnotised into doing it with them. It was absolutely hypnotic.'

The lights came on, the athletes marched from the arena. Hitler left his enclosure, and after he did so all those in the great arena filed out of the Reich Sports Field towards whatever fate had in store for them.

Despite the US domination of track athletics, jumping and diving and Jesse Owens stealing the Führer's limelight, and despite nine Jews winning gold medals, at Games' end, Germany led the medal tally with 89 (33 gold, 26 silver and 30 bronze). This put the Fatherland, which had dominated rowing, boxing, throwing and cycling, well ahead of the United States, which won 56 (24 gold, 20 silver and 12 bronze). Then came Italy, Sweden, Finland, France, the Netherlands, Hungary and Japan. (Australia, with its one bronze medal, languished near the bottom of the list.) Spruiking Germany's success at the Olympics, *Der Angriff* the next day found it 'truly difficult to endure such joy!' The official newspaper of the Games shamelessly licked the Führer's jackboots: 'Must we not conclude that the biggest victor of the Olympic Games was Adolf Hitler?'

It seemed that Hitler *had* pulled it off and the Third Reich had won both the Olympic and the political games. The Berlin Olympics had been more successful than he had dreamed possible. While his Olympics failed to prove Aryan invincibility, he did make a strong case to the world that Germany was a rejuvenated country with a government in firm control, and that his regime could stage a lavish and spectacular Olympic festival—what Olympics chronicler Arnd Kruger called 'the best organised, propagandistically best-prepared, and the best attended Olympic Games up to that point in history'. And the Reich had largely succeeded in concealing its evil machinations from the sports-loving world, sending visitors home with mostly positive impressions.

The influential *New York Times* writer Frederick Birchall wrote on 16 August, in an article headlined 'Olympics Leave Glow of Pride in Reich', that the Olympics had 'humanised' National Socialism and put Germany 'back in the fold of nations'. Germany was 'a happy nation and prosperous beyond belief' and Hitler 'one of the greatest political leaders in the world today'.

Carl Diem and Theodor Lewald wrote—or more likely Goebbels wrote, and put their names to his article—that they had 'observed with pleasure that during the weeks of the Games a genuine Divine Peace prevailed, and that the interest and best wishes of millions throughout the world were concentrated on this event, which contributed substantially towards furthering peace among the nations and developing a nobler and purer type of humanity'.

CHAPTER 16
BEHIND THE MASK

It did not take long for the Nazi Olympics staged by Hitler and his gang to be exposed as the propaganda sham which at its heart it was. These men would soon plunge the world into war.

Hitler had been determined to do whatever it took to realise his territorial ambitions and lay waste to his enemies since he'd snatched power in 1933, if not a decade before then when dictating *Mein Kampf* to Rudolf Hess in Landsberg Prison. By 1936 there would be no turning back. Olympics or not, there would be war. Whether the Olympians of 1936 were truly pawns in Hitler's scheming is academic.

Just two months after the Closing Ceremony, Hitler openly admitted that he had been escalating production of warships, planes, armoured vehicles, bombs and other weapons. In October, Germany and Italy signed the Rome–Berlin Axis Treaty. In November, Germany and Japan became partners in the Anti-Comintern Pact, agreeing to defend each other against communism and other enemies. Italy joined them.

On 5 November 1937, the Führer summoned his lieutenants to the Chancellery and delivered the Hossbach Memorandum, which detailed his plan to plunder European nations to gain living space for the German race. History had proved, he said, 'that expansion could only be carried out by breaking down resistance and taking risks . . . the attacker always comes up against a possessor . . .' Lebensraum could only be achieved 'by means of force'.

Throughout 1937, the news from Germany—for a world that cherished peace and prayed that the horrors of 1914–18 would never be repeated—was bad. Hitler, his Olympics now as done and dusted as the Games of Greek antiquity, made threat after threat as Britain and France tutted and fussed and did nothing to discourage him, and America buried its head in the sand. He left no doubt that he intended to add Austria, Poland and Czechoslovakia to his earlier conquest of the Rhineland, and that Jews had no future in any nation ruled by the Third Reich.

On 12 March 1938, German troops marched into Austria and annexed it. On 9 November came Kristallnacht—Crystal Night, or Night of Broken Glass—when Nazis attacked the homes, businesses and synagogues of Jewish people in Germany and Austria. An estimated 91 Jews were murdered and more than 20,000 were herded into concentration camps.

German forces invaded and occupied the Czech territories of Moravia and Bohemia on 15 March 1939. The Czech capital of Prague fell. On 18 August, Germany occupied Slovakia. A week later, in a development as cynical as it seemed unthinkable, sworn enemies fascist Germany and communist Russia joined in a treaty of non-aggression.

On 1 September, Hitler moved on Poland. The Luftwaffe destroyed airfields, roads, railway stations, offices, factories and military installations, and one million German occupying troops crossed the border.

No longer able to deny that action was needed, on 3 September, Great Britain declared war on Germany and her allies. The same day, on the other side of the world, Australians, undoubtedly including the 1936 Olympians and their loved ones, clustered around their wirelesses as Prime Minister Menzies addressed the nation. 'It is my melancholy duty to inform you officially, that in consequence of a persistence by Germany in her invasion of Poland, Great Britain has declared war upon her and that, as a result, Australia is also at war. No harder task can fall to the lot of a democratic leader than to make such an announcement.'

Many of the young men and women who had engaged in friendly competition on the Reich Sports Field became deadly foes. The exact number of the Berlin competitors who perished in the war can never be known, but it is thought that around 400 of the male and female Olympians did not survive World War II. The lost included German long jumper Luz Long, who had been beaten by his new friend Jesse Owens in the final; and his countryman, the gold-medal-winning shot-putter Hans Woellke. Hungarian swimmer Ferenc Csik, who had won the 100m freestyle, died in a bombing raid in 1945, aged 32. His compatriot fencer Endre Kabos was blown up crossing Budapest's Margit Bridge in an explosives-filled vehicle. Foy Draper, who had run the third leg of the 4x100m relay for the gold-medal-winning US team, perished when his fighter plane was shot down over Tunisia in 1943. Shigeo Arai, who had won bronze for Japan in the 100m freestyle, was slain in Burma in 1944. Silver-medal-winning Austrian handballer Franz Bartl was killed in battle in 1941. British cyclist Alick Bevan fell in 1945. Bronze-medal-winning Italian pentathlete Silvano Abbà died at Stalingrad. There were so many more. In all, 25 German medal winners died in World War II, along with 24 members of the Polish team, some fighting the Germans, others in concentration camps.

One of the most heartbreaking stories is that of German wrestler Werner Seelenbinder, a communist who somehow evaded the

Nazi net and took his place in the German team. He told friends before his event that if he won a medal he would stand tall on the winner's dais and denounce National Socialism. He finished fourth. During the war, Seelenbinder was a dedicated member of the Uhrig underground resistance movement, whose mission was to destroy the Nazis from within. He was arrested, tortured in Brandenburg Prison, then beheaded.

For their crimes, the Nazis received terrible retribution. On 30 April 1945, with Berlin a pile of smoking rubble and Russian forces set to raise the Soviet flag on the Reichstag, Hitler suicided by pistol and potassium cyanide capsule in his Berlin bunker. Fearful that he would suffer the same fate as Mussolini and have his corpse strung up in public view and desecrated, he had ordered his minions to lay his lifeless body and that of his new wife Eva Braun in a shallow pit, douse them with petrol and burn them. The following day, Goebbels and his wife Magda took their own lives, after ordering their six children to be poisoned.

By then, Unter den Linden, the magnificent thoroughfare where the wide-eyed Australian athletes had promenaded, was in ruins, its stately buildings blasted by mortar, shell and rifle fire. The leafy Tiergarten, where they had picnicked and skylarked in boats, was a wasteland, its trees cut down and burned for firewood in the icy winter of 1944, its wildlife slaughtered and eaten by the starving people of the capital of National Socialism.

On 7 May 1945, Germany surrendered.

After being found guilty of war crimes and crimes against humanity at the Allied military tribunals at Nuremberg, Göring snapped a cyanide capsule between his teeth on 15 October 1946, shortly before he was due to be hanged. The strutting German foreign minister Joachim von Ribbentrop and Reich minister Wilhelm Frick, whom Hitler had trusted with the construction of the Reich Sports Field, were executed the following day. Hans von

Tschammer und Osten did not live to see the destruction of Berlin, succumbing to pneumonia in 1943. Theodor Lewald died a broken man in 1947, aged 87, protesting to the end that his devotion to Olympic ideals had blinded him to Hitler's manipulation. Carl Diem fared better. Although he was responsible, as Berlin fell in 1945, for persuading 2000 members of Hitler Youth to sacrifice themselves for the Reich, he, and his reputation, survived the war, and he was a respected sports historian and Olympic official until his death in 1962. Avery Brundage's friend Organising Committee member Karl Ritter von Halt was declared a criminal at the Nuremberg trials in 1946. Werner von Blomberg, the minister for war who presided over the Olympic 'festival of peace' and who had welcomed the Australians to the Olympic Village, was disgraced when Hitler and Göring, who had been guests at his wedding in 1937, learned that his new wife had been a prostitute and posed for widely circulated pornographic photographs. He died of cancer in 1946 after testifying for the prosecution at Nuremberg.

As it had been before the athletes moved in, the Olympic Village was occupied by the German army after the Games, and when they left to fight, the houses where the athletes of the world had gathered now sheltered East Prussian and Silesian refugees fleeing the invading Soviet army. When the Russians converged on Berlin, the refugees evacuated the Village and it fell into decay. Today it is a weed-strewn ghost town, with only a few ramshackle houses remaining.

During the war, the Reich Sports Field was used as a training and parade ground for the Wehrmacht. In Nazi Germany's death throes in March 1945, with its army smashed and Berlin defenceless against the Soviets, 500 children and teenagers of the Hitler Youth were corralled in the May Field and ordered to take up whatever arms they could find and to die for the Führer and Fatherland. To make sure the youngsters got the message, they were forced to watch as 200 Germans who had refused to fight or attempted to desert were lined up against the Dietrich-Eckart Theatre and shot. A distance from the heavy fighting in the Battle of Berlin, the stadium was damaged but avoided total destruction. Diem would write in his autobiography: 'The field where the Olympic youth had once assembled, the buildings and monumental grounds that had once delighted the world, had become a deadly battle-field, revealing nothing but sickening remains and gruesome debris wherever one looked.' The Reich Sports Field was captured by the Russians, and afterwards used as a training ground by the British military. Doris Carter returned there in 1946 and noted that while the arena itself was 'little damaged, other buildings were wrecked. Trees and window frames had been burned for firewood. What was left of the Bell Tower . . . contained damaged machinery . . .'

The women's lodgings, the Friesian House, still stands and provides offices for Hertha BSC, the soccer team whose home ground is the stadium.

Today the bell tower has been rebuilt to its original plans, and the stadium at the Reich Sports Field has been topped with a swooping extended roof of transparent panels to let the sun in; its playing field has been lowered and some seating reconfigured. Known as the Olympiastadion, it has hosted FIFA World Cup games and the 2006 World Cup final. It also doubles as a music venue: Bruce Springsteen, the Rolling Stones, Michael Jackson, Madonna and U2 have all played there.

When I visited the stadium in 2014 I found that much remains as it was in 1936. Large sections of Albert Speer's natural stone structure still stand. Hitler's 'platform of honour', the brazier in which the Olympic flame burned, the engraved names of gold medallists and the external towers remain as ceremonial pieces, although the giant swastikas that once adorned the towers are long gone, shot to pieces by the Russian army. Bullet holes pock the towers. The Olympic bell was recovered from the rubble of the imposing structure built to house it, the Hitler Tower, and is now mounted on a stone pedestal outside the stadium wall. It bears a crack and shell hole. Those who placed it back on display intended the bell to be a memento not of National Socialism but of the enduring spirit of sportsmanship. Still, the bell unsettles. Its swastikas, which have survived attempts to obliterate them, are still visible, supposedly the only swastikas on public display in Berlin. And the Olympic rings are still at the mercy of the Nazi eagle, which clutches them in its razor talons. Also surviving is the inscription welcoming the youth of the world to the Berlin Games.

CHAPTER 17
SIFTING THE WRECKAGE

After the Closing Ceremony, the women athletes returned to Friesian House. Chaperone Mary Fergusson urged them not to linger in the common room and to have an early night because they were to be collected by bus at 8 a.m. the next day and taken to Friedrichstrasse station, where they were to catch a train to Belgium and then take a ferry to England. After a week's rest and recreation, they would board the ocean liner RMS *Mooltan* for the voyage home to Australia.

That last night at their Berlin digs, Pat Norton had the blues. 'The Games finished, and we thought, no more until 1940, Japan!' she wrote. 'The Closing Ceremony had a sad ring to it as the flags of all the nations were marched round the arena accompanied by the sound of rolling guns firing . . . It was saying goodbye to the friends at Friesian House that saddened us. Jeannette [Campbell] from the Argentine who just waved goodbye and did not look back, our giggly little Japanese girls and South Americans. Somehow it didn't seem right—we were very subdued realising we may never see them again.'

In the morning, the Australian men in the Olympic Village

packed their bags, farewelled friends, and waited in line at the gate for their bus to Friedrichstrasse station to join the women athletes. Some were feeling the worse for wear. Dunc Gray told Harry Gordon how the night before the Village was broken up, after the Closing Ceremony, at the Deutschland Hall a couple of the lads 'got sozzled on apple cider. I started to take them back to the Village and one of them puked on the floor and I had to pay so many pfennigs to get it cleaned up and the other bloke wanted to have a go [at the German guards], and I said, "Oh for God's sake, let's get out of here." I got these kids on the bus and back to the Village. I was carrying some beautiful German books they'd given us. I couldn't handle the blokes and the books too, so I asked the fellow at the gate if he'd mind my books while I took the fellas up to bed. When I came back to the gate nobody knew anything about my books. The guard had knocked them off and was going to keep them. I demanded to see the commandant. Next thing the guard "found" my books and gave them back.'

Just before he boarded the bus in the morning, Percy Oliver saw Aussie the kangaroo in his cage. 'He wasn't returning to Australia with us. Because of quarantine regulations he had to remain in Germany, but he didn't seem too worried . . . he was happily chewing away on a big pile of grass clippings. We knew they'd treat him well.' And so they did. According to Basil Dickinson, 'Aussie ended up in Berlin Zoo. Other than that, his fate is a mystery. I've no idea whether he was still alive when the bombs fell on Berlin. I hope not.'

In that last week of Olympic competition, track and field athletes Dickinson, Alf Watson and Gerald Backhouse represented the British Empire against the United States in an athletics meet at London's White City. Jack Metcalfe had opted out, and he and Fred Woodhouse holidayed in France, Switzerland and Italy. They would reunite with teammates on *Mooltan* when it docked in Naples.

At White City, before 90,000 spectators still on an Olympic high, the Empire was vanquished by the United States, despite a distracted Jesse Owens not performing at his best. He was physically and emotionally drained and desperate to go home to his wife and daughter, who were struggling financially in his absence. Spectators at White City did not realise that they were witnessing the great athlete's last outing as an amateur.

At a party in London for the White City athletes, Dickinson found the champion 'sad and bewildered by the position in which he found himself, but philosophical and keen to get back home to his family and see what life turned up. Jack Lovelock was there, too. He was an eccentric man, very private, and at the party he was on his own a lot.'

Owens was never to relive his Berlin glory. After being ousted by Brundage, he returned to the United States to find his reputation tarnished by the blow-up. The lucrative offers of product sponsorship and film and stage stardom were rescinded. Owens was forced to provide for himself and his family by stunt racing against horses, cars and greyhounds. Sometimes he won. Most of what little money he made was taken by the Internal Revenue Service. A heavy smoker in his later years, Owens died of lung cancer in 1980, aged 66. Four years later, Stadion-Allee, the road on the southern boundary of the Berlin Olympic stadium, was renamed Jesse-Owens-Allee.

Owens' nemesis Brundage served until 1952 as president of the US Olympic Association, and then for the next twenty years as the all-powerful president of the IOC.

After the White City meet, Dickinson, Watson and Backhouse caught the Edinburgh Express to Glasgow to compete in another athletics carnival, staged at Hampton Park soccer field. 'The British Olympic Committee paid the bill, and we just had fun,' said Dickinson. 'Nobody cared who won.' Dickinson once more felt acutely alone. 'We boarded at Glasgow University, and the old caretaker insisted I take a book, *The Hunchback of Notre Dame* by Victor Hugo, and I still have it. I had nothing to give him in return. We had no gifts to hand out. Back in London, I stayed at an old-style boarding house at Lancaster Gate.' The boarding house, he recalled, had 'no showers, just uncomfortable baths and the heaters produced as much clanking noise as hot water . . . I had a week in London with no money. I was living on the few pounds Mum and Dad had wired me from Sydney. Breakfast at the boarding house was free and I filled up, but I couldn't eat out, go to the theatre . . . all I did was walk around stopping here and there to gawp at the sights, sit in Hyde Park and watch the people and read *The Hunchback* to while away the hours.'

The police rowers, with Inspector Fergusson in charge, began their two-month taxpayer-funded fact-finding tour of London police stations. One of their more urgent assignments was to 'study London's topography'. In the capital, where they resided at the police barracks, they were forced to wear plain clothes as the suitcases containing their uniforms went missing.

In the week before *Mooltan* sailed away, a number of the other athletes stayed with relatives and friends in London. Bill Kendall continued his world trip with his father in the United States. Evelyn de Lacy pounded the London tourist trail. When she farewelled Doris Carter, who was remaining in London for a few months, both women wept.

On 20 August, the Australians were shocked to hear that the well-regarded former commandant of the Olympic Village, Captain Wolfgang Fürstner, was dead. He had been killed in a road accident, or so they were informed. Later it was revealed that Fürstner had shot himself with his service revolver after attending a party honouring Werner von Gilsa, who had replaced him as commandant.

On learning how Fürstner had really died, Dickinson diarised: 'We were very saddened and realised that the German regime's hatred of non-Aryans had been swept under the carpet for our benefit. It was difficult to understand that such a competent officer who had successfully completed a most difficult assignment could be demoted and humiliated because it was learned that way back he had a Jewish forefather. Here lies the parallel between Captain Fürstner and Jesse Owens: each gave all for his country and was savagely rejected.'

Suddenly, for the athletes who had been away from home for three months now, the lure of the peace, the loved ones and friends, the sunshine and beaches of Australia grew irresistible. Fürstner's suicide heightened Gray's resolve to 'get the hell out of Europe'.

The *Mooltan* steamed out of London's Tilbury Dock on 21 August. Wrote de Lacy in her diary: 'We played tennis and deck quoits, and had a sunbake. Kitty played the piano and Ron Masters the violin and we all gathered round and sang.' Many of the athletes made a beeline to the cabin of boxer Les Harley to see his impressive collection of autographs, including those of American gold medallists Jesse Owens, Cornelius Johnson and Adolph Kiefer. Harley had tried for Hitler's signature. Unlike the Californian woman in the red hat, he could not get near him.

As *Mooltan* steamed down the east and southern coast of Spain, the Australians kept their eyes peeled for signs of the Spanish Civil War. They saw no battles, only tangled barbed wire and refugee camps. Dickinson did see a fighter plane soaring across the deep blue Andalusian sky and thought he could make out a swastika on its fuselage, although the sun was shining into his eyes and he could not be sure.

For long periods on the voyage home, as the athletes stretched their legs in Marseilles, Naples, Port Said, Aden, Bombay and

Colombo, Alderson remained in his cabin writing his official report, *Participation of the Australian Team at the XIth Olympiad*.

After the team members returned to their families and jobs and began training for the British Empire Games in Sydney in 1938, there were recriminations over Australia's performance in Berlin, with its single bronze medal. The catalyst for the bitter words that would fly for months and have a lasting impact on Australian sport was the publication of Alderson's report.

Alderson stressed that his comments were an explanation rather than an excuse for his squad's poor showing, and he pulled no punches: 'I, as manager, and members of the team generally, regret that a greater measure of success was not achieved, but I can assure the Federation and the public of Australia that each and every member of the team trained thoroughly and conscientiously . . . All did their best, as they promised they would . . . but they were not up to the standard of the representatives of some of the other nations who are placed in a more favourable position than Australia. The active participants from Australia numbered 33, out of a total of nearly 5000 competitors, so that our team met far greater competition than at any previous Games.'

What had to be addressed, wrote Alderson, was the issue of the inadequate facilities available to Australian athletes. 'It is absolutely necessary for Australia to provide its representatives with the same facilities as they will compete under overseas at Olympic Games and international contests.' If proper facilities were not provided, no matter how good our athletes, they would be severely disadvantaged when competing overseas, and the gap would grow ever wider because the international standard in all sports was higher than ever before.

Athletes all over the world competed on cinder tracks, so the laying of cinder surfaces in Australia was essential, and the sooner the better if dismal performances in Berlin and the leg injuries sustained by almost all the track and field athletes were not to be repeated. 'Although this team had about six weeks in which to train on the cinders it was not long enough to allow them to gain condition and get used to this class of track.'

It was equally urgent that facilities for swimmers matched those of other countries. Australian swimmers in Berlin had recorded their fastest times, but these were not fast enough when pitted against foreign rivals. 'The swimmers will certainly want indoor fresh water swimming pools which can be heated to allow them to undergo a longer period of training and tuition . . . In the case of our swimmers leaving Australia in May, it is most probable that the selected swimmers [who were largely confined to open saltwater baths] were unable to practise for two months before leaving Australia, as the cold weather had set in. They then had five to six weeks on the steamer, where they could only practise in a small pool which was almost useless; and on arrival at their destination they had to adapt themselves to new conditions: fresh water 50m pools. A good proportion of the time available was then lost getting used to the changed conditions, as there is a vast difference in swimming in salt water and fresh water, which calls for a change in style and technique . . .'

The boxers and wrestlers, Alderson continued, had also been at a disadvantage in Berlin because they competed 'under an entirely different set of rules . . . the International Rules', which penalised attack and defence that would have won the boxers and wrestlers points in Australia.

Specialised coaches and masseurs had to be trained and made a part of future Olympic campaigns. Had Harry Nightingale not paid his own way to Berlin to look after Pat Norton and then been coopted as swimming coach, the only Australian coach in Berlin would have been the rowing coach George Mackenzie, who was paid by the NSW police force.

Australian sport, Alderson said, existed in a state of blissful ignorance. The ways and means had to be found for Australians to compete more often against the best athletes of other nations so that they could learn from the best and be exposed to high-level competition and advances in track and field, swimming and rowing coaching.

Having digested Alderson's report, the media, federal and state governments and the public demanded answers from the AOF and amateur sporting bodies: what needed to be done to ensure that Australia never again returned from an Olympic Games with such a paltry medal haul?

Most responses concurred with Alderson that drastic changes had to be made. Respected sports authority Sir Joynton Smith was scathing of the current situation. 'Viewed from every angle, our efforts at the Olympic Games have been poor. We may, perhaps, find some slight consolation in the fact that, in point of population, [we are smaller] but we have got into the habit of expecting big things of our champions, even when they competed in classic company overseas . . . It takes more than natural ability to win an Olympic championship. Time was when the individual, the competitor, was the only factor in success, but in recent years, the scientist, the doctor, the trainer, have been "the men behind the gun". This trio has helped break more records than all the champions of the last decade.' Yet in Australia, such experts were considered a needless expense and counter to amateurism. Further, observed Smith, the great Lovelock had remarked that it took a year for an athlete to get used to a cinder track. 'Well, our runners and jumpers and hop, step and jumpers were virtual strangers to cinders when they went abroad. Thus handicapped, they were beaten before the Games began.'

The Referee blamed Australia's parochial selection process. 'Whether we like it or not, the British and Dominion sportsmen made a very poor showing in Berlin. Australia, indeed, achieved the unenviable distinction of being near the bottom of the list. The Australian team was surely not the best we could offer for competition in world Games but that is no excuse in the eyes of the world for the humiliating defeats it suffered. However if Australia will only learn from this bitter experience, defeat will not have been in vain. The first and principal lesson of the Berlin Games is that for sport to evolve, modern world champions must be organised on a national basis . . . The moral is that if Australia hopes to compete with success in future Olympiads there must be more co-ordination of effort, and even recognition by the govern-ments—Federal and State—of the importance that sport is playing in raising the status of the modern nation.'

The post mortem continued with cycling authority Claude Spencer complaining that Dunc Gray should have been chosen to contest the sprints, the 1000m time trial and the 1000m scratch sprint, leaving Tassie Johnson to concentrate on the 100km road race. Also, at a time when cyclists around the world were cultivating a faster 'jump', the Australian sprinters had neglected this aspect of racing. And while variable gears were allowed in international cycling events they were banned in Australian racing, so Chris Wheeler had been unfamiliar with the mechanism. Had there been a designated Australian cycling coach to check Wheeler's gears before the 100km road race, the mechanical fault that had brought him unstuck would have been identified and rectified.

The rowing had been lamentable, and the pundits insisted that in future the eight best rowers, rather than the most successful club team, be chosen and blended into a cohesive crew. Rowing authority Sid Middleton said that the NSW Police eight was 'the best club combination in Sydney but they could have been strengthened by the inclusion of men from other clubs in a composite crew. If the selection had been in the hands of the

Rowing Association instead of the Police, three and possibly four of the Berlin Olympics crew would have been replaced.' The main factor in the selection of the eight had been that they would pay their own way (with more than a little help from taxpayers) and sending them cost the AOF no money. There was praise for double scullers Herb Turner and Bill Dixon, who performed meritoriously despite Dixon having hardly sculled before.

'Australia today has faded into insignificance,' summed up swimming writer 'The Captain'. Great technical advances in sport were taking place overseas and we were being left far behind, our outdoor life and climate our only saving graces. Amateur attitudes were out of date. Whether for swimmers, runners, cyclists or boxers, being content to make up the numbers was no longer enough. There had to be instilled in the Australians the desire to be the best. While he was in London, Jesse Owens had been asked why the American athletes at the Berlin Olympics had fared so much better than the British—and by extension other British Empire competitors—and his remarks were picked over in Australia. 'You have splendid material, but you seem to lie down. You don't concentrate. If your boys were to take athletics as seriously as the American boys do there is no reason why you shouldn't do as well. While British athletes go into training for only short spells and do as they please for the rest of the year, they can't expect to compete with the boys who devote themselves to sport the whole time. The British won't be bothered, that's the difference.' The competitors Owens feared most in Berlin had been his own countrymen. 'If I knew I could beat the Americans I knew I could beat the world.'

Alderson thought Owens' comments flew in the face of Olympism. Competing in Berlin had made him aware that the attitude of the competitors of the British Empire differed greatly from that of the nations which won the most medals: 'if we wanted to rise to their level, we would have to abandon the tenets of Olympism that Australian sportsmen and women have always lived by, and is the price of succeeding in the modern Olympics worth it?' Alderson was sure that it wasn't.

'As the British Empire Games will be held in Sydney early in 1938,' he continued, 'this should prove an excellent time for a full discussion on the question of amateurism; and furthermore whether Great Britain and its Dominions are prepared to regard sport and the Games as of national importance and concern, otherwise I am afraid we cannot expect a great measure of success against nations which have already made the Olympic Games and sport of national importance, not merely by providing the means for their athletes to be properly coached and trained, but by . . . educating both athlete and the public in the belief that success at the Games was an outward sign of the strength and courage of the nation.' Government and corporate financial support to athletes, such as had been enjoyed by the German, American and Japanese competitors, according 'to our amateur definition was tantamount . . . to professionalism'.

In all their public statements after arriving back in Australia, Alderson and the athletes were unanimous that staunchly maintaining amateur status and competing in a fair and friendly way—the way the nations of the British Empire had always competed—was more important than following the win-at-all-costs route of the nations that covered themselves in glory, and medals, in Berlin.

Alderson told a press conference in Sydney, 'The nations overseas, or most of them at any rate, have divested sport of its amateur spirit and made it a business. We in Australia cannot compete with them in their intensive organisation, in the vast sums of money they are prepared to spend to ensure success, in the facilities they provide for their athletes to reach world class, or in their fierce determination to win at all costs. Nor do I think we need to. If Australia wishes to win Olympic honours, it can only be done by following the lead of the nations that now lead in sport. I truly believe that our conception of the amateur spirit is truer than that of any nation outside the British Empire, and it is my opinion that we should do everything in our power to keep that spirit alive.'

As an example of the lengths Germany had gone to in their bid for success, Alderson cited the example of Germany's Reichssportführer Tschammer und Osten. 'His rank would be equal to that of one of our cabinet ministers. He is paid a salary in the vicinity of 4000 pounds a year and lives in a mansion compared with which any Government House in Australia would look like a cottage. That official was the head of a huge organisation that dealt only with sport and the preparation for sport. His authority was nationwide. Well, Germany got results, but it was not sport as we know it. The real [amateur] atmosphere was missing. I don't think any Australian would welcome it.'

The following month, Alderson dropped a bombshell: he proposed that Australia should turn its back on the Olympics and concentrate instead on the British Empire Games. Far from the Olympic Games promoting international amity and goodwill, 'the Games now cause international strife, ill-will and bitterness. There are no longer Olympic Games, but international contests in which the different nations regard the results and conduct of contestants as a serious national matter. It is only in the British Empire Games that the amateur status of [Olympism] is genuinely recognised. In most of the other teams, the semblance of amateurism is scarcely maintained.'

Alderson's remarks angered AOF chairman James Taylor, who dressed down the manager. While conceding that other countries had outstripped Australia as a sporting nation and that Germany was 'mass producing' champions, he ridiculed Alderson's suggestion that Australia turn its back on the Olympics. 'As for suggestions that we should withdraw from the Games . . . as one of the pioneer [Olympic] nations, such a thought is a slur on our manhood.'

Taylor's ire caused Alderson's career no lasting harm. Rather than abandoning the Olympics, for the rest of his life he worked tirelessly as a respected senior athletics and rowing administrator, espousing the values of fair and friendly amateur competition, to ensure that the Olympics of Coubertin prevailed over those of Hitler, the manic nationalists, the 'shamateurs' and, in later Olympiads, the marketing opportunists. Today it's clear that he only partially succeeded, but his valiant efforts did not go unnoticed or unrewarded. Alderson received an MBE for managing the 1936 Olympic team, and was knighted in 1956 on the eve of the Melbourne Olympic Games for his pivotal role in winning them for Australia. Till the day he died, in 1978, he always said that the biggest thrill in his life was managing the Australian team in Berlin.

In his fine 1994 history, *Australia and the Olympic Games*, Harry Gordon backed Alderson in ascribing the 1936 team's lacklustre showing to Australia's inadequate facilities, and lamented the lack of specialist coaches, recalling that Fred Woodhouse had taught himself to pole vault from reading a four-and-sixpenny manual and using a backyard clothes prop as his vaulting pole, and Doris Carter also learned to high jump in her backyard by leaping over a carpenter's trestle. 'The truth,' wrote Gordon, 'was that the Berlin experience exposed the sheer innocence of Australian sport.'

It's fair to say that Australian sport learned from its mistakes. At the 1938 Sydney Empire Games, although there was no Owens or Mastenbroek to contend with, Australia won the most medals with 66 (25 gold, 19 silver and 22 bronze), ahead of Canada with 44 and England with 40. Some 17 of the 33 Australian Berlin

Olympians were selected. Of them, the most successful were gold medallists Jack Metcalfe (hop, step and jump), Dunc Gray (1000m match sprint), Ron Masters (3m springboard), Cec Pearce (double scull), Herb Turner (single scull), Percy Oliver (110yd backstroke), Pat Norton (110yd backstroke), Evelyn de Lacy (110yd freestyle), and the wrestlers Dick Garrard (68kg freestyle) and Eddie Scarf (90kg freestyle). Silver medals were claimed by Gerald Backhouse (the mile), Tassie Johnson (1km time trial), Masters (10m platform), Norton and de Lacy (members of the 440yd relay). The Australian bronze medal winners were Basil Dickinson (broad jump and hop, step and jump), Alf Watson (member of the 4x110yd relay), boxer Les Harley (91kg division), Oliver (110yd freestyle), Norton and de Lacy (members of the 330yd medley relay), and Metcalfe in the javelin. The general consensus of the Australians was that competing in Berlin had made them better athletes, and in response to the poor Berlin results and Alderson's crusade, freshwater Olympic-style pools and cinder tracks were becoming available in each state. Why, some of the athletes were even receiving coaching. They couldn't wait to take on the world again in two years at the Tokyo Games.

Thanks to the hosts of the Berlin Olympics, there would be no Olympic Games until 1948, when London staged the Summer Games of the XIVth Olympiad. Australia would win two gold, six silver and five bronze medals. By 1956, when Melbourne hosted the Games, cinder tracks, freshwater pools and expert coaching were commonplace, and Australia's medal haul of thirteen gold, eight silver and fourteen bronze—the third highest in the medal tally—reflected these advances. Australia has been an Olympic powerhouse ever since. Had Alderson been around to see the Sydney Olympics of 2000—by which time his country was a world leader in sporting facilities and reaped 16 gold medals, 25 silver and 17 bronze, and placed fourth in the medal tally—he would have been proud. Today, with such organisations as the Australian Institute of Sport and the Australian Olympic Committee leading the way, it is unlikely that the mistakes of 1936 could be repeated. Australian Olympians are in good hands.

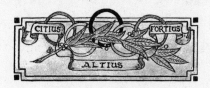

CHAPTER 18
FINISH LINES

The voyage home from Europe in August and September was the last time the Olympians of 1936 were all together. The paths of some continued to cross into their old age. Others never laid eyes on teammates again.

Mooltan docked in Fremantle on Tuesday, 22 September, and Evelyn de Lacy and Percy Oliver disembarked. Between then and 1 October, the liner would offload the other athletes and officials at Adelaide, Melbourne and Sydney. At Fremantle, in a scene to be repeated at the other ports, reporters grilled the Olympians about their great adventure. 'I cannot say enough about the team,' enthused de Lacy. 'We were one big happy family.' She was glad to be home in Western Australia, 'the best state in the best country in the world!' Despite the results, they'd had the time of their lives. As a treat, Oliver's father organised a picnic for the Olympians in a wildflower reserve. At the end of the day, they farewelled their teammates.

Percy Oliver took a job in Kalgoorlie. One day, after his Empire Games gold medal triumph in Sydney in 1938, while diving into the Kalgoorlie pool he hit a lower board and hurt his back. Pain from the injury would last his lifetime, but didn't slow him down. At the Australian Championships in 1940, the 21-year-old won seven events, including every men's freestyle title, the 110yd backstroke and the medley. A virtual one-man team for Western Australia, he won the Barney Kieran Shield for the state with the highest number of first placings. That was his competitive swimming swan song.

Oliver was recruited for the army in 1940. After training at a transport school in Geelong, he taught soldiers to ride horses in army camps at Northam and Karrakatta. He was selected for officer training school, but his back injury, which prevented him from carrying a pack, disqualified him from essential infantry fieldwork. Meanwhile he married, and while with his wife Pat at their home in Perth's Victoria Park on a weekend leave pass, he was stricken by appendicitis that came close to killing him. After being turned away from the field doctor's office in the army barracks because no one was on duty, he finally made it to hospital. He recalled, 'It was about to burst. If it had, it would have been the end of me . . . I was in hospital for a couple of weeks with swelling and bleeding, a haematoma.' Oliver was unable to contact his barracks while hospitalised and so was charged with being AWOL. When he was well enough he returned to barracks, and all was forgiven. He was discharged from service on medical grounds in 1942. After training at Perth Tech, Oliver worked as a machinery fitter, making wheel bearings for Bren gun carriers, and then shells at a munitions factory in North Perth. For a time towards the end of the war, he maintained aircraft engines. 'A chequered wartime career, but it paid the bills,' he said.

At the end of hostilities, Oliver became an advisory physical education teacher and travelled to schools all over Perth and in the south-west of the state. In 1954 he was required to obtain formal qualifications at teacher's college and returned to study at the age of 35. He then taught at Mount Lawley Senior High School and Hollywood High until 1968. Then, he said, 'I was appointed the Education Department's first full-time swimming officer, coaching and administration, and stayed in that role for eleven years until I retired. In the Perth metropolitan area alone, I had 22,000 kids a week swimming, and another 18,000 all over the state. I gave demonstration swims for children into my sixties.'

Oliver sailed his father's boat *Iris* and in time became commodore of Royal Freshwater Bay Yacht Club. He and Pat had daughters Brenda and Anita. Brenda Oliver-Harry says that her father did not often speak about his Berlin Olympics experience— 'For him, once it was over, it was over. Life goes on. Being a champion swimmer was just something that he was in his youth. Everyone asked him about it, and he'd show them his medals, but it wasn't a defining factor in his life. He took satisfaction from coaching, and his greatest achievement was being a good husband and father.

'Competitive sport was Percy's life,' says Brenda. 'He had many sporting interests other than swimming and sailing and was a high achiever in all of them. As a young man he played football for Claremont Amateurs and later was a committed golfer (he scored a hole in one), and played competition snooker and bowls. He was made a life member of many sporting organisations.'

Brenda says that her father taught her and Anita 'to be a doer, not a spectator. He instilled a strong ethic of what was right and that if you put your mind to something you could master it. Life with Dad was filled with sport, fun and outdoors.'

Oliver was not a traveller. Post-1936, he never left Australia again, and after the 1938 Empire Games ventured to Sydney only once. In 2000, the 81-year-old—white-haired now but trim and handsome with an erect bearing and a neatly clipped moustache—travelled with Brenda to Sydney for the Olympic Games. 'Our trip,' says Brenda, 'included corporate hospitality and access to the Olympians Club, which allowed him to meet Olympians. Comparing notes with the current champions was a highlight for Dad. We weren't there during the swimming. We *were* in the front row of the home straight when Cathy Freeman won her nation-stopping 400m race. I have never seen Dad so excited. He was whooping and laughing and crying. Perhaps it brought back memories of his own Olympic and Empire Games experience . . . On 26 September, Dad was a guest of honour at a dinner at NSW Parliament House for pre-war Olympians. It was a special reunion.' At the reunion were 1936 alumni Basil Dickinson, Pat Norton, Merv Wood, Dick Garrard and Bill Kendall, all elderly now, and the memories of their Olympics flowed until late. Oliver had hoped his old friend Evelyn de Lacy would attend. Sadly, she did not.

Over the next decade Oliver's health declined due to an enlarged aorta, and on 9 July 2011 he died aged 92.

Some who knew Evelyn de Lacy, or Evelyn Whillier as she became after marriage in 1940, weren't surprised when she boycotted the pre-war Olympians dinner at NSW Parliament House in 2000. Over the years, the bubbly Berlin diarist soured on the Games. She was turned off by the commercialism and pumped-up patriotism that she believed was marring the modern Games. Says her grandson, Warren Whillier, 'Whenever anyone asked her about her exploits in Berlin and at the Sydney Empire Games, she'd close them down by saying, "That was another life." All she ever said to me about the Berlin Olympics was that she loved being there, seeing how the people lived, and she thought the stage-managed Hitler propaganda was funny and that he was an insignificant little man. She felt privileged to have seen Jesse Owens run.'

Like Oliver, Evelyn didn't bask in her Olympic experiences but locked them away in a compartment in her heart and mind to which only she had the key. She moved on to new things, and whatever she did, she did well and at full tilt. Once she had children and then grandchildren her focus shifted to them. If it was put to her that she must have been disappointed never to have competed in another Olympics after Berlin—she would have been 22 and in her swimming prime at Tokyo, had it happened—she would shrug: 'War came, put an end to that, and I got married instead.'

Ironically, after being one of the most unflappable competitors in Berlin, on returning de Lacy suffered badly from nerves. She would be overwhelmed by negative thoughts and tremble before big races. She won the gold medal in the 110yd freestyle yet was stressed throughout the Sydney Empire Games, and her state of mind wasn't helped when she was carpeted by team management for failing to march in the grand parade of competitors at Sydney Cricket Ground. She had strained her back and thought that standing all day in ranks and tramping around the oval would worsen her injury. She confided in coach J.P. Sheedy, who sympathised but did not defend her. Her only supporter was her Sydney bricklayer boyfriend Albert Whillier.

When the pair became engaged, de Lacy told Sheedy that she intended to move to Sydney after they married in 1940 and would then swim for New South Wales. Sheedy accused her of betraying him and Western Australian swimming and ordered her to remain in Western Australia. She went to Sydney anyway, and would live there with Albert and their children, Lynette, Richard and Christine, for the rest of her days.

Evelyn retired from competitive swimming in 1943, and became a swimming teacher at Bronte baths and the Woollahra pool. 'She was a very giving woman and I loved her very much,' says Warren

Whillier. 'She looked after me when my dad Richard died of a heart condition when I was six and she became my legal guardian, but she became blinkered and, I suppose, hard. She had an iron will. Until she was in her seventies, she rose at 5 a.m. every day, summer and winter, walked to the Bronte pool—the council gave her a key to enter and turn the lights on—swam 30 laps and then walked home again. If she wasn't in the water every day she didn't feel right. She *had* to swim and she had a beautiful style till the end. She was very tall and glided through the water. She still had a faceful of freckles.

'Decade after decade, generation after generation, she taught children to swim, every Saturday for three hours, three or four kids at a time, and did a lot of private coaching around the area. She taught a lot of the older European women in the area to swim, and they had the council erect a plaque in honour of Nan on the promenade at Bronte. I was her guinea pig; she'd drag me out of the surf and make me do breaststroke and butterfly for her pupils. She was tough on me, and on them. She had an amazing eye and could identify and correct faults. I had no interest in competitive swimming but she made me have a try. She told me I had swimming ability but mentally I was lacking and that most of success is mental, focusing and putting everything out of your mind. When I'd daydream and my gaze would wander out to the waves, wishing I was surfing and not swimming in a pool, she'd clip me on the ear.'

Evelyn became a colourful local identity, with her loud voice, brusque manner, her big hat and wetsuit skivvy to protect her fair complexion from the sun. Former swimming pupils were always approaching her and wishing her well. She was special to them. In her stern presence, these adults became kids again. She wrote for seniors magazines, exhorting the elderly to get outdoors and be active, and in her seventies she proved more than a match for the WA Swimming Hall of Fame when they borrowed her medals to display after her induction and forgot to return them. 'Nan got them back,' says Warren Whillier.

Her daughter Lynette was the Australian 220yd breaststroke champion in 1954 and 1955, and Evelyn was the great-aunt of Sally Foster, who swam breaststroke for Australia at the London Olympics in 2012 and who was inspired by her Berlin diary.

Evelyn was being true to her principles when she declined to attend the pre-war Olympians dinner at NSW Parliament House. As she poignantly wrote to the authors of *A Proper Spectacle*, 'My life changed after my Olympic experience. I went away mentally a child and came back mentally a woman. I am disappointed with the Olympic Games these days. It's become a corporate affair, it's too expensive for ordinary Australians. I'll be very happy to see the end of it, as I believe the Olympic movement will collapse within itself.'

Evelyn and Albert Whillier lived a happy 64 years together. They died just nine weeks apart, in 2004. Says Warren Whillier, 'The day we buried my grandfather, Nan said to us, "I think I've got cancer," and she died nine weeks later. If Nan had died first, Pop wouldn't have lasted even nine weeks, they were so close. He relied on her and they loved each other deeply.' When she died, aged 87, Warren took his grandmother's ashes to Perth and joined with her surviving siblings to scatter them in the waters of the Swan River where she'd learned to swim.

For all her history in the west, her home was Sydney's Bronte. When asked why, she replied, 'The beach, the smell of the surf and the sea, the walk back through the park . . . what more could you want in life?'

In 1936, after a day of relaxation in Adelaide, *Mooltan* sailed to Melbourne, where Ron Masters, Alf Watson, Chris Wheeler,

Tassie Johnson, Les Harley and Gerald Backhouse disembarked. 'The Germans were wonderful to us,' enthused Masters, wearing loud checked plus-fours. He told the media, 'It seemed they were keener to look after the Australians than anyone. We were given everything we wanted and the Games were a triumph of organisation. It took us a while to get used to the number of uniformed men everywhere, but despite this we could see the wonderful way in which the youth of Germany is organised and how keen they are to add to their country's welfare.'

Backhouse wondered aloud how, if the Olympics was amateur sport, many of the competitors from other countries were able to train intensively for months before the Games without losing their wages. 'It would be good,' he said, 'if a similar system could operate here, but how it would dovetail with strict amateurism I don't know . . .'

Backhouse lived and trained and competed as he pleased. And perhaps having a sixth sense of what the future held for him, he partied as if there was no tomorrow. Things befell him. He was mauled by a lion in February 1939, when, after winning his silver medal in the mile at the Sydney Empire Games, he voyaged across the Tasman Sea to compete in an athletics competition in New Zealand. The Australian athletes were sharing the steamer with a travelling circus, and Backhouse patted the lion through the bars of its cage. The lion lashed out and clawed his arm badly.

When war broke out, buoyed by his spirit of adventure and his strong religious faith, Backhouse continued to live dangerously. He joined the Royal Australian Air Force in February 1940, and after learning to fly fighter planes, Sergeant Backhouse sailed to England in October 1941 to train for combat with the Royal Air Force.

On 13 January 1942, a telegram arrived at the home of Gerald's brother. The Royal Air Force wrote to advise that Sergeant Gerald Ian D'Acres Backhouse had been killed on 20 December 1941 in an aircraft accident. He had just turned 29. To honour him, his old running club St Stephen's Harriers added a new event to their calendar, a 10,000m race; the winner to be presented with the Gerald Backhouse Memorial Shield.

As *Mooltan* plied its way to Sydney, those who had chosen not to make the voyage were busy at work—the NSW Police rowers in London—or holidaying: Doris Carter in England, Bill Kendall, Dick Garrard and Jack O'Hara in the United States.

The rowers were learning the intricacies of policing, London-style. If true to form, they would have been playing as hard as they toiled. Only one of them would continue to row at the highest level on their return to Australia. Merv Wood, just nineteen when he was the baby of the eight in Berlin, has claims to being Australia's most illustrious Olympian. He competed at four Olympic Games. As well as Berlin, he rowed at the 1948 London Olympics, the 1952 Helsinki Games and, aged 39, at the Melbourne Olympics of 1956. He won a gold medal in the single sculls in London, silver in the same event in Helsinki and bronze in the double sculls in Melbourne. He is the only athlete to be Australia's flag-bearer at two Olympics: Helsinki and Melbourne. He won four gold medals and one silver at British Empire/Commonwealth Games, and was an eight-time Australian national sculling champion. In his other life, as a policeman, he rose to be police commissioner of NSW.

Wood was interviewed about his time in Berlin and reflected, 'Until 1936, sports used to be not more than pastimes, but suddenly you could see what a critical role training played. You could see that the human body could be forced to do better. In some sports, the professional kind of sports, people had always trained hard. But in others they had just dabbled. One of the reasons the Australians didn't do well was that they were not putting a total effort into sport, they were still regarding it as a pastime. And transport was an awful problem. They were coming from the other side of the world on a boat for five or six weeks, losing their condition, then trying to compete against superbly conditioned athletes.'

It was after marvelling at the crack German scullers in Berlin, and especially single sculls gold medallist Gustav Schäfer, that Wood decided he would quit rowing in eights and become a sculler. (The reported constant bickering and brawling among the policemen may also have had something to do with strictly-by-the-book Wood's decision.) 'In that one season I went from maiden sculler to NSW champion. I don't think that's been done before.' Throughout his sculling career, Wood never had a coach.

In the 1950s he would write that he could see the day when 'professionalism', 'amateurism' and 'shamateurism' 'are words that no longer exist', as regards sport. In time, he predicted, every sportsperson would be what we now call a professional. 'It's well-known that some countries give their so-called amateur athletes grand rewards, money, houses, all sorts of things . . . in Australia we know nothing of this world, officially anyway. In the years to come we won't be able to stay remote if we want to succeed. Australia will have to treat its athletes as other countries treat theirs, look after them, pay them to compensate for the careers they are missing out on while training and competing for nothing.' He believed that Coubertin's 1896 vision of the Olympics had been dashed. 'There is a good argument that the present Olympic Games do more harm than good. They are too big, too corrupted by nationalism and politics.'

Nicknamed 'the Cary Grant of rowing', Wood married in 1942, shortly before he served in the RAAF. His wife Betty said that he rarely spoke about himself and it was ages after they met before she even knew he was an Olympian. No family member can recall him so much as mentioning the 1936 Olympics. 'Dad was Dad,' remembers his son John Wood. 'He was not what you'd call a regular father. The only time he ever babysat my brother and me, I hit my brother on the head with a golf club. That was enough for Dad. His babysitting days were over. Mum's role was to look after the children. Dad rowed and worked. He was a fine detective. Although he never discussed them with us, I know that there were aspects of police work he didn't enjoy, the enemies you inevitably make, the phone calls in the middle of night, the forensic work with corpses . . .'

When, in later years, Wood was asked to tell of his more remarkable experiences, his pride in defending the World Single Sculling Championship in Philadelphia in 1950 helped him overcome a lifelong reluctance to talk about himself. 'Having won the gold medal at the Olympics in 1948,' he wrote in his diary, 'I was recognised as the world single sculling champion, and Jack Kelly, the brother of Princess Grace of Monaco who was a fine sculler, challenged me for the world title. He had already won a Diamond Sculls and in 1949 won the European sculling title. This gave him credentials to challenge me. Now, as the holder of the world championship, I could have nominated the venue but Jack put out the old carrot and said, "Now, if you'll come to America and row against me on my home ground in Philadelphia, all expenses will be paid and your trainer or your wife can come to America with you." . . . I'm happy to recall that I was fortunate on that occasion to defend successfully my world title.' Years later, when Wood was honoured on TV's *This Is Your Life*, Jack Kelly paid his own way to fly to Sydney to sing his old rival's praises. Wood received the Member of the British Empire (MBE) in 1957 for his services to rowing.

After he retired from competitive sculling in 1958, Wood's brains and doggedness propelled him quickly through police ranks. He became a detective and a fingerprint expert who pioneered new techniques for identifying decomposed bodies and helped to solve high-profile murder cases. In 1975 he was named NSW assistant police commissioner, then in 1977, commissioner. That year he was summoned to a private audience with the Queen on the royal yacht *Britannia*, where she presented him with an LVO (Lieutenant of the Royal Victorian Order), given to those who have given distinguished personal service to the sovereign. Sadly, Wood's tenure as commissioner was turbulent and short, lasting only until 1979. He was dogged by criticism from political enemies and foes within the force that he turned a blind eye to organised crime. And he was tainted by his association with Murray Riley, a fellow policeman who was his 1956 Olympic double sculls partner and friend but went bad and became a drug dealer. It was said that Wood's old-school style of policing was outdated. Wood resigned after being charged with perverting the course of justice in the case of two drug dealers. After a decade's argument, he was committed to stand trial in 1989; then two years later the district court ruled that there was no need for him to do so.

The stress took a toll on the now white-haired and thin ex-athlete, who grew even more taciturn than he was when young. He bottled things up. Son John believes 'the pressure made him ill after a lifetime of good health'. In his final years Wood had operations to remove his spleen and gall bladder and suffered blood clots in his legs. Then came the cancer that would kill him, but not before he ran with the Olympic Torch through his home suburb of Maroubra before the 2000 Sydney Games. 'I was proud of my dad, and I still am,' says John. 'He would have been happier not being the top policeman. He would have been content to sit back and do what he was good at and let others take the limelight, but he answered the call. Dad was a remarkable man, and he had a remarkable life.'

When Wood died aged 89 on 19 August 2006, the Australian rowing team was competing in the World Championships at Eton in England. The day the news broke, the Australians won seven out of their eight races, and dedicated the victories to him.

Another member of the rowing eight had a distinguished career in the force before a tragic end. Don Fergusson, whose mother Mary was the women athletes' chaperone in Berlin and father George was an inspector of police who also travelled with the team, worked his way from beat cop to chief of the Criminal Investigation Bureau. Described as articulate and well dressed, with 'nerves of steel', Fergusson was just weeks away from being appointed metropolitan superintendent of police when, on 15 February 1970, he apparently committed suicide in the toilet of his office at Sydney police headquarters. Colleagues found his service pistol by the body and a note revealing that he was suffering from incurable brain cancer. Investigators ruled out suspicious circumstances, which has not prevented speculation ever since that Fergusson was murdered.

And what of the wild man of the rowing eight, Wal Mackney? 'Age never mellowed my father,' says his son Kim Mackney.

In the 1930s and '40s, Mackney was a much-feared policeman. His son says he was known as 'a nasty bastard, a mercenary for the state. His superiors would say to him, "Take your uniform off and go down and clean that place out."' He liked to wade into a street melee, winding wrongdoers by jabbing his truncheon into their solar plexus, flailing his fists, and making skin, hair and blood fly. Mackney's career in the police force did not end well. Kim Mackney tells how his father refused orders to stop pursuing a certain criminal. 'I don't know if he resigned or was sacked. I do know he sat the police commissioner on his arse. He liked to say, "You know why there's no Mafia in Sydney? Because the blue shirts [the police] run all the crime."'

For a while Mackney donned a mask and wrestled as a villain at Sydney Stadium, then bought market gardening land in Sydney's north and grew vegetables and flowers. He opened a corner store, and loaned money to needy people, keeping all the records in his head. 'After he died, my mother and I had no clue who owed us what,' says Kim.

Mackney's store came under threat in the mid-1950s when the Fairfax newspaper company threatened to sell its papers through alternative outlets. On the verge of going broke, Mackney swallowed his pride and sought help from his old boxing foe Frank Packer, who by then was chairman of Australian Consolidated Press. 'My father and Packer *hated* each other,' recalls Kim. 'Apart from fighting in the ring, they had a memorable back alley brawl in The Rocks that ended in a draw when neither man could continue. My father's business must have been at crisis point, and I can remember when I was five or six, Dad sitting at his desk at home and telephoning Australian Consolidated Press. "I want to talk to Packer. Tell him it's Mackney." There was a short wait, then, "G'day . . . the business with Fairfax . . . yeah . . . yeah . . . right." Then *click*. Mum asked, "What's happening?" and Dad said, "He'll fix it." Packer was true to his word. My old man went to his grave resenting that he'd had to accept Packer's help.'

Mackney, says his son, was a communist in the sense that he lived by 'the Christian ethos of doing the right thing by the masses'. In his forties, when he was still playing rugby for Northern Suburbs, he and his teammate Eric Bardsley were censured by the club for supporting the sending of food parcels to Russia. Both men quit the club in protest (and Mackney married Bardsley's sister). 'My father hated fascists,' says Kim. 'He very nearly went to fight in the Spanish Civil War with the International Brigade after he returned from the 1936 Games. He was not a man who communicated easily, and never said much about being at those Olympics, certainly nothing about the brawls the Australian rowers are supposed to have had with other teams, or about Hitler or Goebbels, and he was at close quarters to them. About all he told us was how he'd stolen a flag from a sleeping German officer, and he added, "I could have had his gun, too, if I'd wanted it." He did admit to being impressed with the German rowers.'

Kim Mackney admired his father, despite learning when young 'to stay away from him. He had a volcanic temper. He would erupt and there seemed no rationale to his anger. The first time I kissed my father [was when] he was dead.'

Mackney literally ate himself to death. 'My father *over*-enjoyed food,' says Kim. 'Looking at him from behind you'd think he was a thin man, but from the side you could see his big, hard midriff. He ate animals from top to bottom. As a country lad, he'd learned not to waste any part of a beast. Mum had a big pot to keep the fat from the meat she cooked, the dripping. The blood settled at the bottom of the pot, and Dad cut huge door-stops of bread with his knife and dug down to the dripping and spread it on the bread. The blood drooled down his chin. He had a special relationship with the local butchers, so they sold him huge 50mm thick T-bone steaks too big to fit on any plate. The fat was like a mountain bike tyre. He ate the lot, and sucked all the marrow from the bone. He died at 72. He could have lived a lot longer if he'd just put the knife and fork down.'

Doris Carter returned to Victoria from her European sightseeing trip following the Olympics to teach at Moreland Central State

School. Carter, who would never marry or have children, was appointed to the Victorian State Schools Athletics Association committee. Her hopes set on representing Australia at the 1938 Empire Games, she also continued to compete at the highest level in high jump and discus, remaining Australian champion in the former and setting new records in each. Her national high jump record of 1.609m, set in 1936, stood for twenty years. She also played hockey for Victoria and Australia.

In 1941, with World War II being waged, Carter joined the Women's Auxiliary Australian Air Force (WAAAF), which supplied women to do the work of male personnel serving overseas. All her life, Carter had blazed trails. She was the first Australian woman to qualify for an Olympic track and field final when she high-jumped at the Berlin Olympics; the first Australian woman to compete in athletics at an Olympics and a British Empire Games; and as chief instructor of WAAAF officer trainers, Wing-Commander Carter was the first Australian woman to serve on a warship and the first to fly a Canberra bomber and a Vampire jet.

Carter was assigned to London in 1946 as officer-in-charge of the WAAAF Victory Contingent, and for the next two years lent her administrative skills to helping Britons recover from the trauma and destruction of the conflict. That done, she accepted a three-year posting as officer-in-charge of child and youth immigration at Australia House in London. Small wonder that she was awarded an Order of the British Empire (OBE) in 1957. She returned to Australia in 1961 to be director of the Women's Royal Australian Air Force.

The Melbourne Olympics were staged in 1956, and as an Olympian, a proven leader, and member of the organising committee for Melbourne, she was the obvious choice to manage the Australian women's team. She may have smiled wryly when she learned that there were 44 women in the team, when in 1936 she had been one of just four. Australia's new-generation Olympians Betty Cuthbert, Dawn Fraser, Lorraine Crapp, Shirley Strickland and Marlene Mathews could have had no wiser or more understanding mentor. As she joined the 325 Australian athletes marching around the Melbourne Cricket Ground at the Opening Ceremony on 22 November, her 1936 teammate Merv Wood carrying the flag, her mind must have harked back to Berlin, when the VIPs were not Prince Philip, Prime Minister Robert Menzies and Governor-General Field Marshal Sir William Slim, but Hitler, Goebbels, Tschammer und Osten, Lewald, Diem and Baillet-Latour. The only survivor of the 1936 official party in 1956 was Avery Brundage.

There would be other honours in Carter's life. She served as general secretary of the YMCA, Melbourne; in 1963 was made a member of the board of trustees at the Australian War Memorial in Canberra; and in 1971 became a member of the National Fitness Council, Victoria. Yet she said that her greatest honour was, at 84, being chosen to head Melbourne's Anzac Day march in 1996. She was the first woman to lead the procession. Standing tall in the front seat of a jeep, her now grey but still wild and curly hair crowned by a wide-brimmed black hat, her jacket front weighed down by medals, and waving energetically to the crowd, she received the loudest cheer of all.

For some time, she had corresponded with the authors of *A Proper Spectacle*. In 1999, she wrote to them from the nursing home where she had lived for the past twelve years, hoping sincerely that next year's Sydney Olympic Games 'would be a huge success'. That was her last letter. Carter died on 28 July 1999.

Wrestlers Dick Garrard and Jack O'Hara were lucky to make it home to Melbourne after they parted company with their teammates and sailed to New York. Many years later, Garrard recounted their near-death experience to Harry Gordon. 'We bought an old Chrysler for the equivalent of 20 pounds in New York, and drove as far as Denver where we wrapped it around a pole. Jack finished up in hospital with a broken jaw and I was a mess too. [His doctor told him he would never wrestle again.] So we were in hospital, had very little money, no car, and needed to be in San Francisco (or Los Angeles, I've forgotten which) to catch our ship to Australia.' The resourceful Garrard left hospital to buy a car and found another Chrysler for the equivalent of nine Australian pounds. When Garrard and the rattletrap arrived in the hospital car park, O'Hara checked himself out with a broken jaw that was still wired, and the pair continued west. Somehow they arrived at the dock on time and boarded SS *Monterey*, bound for Hawaii and Sydney. 'When we arrived in Sydney we were stony broke so I borrowed a pound from an old mate . . . to get home to Melbourne.'

Had Garrard not survived the car smash in Denver, Australia would have been deprived of one of its finest sportsmen. In the punishing bone- and muscle-grinding world of wrestling, Garrard enjoyed success over many years. After he limped home from America, he continued to compete as a lightweight. He found that the best training was against heavier men, and he boosted his strength by becoming a champion weightlifter and increased his heart–lung capacity by competing for Victoria in the Australian Surf Life Saving Championships. His willingness to punish himself bore fruit at the Sydney Empire Games when he won the gold medal.

Neither the war nor his ageing body could slow down the terrier-like grappler. At 37, he placed second in the welterweight freestyle event at the London Olympics of 1948. At a reception for the Empire's athletes at Buckingham Palace, the Queen could not help remarking on Garrard's battered visage. Prince Philip, who understood that six bouts in three days were going to cause some facial injuries, explained, 'This man has just had a torrid time on the mat.' He followed his Olympic silver medal with a gold medal at the 1950 Auckland Empire Games and, at age 53, a bronze medal at the Vancouver Empire Games of 1954 (where he was flag-bearer).

Once likened to 'the old circus horse which just can't keep out of the ring when he hears the band', Garrard set his sights on wrestling at the 1956 Melbourne Olympics. After he dislocated his left shoulder in the trials, he decided to retire. 'My body is finally giving me the message,' he chuckled.

In his 30-year career of 483 contests, Garrard lost just nine and was Australian champion ten times. He took time off from his job as driver-manager of a taxi company to officiate in wrestling events at five Olympic Games and was manager of the wrestling team at the 1972 Munich Olympics. He mourned deeply when four wrestlers were among the eleven Israeli team members slain by Palestinian terrorists at the Munich Games. 'It was terrible, I couldn't comprehend it,' Garrard told Harry Gordon. 'After the massacre, everything went from gaiety to gloom. Before it happened, the boys and girls were all dancing and having fun together, afterwards it was lights out. Everything was miserable.'

For his efforts as a wrestler and administrator Garrard received an MBE in 1970 and an OBE six years later. In 1976 at the Montreal Olympics, the International Amateur Wrestling Federation gave him its highest award, the Grand Cross. Three years before his death aged 92 in 2003, he was awarded an Australian Sports Medal, and he remains the only wrestler inducted into the Australian Sports Hall of Fame. In 2000, Garrard carried the Olympic Torch through the streets of his hometown Geelong. His stoop was the legacy of numerous shattered ribs over many decades, and by then his hands were so gnarled by arthritis that it was hard for him to grasp the torch. He limped and needed to rest from time to time, but he battled on proudly. After lighting the community cauldron, he addressed the crowd. 'To walk down in front of all you people before I lit the cauldron is something I'll never forget. I'm a Geelong person, like all of you . . . I've been in a few Olympic teams and won a medal, but I'm just like you.'

'Jack Metcalfe and I remained friends until his death in 1994, when he was 82,' said Basil Dickinson in 2013. 'We stayed in contact by letter and phone. A constant refrain of our conversations was that the old Olympic ideals had changed, and not always for the better. How it seemed the only time the athletes of the world mingled these days was during the Closing Ceremony, when in the days before media intrusion and high-level security to thwart terrorism turned Olympic villages into fortresses we befriended fellow competitors. Jack also regretted the bungling that went on when we were hitting our straps as athletes in the 1920s and '30s. He resented the poor preparation of the 1936 Olympians. Jack wrote me a letter just before he died . . . and he said, "Basil, we might have all done so much better."'

While running a busy legal practice, Metcalfe continued to compete with some success at national athletics meets after the war, and at Sydney inter-club carnivals well into the 1950s, when he was in his forties. Intelligent, well-respected and devoted to athletics, he became an effective administrator. At the 1948 London Olympics he managed the male athletes, and joined Carter on the 1956 Melbourne Olympics organising committee; during the Games he was chief jumps referee. As an administrator and coach at state and national level, he exhibited an expertise and fair-mindedness that would have come in handy back in the parochial 1920s and '30s.

In the late 1930s, Metcalfe wrote a paper that was distributed to young athletes, telling them how to prepare for an athletics meet. Sound sleep on the nights before the event was a must, so too 'a good meal [of] eggs and underdone steak'. It is interesting to read his thoughts on stimulants. He warned 'the athlete against taking stimulants before his event. Most stimulants, such as brandy, have a very short effect which lasts but a few minutes and which is followed by a reaction which leaves the athlete worse off than before. The taking of the stimulant becomes a practice and even for that short-lived effect it has to be taken in increasing quantities and becomes harmful. Avoid it.'

Two years before his death, Metcalfe told Harry Gordon of the day he was coaching primary school children on an oval at Bermagui on the NSW south coast. 'I said to the kids, "I want you all to run around the oval and I'll watch your running style." After she had done her lap, I called over a youngster who had run all the way with her arms held tightly to her sides. With all the children gathered around me in a circle I gave them a talking-to on body posture, how you pump your arms in rhythm with your legs to help your drive forward. I asked the girl to run another lap and this time to try to follow my advice. She ran exactly the same way, with her arms glued to her sides. I brought them together again and gave a long lecture on the need for athletes to rid themselves of bad habits and adopt good ones that would make them run faster. "It all takes practice and time," I told them. At this point, another little girl came up to me and said, "Mr Metcalfe, she can't run the way you want. The elastic has broken in her shorts and if she doesn't hold them up they'll fall down!"'

Despite Metcalfe's kind and caring nature, he could be tough. To him, amateur track and field was the purest of sports, and he came down hard on anyone who sullied its name. When Frank Delaney, secretary of Sydney's Campbelltown Club, was found guilty of bringing the NSW Amateur Athletic Association into disrepute in 1949, other officials felt that a twelve-month suspension was an adequate penalty. Not Metcalfe, who demanded that Delaney be suspended for life. Proof of Metcalfe's stature as a giant of Australian track and field was that he received the Helms Award for the most outstanding figure in Australasian athletics twice, 21 years apart, in 1934 and 1955.

When he arrived back in Sydney after his world holiday, swimmer Bill Kendall thought hard about his performance in Berlin, and concluded that he wasn't meant to be a sprinter. Attending Harvard University in Boston, he benefited from its intensive training regime, and transformed into a 220m and 440m swimmer. He captained the prestigious university's freshman team. 'The back swimmer on our team was John F. Kennedy. He won his share of races too,' recalled Kendall in 1990 in *Mature Living* magazine.

Kendall was studying and working overseas when the Sydney Empire Games rolled around in 1938, and there was no Olympics in 1940, so he concentrated on his career. After two years at Harvard, he decided to be a geologist, then realised that his future lay in the Sydney steel-making factory his father had co-founded. To gain experience he went to England and worked for a year in a steel plant. After his father died, 26-year-old Kendall returned to Sydney and took charge of the company.

Kendall married and became a father, followed the Olympics and the Commonwealth Games, and after he retired, aged 60, swam year-round at the idyllic Sydney Harbour tidal pool at Nielsen Park. 'He was not a flashy man,' says his daughter, Brooke Ryan. 'He was from another era, humble and stylish.'

Thirty years after the Games, Kendall's Japanese opponents visited Australia and he invited them to the exclusive Cabbage Tree Club at Sydney's Palm Beach. Brooke Ryan says there was 'an incident that mortified Dad. When they arrived at the club, his guests were informed that, being Japanese, they were not welcome.'

Kendall was a good advertisement for an active old age until he suffered a stroke. 'He lingered for a week unconscious, and then passed away,' says Brooke Ryan. 'He had no regrets. What a life he had.' She has some of her father's precious mementoes in her safekeeping: the photograph signed for him by Johnny Weissmuller, a photo of Kendall taken in Berlin by Leni Riefenstahl, and a telegram his father sent him on the eve of his Olympic event telling him to be sure to have Epsom salts and a big, juicy steak before he swam. Sadly, some of Bill's medals were stolen when his daughter's home was burgled. 'That's about my only regret,' she says, 'along with Dad not being able to compete in 1940 in Tokyo when he would have been in his prime. Bloody Hitler.'

On 1 October 1936, two months to the day after the Berlin Opening Ceremony, when the athletes disembarked *Mooltan* in Sydney, Pat Norton told reporters she hoped that Berlin would be only the first of many Olympic Games for her and how she was counting the days until Tokyo in four years' time. 'I'll still be only 21,' she chirped.

At Circular Quay, Kitty Mackay told how she had been amazed by how hard the foreign athletes trained and that some of the 'coloured athletes had been primed up like race horses'. And, echoing coach Harry Nightingale, in swimming, 'style was bunkum!' The most beautiful athletes at the Games, she observed as the reporters jotted down her thoughts, were the Dutch swimmer Willy den Ouden, Jeannette Campbell from Argentina and the disgraced Eleanor Holm. German girls, she concluded, 'were very healthy but as far as appearance went, had little individuality'. And as far as she was concerned, no foreign men could compete with Australian men for good looks and physique.

When Kitty Mackay disembarked *Mooltan* that first day of October 1936, clamouring reporters wanted to know her impression of Hitler and she replied that 'he looks just like an ordinary man . . . You'd never know he was a dictator. He seems very fond of children and was always patting them on the head. Whenever we saw him he was in uniform and had a large guard around him. Certainly he inspires the German people. For instance, when we asked the German girls whether Hitler was likely to marry, they reverently replied, "Hitler is married to his country. He has no time for love."' She did notice, however, that while Germans seemed enamoured of Hitler, Göring and Goebbels, when she had tried to get them to talk about their leaders they seemed 'afraid to talk'. Perhaps they had been ordered not to, 'and orders are orders in Germany'.

On returning from Berlin, tall, elegant, life-loving Mackay continued swimming for a year, recording freestyle and back-stroke wins and losses over her friends and rivals Norton and de Lacy. She would have qualified for the Empire Games in 1938, but her heart was elsewhere. In July 1937 she announced that she would marry Bondi lifesaver and Australian surf team representative Bruce Hodgson the following year, and promptly retired from competitive swimming. Their wedding was a Sydney social event. In 1939, she gave birth to a son, Robert. She died in 1974, aged 59.

Disembarking from *Mooltan*, Harry Alderson typically was a good sport in his quay-side remarks: 'We have been far from disgraced. We have all done our best. We went down fighting, beaten by better people training under very different conditions than Australia.' He had no doubt that the Berlin Olympics were 'the greatest festival of sport ever held in the history of the world'.

One wealthy sportsman who travelled with the team to Berlin and found himself on the end of a microphone when *Mooltan* docked in Sydney had only good things to say about the Führer and his New Germany. James A. Burke, a gullible victim of Nazi propaganda if ever there was one, felt Hitler was misunderstood. 'Most of the stories about him are wrong,' declared the president of Northern Suburbs Rugby Club and member of the Australian Billiards Council. 'I was seated a few yards from him on several occasions for three hours at a stretch. He is a quiet, unassuming, human man who is loved and adored by the people, whom he has lifted out of the slough of despond. When he came into the stadium, almost unattended [*sic*—he had an entourage of 100], in the old khaki uniform similar to that which he wore in the war, without any adornment, the 100,000 people (men, women and youths) rose as one and cheered him again and again. He is the most popular man they have ever had in Germany. Those stories about the oppression of the Jews are not correct. I spoke to many Jews in the big stores, and they all praised him.'

Basil Dickinson disembarked *Mooltan* at Sydney's Circular Quay and fell into the arms of his parents and sisters who were there to meet him. 'I returned, like a number of us, excited yet unsettled by what we'd experienced in Berlin.'

Finding work was his top priority. 'My family couldn't help me. They had little money, having just survived the Depression, and they'd already somehow come up with my spending money for the trip.' So Dickinson swallowed his pride and approached his old company, Royal Insurance, and was informed that since his job had not been filled he was welcome to reapply for it, 'but

I would be reappointed from scratch, my four years of service and accumulated benefits would be wiped and I would be paid only a novice's wage of three pounds, seven shillings and sixpence a week. Take it or leave it. With no other prospects, I took it.' Then they hypocritically cashed in on Dickinson's athletic prowess. He was ordered to travel all over Sydney introducing himself to strangers as an Olympian and to talk them into buying insurance. 'It was degrading,' he said.

In 1938 he was offered a job with a rival insurance company, Bankers and Traders. His new firm had no objection to Dickinson taking a week's leave to compete in the 1938 Empire Games, where he won bronze medals in the hop, step and jump (bettering his 14.48m Berlin effort by almost 1m) and the broad jump. 'When I stepped onto the podium to receive my hop, step and jump bronze medal, they'd run out and all they had left was gold, so a gold medal was placed around my neck.' His athletics swan song was winning the NSW decathlon title in 1939. 'By then I'd had enough of athletics. I wanted to play rugby union.'

With the outbreak of World War II, Dickinson enlisted, but weeks before he was due to join the army he badly broke his leg playing winger for St George first grade rugby team. It was his first and last game of senior football.

In 1939, he became engaged to Elizabeth, known as Bettie to her friends, whom he'd met while bush-walking. 'I'd met Bettie at the end of 1938 when I joined the Coast and Mountain Walkers bush-walking club. She was a lovely girl with long plaits and during the walks we found it easy to talk. We saw more and more of each other and gradually it dawned on us that we'd fallen in love.'

By 1941, Dickinson's leg had mended and he was passed fit for active service. He enlisted again for overseas duty with the army. 'The recruitment fellows gave me three weeks to finish up my work and report to barracks. I hadn't told my fiancée that I'd enlisted. I don't know why. I was determined to fight in the war but I suppose I knew how upset Bettie would be and I wanted to avoid a scene.' Upset was an understatement. 'She angrily accused me of trying to escape from her and I protested that I loved her and would never do that. She said, "Right then . . . how quickly can we get married?" We were married within a fortnight, just a sermon and a handful of friends at a local church.'

Three days after their honeymoon, Dickinson reported to army headquarters. After three weeks he was made a lance corporal with orders to improve the troops' fitness. He underwent physical education training, then 'I was sent to the north of Western Australia to knock the soldiers there into shape because there were fears of a Japanese invasion. That didn't happen and for the rest of the war I crisscrossed Australia putting troops through their paces.'

After more years with Bankers and Traders as a regional branch manager in Bathurst, Dickinson accepted a job with Mercantile Mutual. 'It was hard to leave Bankers and Traders because they'd been good to me, but Bettie and I had had our children, Pauline and Michael, and Mercantile offered more money and opportunity.' In 1966, aged 51, he became manager for Queensland, and he and Bettie moved to Brisbane's Holland Park and remained there until his retirement in 1980, smack on 65.

While progressing through the ranks at Mercantile, Dickinson continued in athletics as an administrator and judge. 'In 1956 at the Melbourne Olympics I was the major judge for the men's long jump [it had become known as long jump, rather than broad jump, after Berlin] and triple jump [formerly hop, step and jump], the women's high jump and the decathlon high jump . . . Nothing much had changed in twenty years. I had to pay my train fare to Melbourne and buy my own uniform.'

In 1972, Bettie and Basil visited Munich for the Olympic Games. In Munich, he reunited with Berlin Olympics alumni

Sir Harry Alderson, now president of the Australian Olympic Committee, wrestling team manager Dick Garrard, and Heinz Schweibold, the German attaché at Berlin Olympic Village. 'We all met and had a lovely time.'

The Dickinsons were sightseeing in Salzburg when they heard news of the Olympic kidnappings and murders. 'Bettie and I rushed back to Munich and I went straight to the Village. I wasn't allowed in. I asked the bloke who was barring my way to get in touch with the Australian chargé d'affaires whom I knew well, and he organised for a German guide to admit me. Security was on red alert. Once inside, I was continually asked to show my entry pass and passport. Dick Garrard took me to the press conference. Everyone there was in shock. Dick and I sat numb as word came about the developing tragedy, which ended at Fürstenfeldbruck airport. In all, eleven Israeli athletes and officials and five terrorists were killed.' The German Olympic Committee had called the Munich Olympics 'the Happy Games' to try to expunge memories of Hitler's cynical manipulation of them in 1936. After the Munich massacre, the days of free and easy Olympic Villages were over.

Dickinson and Schweibold met one last time in 1990. 'Heinz wrote to me: "Basil, we're getting old . . . let's get together and say our auf Wiedersehens while we still can." Heinz had become a lonely man. His wife had died and his children were in other countries. I wasn't affluent and my older sister helped me pay for my airfare, and it was all worth it. Heinz and I had a wonderful reunion.

'We had both skirted around our war experience when we were together in 1972, and [one] night at his home on Lake Constance we talked about the war. Heinz had been a lieutenant in the Wehrmacht's anti-aircraft division and was in Rostok when it was bombed by the Allies. We talked for some hours, sharing a bottle of his good red wine. Heinz was still bitter about the British and

American bombing of German cities and towns, and at the risk of offending him I had to say, "Yes, that was truly dreadful, but Heinz, your side started it."'

Dickinson had been profoundly moved by the destruction of Berlin in 1945. 'I followed the newspaper reports, and watched the newsreels, and seeing that magnificent city obliterated like that was devastating,' he said. 'I knew those beautiful palaces and buildings, Unter den Linden, the Tiergarten, the Opera House, the Reichstag, Brandenburg Gate, the department stores selling every product imaginable. It all made me wish there was no such thing as war. I saw a photo of the stadium with soldiers marching where we had competed, where Leni Riefenstahl in her big overcoat and beret had busily directed her cameramen. It still makes me sad.'

Later that evening, after he and Schweibold had bid each other goodnight, Dickinson fell and injured himself trying to find the way to his bedroom. 'I stress it had nothing to do with the red wine,' he chuckled. 'I fell headfirst down a flight of fourteen stairs. I split open my noggin and bruised my ribs. There was blood everywhere. Heinz took me to hospital where my head was stitched, and I was kept for observation. I was 75 years old. I had planned to travel north to Berlin to take a final walk through the Reich Sports Field and the city and see how it had been divided into east and west by the Allies and the Russians and rebuilt, and what memories it brought back. After my fall I wasn't well enough. That was my last time in Germany.' In 1992, Dickinson received a letter from one of Schweibold's children telling him that his old friend had died.

Bettie and Basil's hearts were shattered when their architect and journalist son Michael died in 1994 when he was 46. Said Dickinson, 'Mike was homosexual. I don't like the word "gay" . . . He took very ill and died and it was a shame because he was a remarkable, thoughtful and well-liked young man.'

Dickinson was feted at the Sydney Olympics in 2000, attending the Parliament House function for pre-war Olympians and sitting in a reserved seat at the stadium. At Sydney, Englishman Jonathan Edwards won the gold medal in Dickinson's event, the triple jump. When Edwards leapt 17.71m, which was 3.1m further than Dickinson had achieved at Berlin and 1.71m greater than Naoto Tajima's 1936 gold-medal-winning 16m, Dickinson cheered as enthusiastically as anyone else.

For as long as he lived he was a treasured guest at Australian Olympic Committee functions and at his home athletic club St George, where the broad jump record he set in 1935 remains unbroken to this day.

On retirement, the Dickinsons returned to New South Wales, buying a home in a bush setting in the Blue Mountains. With time on his hands and his mind as active as ever, Basil completed an external studies Bachelor of Arts degree at the University of New England. When not studying and writing essays he read the bush poets, Oodjeroo Noonuccal and Banjo Paterson especially, and spent time with his family and, with his darling Bettie, travelled widely throughout Australia and took long walks in the Blue Mountains bush. They were members of the Australian Historical Society and custodians of the Norman Lindsay Gallery. 'We were married for 68 years and that was a blessing. We were lucky to have had a wonderful marriage. We had the usual arguments. I laugh when I hear married couples say, "Oh, we've been married for 65 years and have never had a disagreement and never had too much to drink or did something really stupid, and of course we brought up our children perfectly." Well, Bettie and I weren't like that. We made mistakes and our marriage was blessed for all of that. We lived quietly. We were both private people and enjoyed being so. It was a real marriage.'

After Bettie's death, Basil lived alone in their home. He cooked all his own meals, because after a week's trial of Meals on Wheels fare he wrote them a polite note saying he preferred to cook for himself.

After three hospitalisations for ageing ailments in 2011, Dickinson moved to an aged care facility where he was an active and opinionated participant in current affairs meetings.

For a while after the Berlin Olympics, Pat Norton moved back in with the Nightingale family in Bondi. She worked in a bank while training for her triumphant Empire Games. In her early twenties, seeing no future as a bank clerk, she moved to Tasmania to teach swimming to underprivileged children. There she met and married Bill Down, a pilot. On 27 January 1944, Bill perished when his plane crashed. His grieving wife lost their unborn child.

As she had always done, Pat Down fought back. She taught swimming in Melbourne, and learned to fly. To honour her late husband's memory, she bought a Tiger Moth and with a friend, Nan Watts, flew around Australia. They were the first women to fly across Bass Strait, and survived an emergency landing in a field of large and truculent bulls. The adventure bug still biting, she attached a motor to a bicycle and rode from Melbourne to Sydney and back. Down ran a guesthouse and a driving school and swam in masters events. She adopted a six-year-old boy, Laurie Kingsley, from an orphanage. In time, Kingsley married, and he and his wife Jean had children who in turn had children of their own. All have much to thank Pat for.

The last time Harry Nightingale junior saw his father's protégée was in the mid-1960s at a rugby union match in which young Laurie Kingsley was playing against Nightingale's school, Waverley College, and she was barracking for him. 'Pat was in her forties, and still had that baby face.'

She stayed in touch with a handful of her Berlin teammates, including de Lacy, Mackay and Dickinson, and maintained a life-long correspondence with Jeannette Campbell in Argentina.

One year shy of 60, Down renewed her daredevil credentials when she took up gliding. The challenge she gave herself at 69 was to go white-water rafting. At 79 she began writing her remarkable life story, and she was a volunteer and honoured guest at the 2000 Olympics.

'Pat was quite a girl, a game girl, she would have a go at anything,' said Dickinson. 'Losing her husband and her unborn babe, she experienced more tragedy in her life than anybody deserves. I saw a lot of her . . . we were good friends and then life went on for us both and we lost touch. One day I decided to find out where she was living and I wrote to her, and just before the Sydney Olympics my wife Bettie and I had dinner with her in Sydney. By then she was living in a nursing home. We talked on the telephone, but she had a cleft palate and her speech was not easy to understand. I told her I'd prefer it if we wrote to each other than spoke on the phone. She said, "Bad luck, Basil, I'd rather talk." I wanted to write her obituary in *The Sydney Morning Herald* when she died in 2007, but it needed a pro. I contacted Harry Gordon who wrote a wonderful obit. I thought that was the least I could do for Pat. I helped organise her funeral and had the Olympic Committee send a flag for her coffin. She deserved that.'

On his return, Harry Nightingale continued to win Australian Rescue and Resuscitation (R&R) championships; he had won the title in 1932, 1935 and 1936, and would hold it again in 1940 and each year from 1958 to 1963. Nightingale distinguished himself along with Bondi's other lifesavers on 'Black Sunday', 6 February 1938, when they saved all but seven of around 250 swimmers who

DANGEROUS GAMES

were swept out to sea by the backwash from a series of large, thumping waves. He coached R&R teams into the 1970s, and for his work as chief instructor at Bondi was granted life membership of the club. To this day, the open six-person R&R trophy at the NSW Surf Life Saving Titles is named in his honour.

As well as Salty, Nightingale's nickname was 'Relaxation'. 'Dad was a master relaxer. He was Zen before people in Australia knew what Zen was,' says his son Harry 'H-Man' Nightingale, who has followed in his father's footsteps as a surfer, lifesaver and free spirit, and has been a sometime TV star on *Bondi Rescue*. 'He believed that God and spirit are everywhere, but he'd clip me for even talking about it because he was an old-school tough guy.'

Nightingale senior was one who didn't mind regaling others about his adventures in Berlin, and he enjoyed telling how he'd been '*this close*' to 'Adolf the arsehole'. 'I've got a photo of Dad at the 1936 Games,' says H-Man, 'getting off the train with Pat Norton at the station when they arrived in Berlin with all the Nazis standing to attention and the brass bands playing.'

As Nightingale grew older, eight decades in the sun took a toll. He had many skin cancers removed and in 1980, when he was 79, he suffered a cerebral haemorrhage. 'He was taken to hospital and I never saw him again,' says his son. 'I was surfing in the south corner of Bondi when a mate told me Dad had died. I said, "I have to go for a swim," and I swam out a long way and I cried and cried.'

The irascible, outspoken but endearing Dunc Gray greeted the reporters at Circular Quay in 1936 with a cheery, 'It's bloody great to be home.'

After Berlin, Gray retained his mantle as Australia's premier cyclist until he retired in 1942, citing the probability that he'd be called up for military duty and, as a churchgoer, his disinclination to race on Sundays. Gray won the 1000m sprint at the 1938 Sydney Empire Games to add to the gold medal he had won at the London Empire Games in 1934, and won twenty Australian titles, 36 NSW titles, and 36 club championships. He never added to his Olympic medal tally, which included a bronze in the 1000m time trial at Amsterdam 1928 and a gold in the same event at the Los Angeles Games in 1932. Unlike most 1936 Australian Olympians, at 34 he would probably have been past his prime had the 1940 Tokyo Games been staged. Despite his predilection for pilfering sporting souvenirs, he was flag-bearer at both the 1936 Olympics and the 1938 Empire Games. After he retired from the velodrome, he continued to cycle to and from the Sydney showrooms of Bennett & Wood, where he sold his beloved Speedwells.

Gray and his wife—who first met, fittingly, in a bicycle shop—had four children. In later years he manufactured fibreglass, yet his true occupation was promoting cycling and the Olympic Games. Writers always found him good for a memorable quote. Four years before his death, he expressed his enduring bitterness that he was forbidden by Australian cycling officials from riding in his favourite event, the 1000m time trial, in Berlin. 'I was a better rider than Tasman Johnson [who rode the race]. Very seldom did he ever get his wheel in front [of mine]. When you win a race in one Olympics, why can't you be in the same race at the next Olympics if you're good enough?'

Gray despised cyclists who took performance-enhancing drugs, which had been around cycling since his day. 'There was dope-taking—I don't know if they were amphetamines or pep pills—in Berlin in 1936. There was no testing then. The little German bloke who was looking after us came to the track one day and he had a bottle of pills and said, "Take one of these, you must take it to win." And he was right. I didn't take it and I didn't win!'

The grand old man of Australian cycling was 90 when he died on 30 August 1996. There to say goodbye at his funeral were his Olympic peers Dawn Fraser, Murray Rose, Raelene Boyle, Kevin Berry, John Devitt, and his 1936 Olympics teammate Merv Wood. As is the custom with fallen Olympians, a five-ring flag was draped on his coffin, and propped proudly beside it at the chapel was the Speedwell bike he rode to glory in Los Angeles 64 years before.

Today that bicycle is displayed in a showcase at Australia's premier cycling venue, built for the 2000 Sydney Olympics: the Dunc Gray Velodrome.

EPILOGUE

'Berlin was very, very long ago, and we were all so young . . . I'll try to remember how it was,' was Basil Dickinson's response when I first asked to interview him about his experiences as an Olympian in 1936.

Late in 2012—having written on sport for 30 years and after viewing Leni Riefenstahl's *Olympia* and reading Guy Walters' *Berlin Games*, Christopher Hilton's *Hitler's Olympics* and David Clay Large's *Nazi Games*—I came to believe that there was room among this excellent literature on the XIth Olympiad for a book about the seldom recounted experiences of the Australian team who competed. Who was in the team? How did they fare? What did they think of Hitler and his Nazis, and of Jesse Owens? Of each other? What was it like to be in old Berlin before it was destroyed by war? Were the athletes different from, or similar to, modern-day Australian champions? To answer my questions and perhaps, if the information was available, write the story of Australia at the Berlin Olympics, I knew I could search for official documents, diaries and mementoes kept privately or donated to libraries. The reports of sports experts, journalists and eyewitnesses written and broadcast before, during and after the Olympics were all available in libraries or newspaper archives. I could travel to Berlin and be guided by experts through what remained of Berlin circa 1936 and the Reich Sports Field, and steep myself in local records of the time. Yes, but what would make my book really worthwhile would be to find a primary source, to interview at length an athlete from that 1936 squad. Any such person would have to be well into their nineties. Perhaps, I worried, there was nobody left alive.

After some sleuthing, I learned that there was: Basil Dickinson. His daughter, Pauline Watson, told me that Basil was 98 and in an aged care facility, but his mind and memory were sharp.

Basil and I met for the first time in his room at the nursing home in Kingswood, west of Sydney, in June 2013. He was sitting on the edge of his bed, a trim man with a shock of wiry white hair atop an intelligent face. His manner, though friendly, was formal and courtly, befitting a man of his vintage. He was impeccably dressed in slacks and sports shirt and his shoes were polished. His room was neat. Bright winter morning sunlight flooded through his window onto his perfectly made bed, his furniture and shelves, which held books on sport and poetry (Oodjeroo Noonuccal, Henry Lawson, Banjo Paterson, the *Rubaiyat of Omar Khayyam*, the very book he purchased in Aden when *Mongolia* dropped anchor there in 1936 bound for Europe). By his bed were recent and past photographs of Basil and his family, and stacked on a tape player, cassettes of classical music, Leonard Teale reading the works of Paterson, Lawson and other bush poets, and Geoffrey Gurrumul Yunupingu's *Gurrumul*. By his bathroom door was his walking frame, an ironic aid for one who was once a world-class athlete. On a bedside table was that morning's broadsheet newspaper, which Basil, a voracious reader of political news and arts features as well as the sports pages, had already read from cover to cover. 'Well, what can I tell you?' he said before we began our first interview. 'I want this to be accurate, exactly the way it was.'

I recorded Basil's recollections and insights about the 1936 Olympics and his life during a dozen or more meetings at the nursing home. When I arrived he would have his Olympic books, pamphlets and photographs arrayed on his bed and bedside chair as ready references. Speaking softly and thoughtfully, Basil brought vividly to life long-ago events and memories, some of which he had forgotten, perhaps repressed, until encouraged to delve into his past to reclaim them.

I like to think he looked forward to our weekly interviews. Although he insisted he wanted no gifts—'my needs are simple, I have all I want'—he swiftly stashed away in his bedside cupboard the packets of soft jubes and occasional bottle of red wine that I would spirit into his room.

Our meetings, which began in June 2013, followed a pattern. He would update me on his health—the heel he injured jumping on cinders in Berlin remained painful on cold days—and perhaps grizzle a little about the nursing home food and the others' inability to appreciate poetry. Then would follow our interview, which would last until he grew tired, usually 60 or 70 minutes.

At one interview session, Basil asked me to be sure to try to work what he was about to tell me into the book, because he'd spent much of the last days wrestling with his thoughts. This is what he said: 'I'd like it on the record that apart from losing my son Michael, I've had a most happy life. A good life. I've repre-sented my country and won medals. I've loved my family and they've loved me. So many wonderful things I've seen and done. My experiences as an Olympian in Berlin helped turn me from an immature boy into a man. After Berlin I knew that life was about more than running and jumping. Although it all happened nearly 80 years ago, I can easily close my eyes and bring to mind that crowd at the stadium yelling, *"Yess-say O-vens! Yess-say O-vens!"* and my teammates Jack, Pat, Evelyn, Merv, Harry Cooper, all kids then, and all gone now. The competitors from other nations, many of whom didn't survive the war, and up in his box, with his Nazi mates in their battle dress and the Olympic dignitaries in monkey suits, Adolf Hitler.

'We Australians did not all fail individually, as many of us bettered our personal best performance. Where we were lacking was in our preparation and our attitude. There was no intensity, just a belief that if we did our best, whether we won or lost, competed fairly and didn't disgrace Australia, well, that was okay. To me, then and today, that sums up the Olympic spirit, but only in rare cases does it win gold medals.

'I didn't look on the political side till I returned home. [In Berlin] I blanked out Adolf Hitler's evil and that he was using us as part of his propaganda. I tried hard to find positives. I was genuinely impressed with what National Socialism was doing for the youth of Germany with such programs as the Strength Through Joy movement which promoted sports and life in the open air. After I came home and things got hot in Europe, the blinkers fell from my eyes and I realised that the Nazis had an ulterior motive for staging the Olympics and that we athletes had been ruthlessly used. Still and all, as long as we were competing well and living up to the Olympic ideals, does it matter? I don't know. I would never swap my Berlin experience for anything. What I do know is that that little fellow Hitler certainly buggered things up.

'For all the faults, I put the Olympic Games at their best on a pedestal. Some of the best moments of my life have been Olympic moments, mine and others'. I've always been upset when I've seen the Olympic ideals of excellence, friendship and respect being undermined by extreme nationalism, politicisation, commercialism and the demand with each Olympics for an ever more extravagant spectacle.'

Sometimes Basil would say he wanted to live at least another two years, when he would turn 100 and receive a letter from the Queen. 'I've lived so long because I've tried to be physically and mentally fit. I have good genes. I'll go quietly at 100.'

On 1 September, I arrived and found Basil's bed empty. I feared the worst, until a nurse told me he'd fallen ill with a staph infection and been transferred to hospital for treatment.

When he returned to the home I telephoned Basil and he assured me that he felt well enough to continue our interviews in his room. I arrived on 24 September and found him lying still on his bed with his eyes staring open and his mouth agape. I ran out into the corridor and alerted a nurse: 'Something's wrong with Basil, come quick!' The nurse gave the old man a hug and he woke. 'He's fine, this one, he just likes to nap with his eyes open. He'll be with us forever.'

Our interview went ahead that day, although Basil had become shockingly thin and his mind now wandered. His once mellow voice was a cracked rasp. He sometimes writhed in pain and explained that his heel was really hurting. He seemed sad, and instead of rejoicing in his positive experiences he began to dwell on the disappointments of his life. He spoke longingly of his lost loved ones Michael and Bettie. Again and again, he ruminated that he hadn't performed as well as he could have in Berlin because he had felt lonely and ostracised, inferior to the other athletes, and had convinced himself that he was at those Olympics on false pretences. 'I didn't have the confidence to converse with the more self-assured athletes like Dunc Gray and Gerald Backhouse. I even found my friend Jack Metcalfe intimidating, good old Jack who did everything to help me . . . It wasn't until I found success at work, and Bettie, that I realised I *was* as worthy as the next bloke, and had something to offer.'

On 6 October when I visited, Basil lay on his bed too weak to acknowledge my presence, let alone talk, so I read to him from his poetry books and we listened to music and a tape of bush bird calls. After two hours, I grasped his hand and even though I'm sure he couldn't hear me, I said goodbye.

The following day Pauline called to say that Basil had passed away and that his funeral would take place in the Blue Mountains. Basil's coffin, as was his right, was draped with the five-ringed Olympic flag. At the chapel on 21 October 2013 were his family and friends and a sprinkling of old Olympians. 'Marrandil' by Gurrumul was played, and so too at the end was the great hymn 'Jerusalem', from the soundtrack of *Chariots of Fire*, the film that celebrated the 1924 Olympics and the English champions Eric Liddell and Harold Abrahams, both of whom Basil had met in Berlin in 1936. Australian Olympic Committee president John Coates sent a message calling Basil Dickinson a gentleman and a credit to his sport and country. 'He was our most senior Olympic competitor and one who we all treasure for the standards he set for the Olympians who followed him over the next 70 years.'

It was a dignified and low-key service, one of which Basil Dickinson would have approved. Sadly, the bushfires that were threatening to cut off the highway from Sydney to the Blue Mountains kept many away. Smoke that had drifted into the Leura Valley from the blazes hung over the memorial park where, in a small family plot overlooking the valley among the gumtrees and native plants, the last of the 1936 Australian Olympians was laid to rest.

ACKNOWLEDGEMENTS

I cannot adequately convey my gratitude to and admiration for the late Harry Gordon, Australia's finest Olympic historian, who, despite battling illness from which he would not recover, vetted my manuscript for accuracy and allowed me to delve into his taped interviews with Berlin Olympians Cec Pearce, Dick Garrard, Dunc Gray, Jack Metcalfe and Fred Woodhouse, all of whom had died before I embarked on this project. Harry's generosity was above and beyond.

My deep thanks, too, to Tony Baine, whose sporting knowledge and contacts were invaluable; Ryan Balmer, my guide in Berlin and at the Reich Sports Field; Lucy Carter, ABC broadcaster, who sent me a CD of her insightful radio interview with Basil Dickinson; Stephanie Daniels and Anita Tedder, who generously allowed me access to their interviews with Doris Carter, Pat Norton and Evelyn de Lacy (to purchase a copy of their fine book *A Proper Spectacle: Women Olympians 1900–1936*, contact steph8554@googlemail.com); John Devitt, an Olympic champion himself, who was wise and supportive throughout the research and writing of *Dangerous Games*; Basil Dickinson, who lived long enough to be the heart

331

and soul of this book; Tony Dixon, who spoke to me about his uncle, the sculler Bill Dixon; Jennie Fairs, a brilliant and dogged researcher; sportswriter extraordinaire Ian Heads, who has been a friend and adviser for 30 years; Rod Laver and John Newcombe, for speaking to me at length about the particular and peculiar psyche of elite sportspeople; Gary Lester; Brenda Oliver-Harry, Anita and Vinka Hutchinson and Basil Twine, who enabled me to profile swimmer Percy Oliver; Kim Mackney, for sharing hilarious yarns about his remarkable father, the rambunctious rower Wal Mackney; my agent Fran Moore; Harry Nightingale junior, a true character, for speaking to me about his equally fascinating father Harry Nightingale and Harry's protégée, backstroker Pat Norton; Brooke Ryan and Cashel Ardouin, daughter and granddaughter of Bill Kendall and Dominic Ryan; Mike Tancred of the Australian Olympic Federation, who put me in contact with Pauline Watson, Basil Dickinson's daughter; Pauline Watson, who introduced me to her father and somehow persuaded him that 40 hours of being interviewed might be therapeutic and even enjoyable; Warren Whillier, for speaking to me about his grandmother Evelyn (de Lacy) Whillier and giving me her diary, which allowed me, and the readers of this book, to time-travel to Berlin circa 1936; and John Wood, who regaled me with stories on the life and times of his father, rower Merv Wood.

My gratitude to those who embraced and then steered this project at my publisher Allen & Unwin—publisher Elizabeth Weiss, editorial manager Angela Handley, and publishing director Tom Gilliatt—for their wisdom and professionalism and for understanding that the experiences of an Olympic team which won just one medal, and a bronze at that, can be more compelling than those of a squad that covers itself in glory (although it must help when the athletes were a remarkable group whose experiences occurred in such a turbulent and terrifying time and place). I am also deeply indebted to my editor, Meaghan Amor, who so skilfully and sensitively whittled a massive manuscript down to its present size, and in doing so made my book better. It wasn't easy for her . . . or for me: killing my darlings is not a strong suit. Praise too to Clara Finlay for her peerless proofreading and suggestions.

Finally, thank you to my family, Carol, Tom and Casey Writer, Lenore Adamson, and Maddie and Winston, for so much love and so many good times.

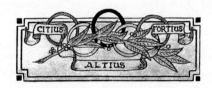

BIBLIOGRAPHY

BOOKS

Alderson, H. and Eve, James S.W., *XIth Olympiad—Berlin, Germany—August 1 to 16, 1936—Participation of the Australian Olympic Team*, Australian Olympic Federation, 1936

Bach, Steven, *Leni: The life and work of Leni Riefenstahl*, Vintage, 2008

Bachrach, Susan D., *The Nazi Olympics: Berlin 1936*, United States Holocaust Memorial Museum, Little, Brown and Company, 2000

Benjamin, Walter, *Berlin Childhood Around 1900*, The Belknap Press of Harvard University Press, 2006

Berg, A. Scott, *Lindbergh*, Macmillan, 1998

Bloch, Michael, *Ribbentrop*, Bantam Press, 1994

Brown, Daniel James, *The Boys in the Boat: Nine Americans and their epic quest for gold at the 1936 Berlin Olympics*, Viking, 2013

Clay Large, David, *Nazi Games: The Olympics of 1936*, WW Norton & Company, 2007

Daniels, Stephanie and Tedder, Anita, *A Proper Spectacle: Women Olympians 1900–1936*, ZeNaNa Press and Walla Walla Press, 2000

Dickstein, Morris, *Dancing in the Dark: A cultural history of the Great Depression*, WW Norton & Company, 2009

Diem, Carl (author), Richter, Friedrich (ed.) and Wasner, Fritz (statistics), Organising Committee for the XIth Olympiad Berlin 1936, *The XIth*

Olympic Games Berlin, 1936—Official Report Volumes I and II, Wilhelm Limpert-Verlag, 1937

Donald, David Herbert, *Look Homeward: A life of Thomas Wolfe*, Bloomsbury, 1987

Evans, Richard J., *The Coming of the Third Reich: How the Nazis destroyed democracy and seized power in Germany*, Penguin Books, 2004

Friedrich, Otto, *Before the Deluge: A portrait of Berlin in the 1920s*, Harper Perennial, 1995

Gardner, Juliet, *The Thirties: An intimate history*, Harper Press, 2010

Gordon, Harry, *Australia and the Olympic Games*, University of Queensland Press, 1994

Gordon, Mel, *Voluptuous Panic: The erotic world of Weimar Berlin*, Feral House, 2000

Hilton, Christopher, *Hitler's Olympics*, Sutton Publishing, 2006

Hitler, Adolf, *Mein Kampf*, CreateSpace Independent Publishing Platform, 2014

Hohne, Heinz, *The Order of the Death's Head: The story of Hitler's SS*, Penguin, 2000

Kershaw, Ian, *Hitler: 1889–1936 hubris*, Allen Lane, The Penguin Press, 1998

——*Making Friends with Hitler: Lord Londonderry, the Nazis and the road to war*, The Penguin Press, 2004

——*The End: The defiance and destruction of Hitler's Germany, 1944–1945*, The Penguin Press, 2011

Klemperer, Victor, *I Shall Bear Witness: The diaries of Victor Klemperer 1933–1941*, Phoenix, 1998

Kruger, Arnd, *Die Olympische Spiele 1936 und die Weltmeinung: Ihre Aufsenpolitische Bedeutung unter Besonderer Berucksichtigung der USA*, Bartels & Wernitz, 1972, in English translation

Larson, Erik, *In the Garden of Beasts: Love, terror and an American family in Hitler's Berlin*, Crown, 2011

MacLean, Rory, *Berlin: Imagine a city*, Weidenfeld & Nicolson, 2014

Manvell, Roger and Fraenkel, Heinrich, *Goering*, Greenhill Books, 2005

Nagorski, Andrew, *HitlerLand: American eyewitnesses to the Nazi rise to power*, Simon & Schuster Paperbacks, 2012

Persico, Joseph E., *Nuremberg: Infamy on trial*, Penguin Books, 1994

Pryce-Jones, David, *Unity Mitford: A quest*, Phoenix, 1995

Read, Anthony, *The Devil's Disciples: The lives and times of Hitler's inner circle*, Pimlico, 2004

Reuth, Ralf Georg, *Goebbels*, Harcourt Brace, 1990

Riefenstahl, Leni, *Leni Riefenstahl: A memoir*, Picador, 1992

Romer, Willy, *Berlin as a Cosmopolitan City: Photographs by Willy Romer 1919–1933*, Braus, 2013

Roth, Joseph, *What I Saw: Reports from Berlin 1920–1923*, Granta, 2003

Shirer, William L., *The Rise and Fall of the Third Reich*, Mandarin, 1960

——*The Nightmare Years*, Little, Brown, 1984

Walters, Guy, *Berlin Games: How the Nazis stole the Olympic dream*, Harper Perennial, 2007

Wick, Steve, *The Long Night: William L. Shirer and the rise and fall of the Third Reich*, Palgrave Macmillan, 2011

Wolfe, Thomas, *You Can't Go Home Again*, Penguin Books, 1984

FILM

Berlin: Die Sinfonia der Grosstadt, directed by Walther Ruttman, Edition Film Museum

Die Melodie der Welt, directed by Walther Ruttman, Edition Film Museum

Olympia: The complete original version, directed by Leni Riefenstahl, Pathfinder Home Entertainment

Triumph des Willens ('Triumph of the Will'), directed by Leni Riefenstahl, Pathfinder Home Entertainment

NEWSPAPERS

The Advertiser
The Advocate
The Argus
The Australian
The Australian Women's Weekly
Cairns Post
The Canberra Times
The Courier-Mail
The Daily Telegraph
Goulburn Evening Post
The Mercury
The Mirror

The Morning Bulletin
The New York Times
The New Zealand Truth
The News
The Referee
The Singleton Argus
The Sun
The Sunday Times
The Sydney Morning Herald
The Times (UK)
Townsville Daily Bulletin
The Truth
The West Australian